THE AGE OF ANXIETY

32-6457   JN6511   94-9874 CIP
Galeotti, Mark. **The age of anxiety: security and politics in Soviet and post-Soviet Russia.** Longman, 1995. 219p bibl index ISBN 0-582-21853-5, $36.95; ISBN 0-582-21852-7 pbk, $16.95

When great multinational states crumble, the shock waves spread across the international system. In the case of the analysts immediately turned their attention to the military, the KGB, and the police for signals about the new Russian state's domestic and foreign policy. Some have warned of civil war and anarchy. Others see a new dictatorship capable of reviving Russian hegemony over the former Soviet Union. Understanding military and security issues in contemporary Russian politics requires knowledge of Russian history and sophisticated information about the previous 20 years. It takes a clear mind that avoids Cold War and post-Cold War propaganda and concentrates on realistic political analysis. Galeotti has more than met that standard. He is a specialist in Russian security affairs. His work is an excellent analytical political history that will have broad appeal. He explains how and why the Soviet leadership launched and then lost control over a serious reform intended to strengthen the Soviet state. The book's core is Gorbachev's rise and fall. It provides rich detail which gives the work credibility. However, the author does not cite the sources for the evidence he uses, an omission that decreases this book's appeal to academic libraries. Nevertheless, the analysis is at as high a level as the best work in the field, and the writing is clear and understandable to the general reader. It will make an excellent edition to general collections and cannot be ignored by specialists.— *R. V. Barylski, University of South Florida*

THE AGE OF ANXIETY
SECURITY AND POLITICS IN
SOVIET AND POST-SOVIET
RUSSIA

MARK GALEOTTI

LONGMAN
London and New York

Addison Wesley Longman Limited
Edinburgh Gate,
Harlow, Essex, CM20 2JE, England
and Associated Companies throughout the world.

*Published in the United States of America
by Addison Wesley Longman, New York*

© Longman Group Limited 1995

First published 1995
Second impression 1996

ISBN 0 582 21853 5 CSD
ISBN 0 582 21852 7 PPR

British Library Cataloguing-in-Publication Data

A catalogue record for this book is
available from the British Library

Library of Congress Cataloging-in-Publication Data
Galeotti, Mark,
    The age of anxiety : security and politics in Soviet and post-Soviet Russia /
    Mark Galeotti.
        p.   cm.
    Includes bibliographical references.
    ISBN 0-582-21853-5. -- ISBN 0-582-21852-7 (pbk.)
    1. Soviet Union--Politics and government--1985-1991. 2. Russia
(Federation)--Politics and government--1991-   3. National security--Soviet
Union. 4. National security--Russia (Federation)
I. Title.
JN6511.G35 1995
320.947--dc20   94-9874
                                                                      CIP

Set by 7
Produced by Longman Singapore Publishers (Pte) Ltd.
Printed in Singapore

CONTENTS

PREFACE

An empire founded by war has to maintain itself by war.

Montesquieu

Security policy taken at its broadest, to include foreign relations and internal control, was to prove at the heart of the process of reform in the Soviet Union of the 1980s. The very first impetus for reform came from the military, KGB and foreign policy establishments, worried about falling behind the West, about the decay of their Eastern European buffer states. Ultimately, it was elements within these same interests which pressurised Gorbachev, limited any hopes of radical change, and – by launching the August Coup in 1991 – doomed the Soviet state. Yet the end of that state has not changed many of the dilemmas facing Moscow – indeed, with the independence of the former satellites of Eastern Europe and the new successor states of the former Soviet Union, security policy is still critical and will remain so. What is more, the figures shaping security and foreign policy are all products of the old thinking and the old orthodoxies.

This is hardly surprising, because the traumas and uncertainties which racked the USSR in its dying years were in essence very similar to those which tore at the heart of tsarist Russia, and which are already beginning to trouble the new Russian Federation. If there is one basic approach underpinning this book, then it is that there is no escaping the intellectual legacy of history or the challenges posed by culture and geography. Of course, states and societies change over time, but only gradually. Despite the utopian dreams and seeming successes of radicals and revolutionaries, change is a slow process akin to the reshaping of the landscape. Over the years, mountains can be eroded by the elements and continents torn in two by the movement of the earth, but this is a gradual and incremental business, and not one easily hurried. Modern technology may now give us the means to level mountains, but it has yet to unlock the secret to reshaping societies and resolving international rivalries.

USING THIS BOOK

Not only is this a complex time in the evolution of Russia, itself a nation of great political, cultural and historical intricacies, but this book inevitably spans several disciplines. By interpreting the term 'security' so widely, it incorporates military doctrine, political skulduggery, international relations and economic stability, and seeks to knit them together in some coherent whole. The chapters follow a broadly chronological line, with the exception of the first two and the last chapters, which explore general themes in Russian history, the main interests involved and, finally, Russia's prospects for the future. Chapters 3–7 have a capsule chronology, but in the appendices the reader will find a rather more detailed one, as well as a guide to key people, terms and abbreviations used in the text and some suggestions for further reading.

The transliteration of Russian names and terms in this book represents an unholy compromise between my own pedantry and my publisher's eye for general accessibility. While precise transliterations are used in most cases, where some other form has become generally accepted, then I have followed the herd. Russia's President is thus – as of writing, I suppose I should add, given the volatile nature of politics in Moscow – rendered as Boris *Yeltsin*, and not the more accurate but less recognisable Boris *El'tsin*. In addition to which, several of the post-Soviet states abandoned old, Russian versions of their names. The reader should bear in mind, then, that Moldavia becomes Moldova, Belorussia becomes Belarus and Kirghizia becomes Kyrgyzstan.

***

All works are collaborations, even if most of the people whose ideas we gleefully adopt or whose views trigger off our own thought processes never know the part they play. In particular, thanks are due to Martin McCauley for his helpful and perceptive comments and to Dominic Lieven for first alerting me to the fascinating interconnections between politics, policing, security and empire. To my wife-to-be Mickey, thanks and love for her support, companionship and lemon tea.

MAPS AND TABLES

PART ONE

THE CHALLENGES OF RUSSIAN SECURITY

Part two

THE CHALLENGES TO RUSSIA'S
sovereignty

1 RUSSIA'S SECURITY DILEMMAS

I cannot forecast to you the action of Russia. It is a riddle wrapped in a mystery inside an enigma; but perhaps there is a key. That key is Russian national interest.

Winston Churchill, 1939

'National security' is a complex and intangible concept. It means a lot more than just the security of a nation's borders – military security. It necessarily incorporates safeguarding a country's vital economic interests – economic security. Yet already, the question arises of where to draw the line? To the imperial leaders of Britain and France, attempts by China to keep out cheap Indian opium represented a threat to their economic interests and thus reason enough to send in the gunboats and fight the 1839–42 and 1856–68 Opium Wars, to keep China addicted. Beyond that, there is internal security, the maintenance of the status quo and thus, by extension, the rule of the dominant class, system or group. Hence, security is an intrinsically political issue, in which the general and the private, like the policeman, the secret agent and the diplomat all play their role:

Nowadays it is impossible to ensure security merely by improving one's sword and shield.

Chief of the General Staff Akhromeev, 1987

Russia's concept of its security – what it entails, from whom it needs to be guaranteed and how this best is done – has been and still is dominated by three challenges: its geography, its history and its empire. Together, they go some way towards explaining those characteristics the USSR shared and Russia shares with other nations, and those features which are much more distinctively Russian. After all, one can draw all sorts of comparisons. The USA is another frontier state – both were born from expansion across

3

largely virgin territory – and like Russia has a strong tradition of patriotism and a sense of historical mission. To understand the differences between the two one must look at the extraordinary problems the Russian state has had to face, and the strategies she has adopted across the years and centuries.

THE CHALLENGE OF GEOGRAPHY

Geography is probably the single most important factor in determining a nation's concept of war.

Chris Donnelly, *Red Banner* (Coulsdon: Jane's, 1988)

Even a cursory glance at a map reveals the problems facing Russia. For a start, consider the size of this nation, whether the Tsarist empire, USSR or post-Soviet Russia. The USSR was the largest nation in the world, spanning eleven time zones – almost half the circumference of the globe – and larger than the USA and China put together. With that size came great strategic vulnerability and difficulties of rule. How could the USSR secure a border 67,000 km in length? How do you centrally control such a huge nation, over twenty-two million square kilometres in size for the USSR, seventeen million square kilometres for Russia?

The answer, in short, is that you do not. Even modern communications technology failed to tighten the centre's grip on the country to the extent it desired. The USSR was just too huge and varied a nation for centralisation to be anything more than a crude instrument. It spanned the baking Islamic republics of Central Asia and the ice-locked northern ports of Archangel and Murmansk, the advanced and disaffected Baltic states (incorporated by conquest in the Second World War) and the traditional *Rus* heartlands; as the sun set on Kamchatka, it was rising over Moscow, 6,700 km to the West. As the archives are opened, it becomes clear just how far even the excesses of Stalinism could not impose unitary control over this nation. Instead, the state has always had to rely upon two basic strategies: delegation and deterrence. Delegation in the sense that local élites and administrators had to be relied upon for much day-to-day governance of the country, deterrence in maintaining a suitable apparatus to monitor their execution of the orders of the centre and exact a terrible penalty when transgressors are uncovered.

Thus, the tsars had to put their faith in the aristocrats and provincial governors, and while elaborately codified laws could be and were drawn up, their application out in the localities was often haphazard. Instead, the tsars relied upon their spiritual and mystical role as monarchs by divine right to bind the country together, while creating a variety of political police forces, from Ivan the Terrible's black-cloaked *Oprichniki* to the cavalier-investigators of the Third Section, whose symbol was a handkerchief 'to wipe away the tears of Russia'. In the Soviet era, it was the local Party committees which increasingly came to dominate politics, especially in the Brezhnev era of the 1960s and 1970s, while the KGB provided the deterrent arm of the state.

Not only is Russia large, it has been isolated from the cradles of civilisation. It has been bypassed by the great world trade routes and the importance, wealth and cultural influences they brought. Within its bounds it is distinguished by poor soils and an inclement climate: less than a third of the USSR's area could be farmed, and of that only about a third was decent arable land. The result is that the farming season is short and poor harvests regular. No wonder Russians refer to life as *bor'ba*, 'struggle'. One result is to ensure that, for all its natural resources, Russia has been poor. The industrial revolutions of Europe were sparked by improving productivity in the farms, producing surpluses to support growing urban populations, trade and investment. Yet while agrarian productivity in Britain grew by anything from four to six times between the fifteenth and nineteenth centuries, in the same period, Russia's stayed the same.

Economic backwardness meant military vulnerability. Most of Russia's borders were not 'natural' in that they were not marked by seas, lakes, rivers, swamps, mountains or similarly convenient obstacles. Instead, the borders were open to any invader. From the east came the Huns, Avars and Khazars, the Mongols in the thirteenth century and the Chinese in the eighteenth. From the West came Teutonic Knights in the thirteenth century, Lithuanians in the fourteenth, Poles and Swedes in the seventeenth, Napoleon in the nineteenth, the Kaiser and then Hitler in the twentieth. They were also to prove all too permeable the other way, open to serfs fleeing their masters or stubborn Cossack raider-traders, eager to find new sources of wealth far from tsarist tax-collectors. In the twentieth century, barbed wire, helicopters and radios helped close the border to much incidental traffic, but Soviet military planners were to have to face the headache of devising a strategy which could cope with their nightmare scenario: war at once in Europe and in Asia. What is more, they were being asked to cope without having to rely on 'defence in depth', retreating across Russia's vast plains until the enemy's supply lines become over-extended – as had happened to Nazis and Napoleon alike. In both those cases the wars had eventually been won, but at terrible cost in terms of deaths and devastation.

THE CHALLENGE OF HISTORY

One feature of the history of Old Russia was the continual beatings she suffered for falling behind, for her backwardness. She was beaten by the Mongol khans, she was beaten by the Turkish beys, she was beaten by the Swedish feudal lords, she was beaten by the Polish and Lithuanian gentry, she was beaten by the British and French capitalists, she was beaten by the Japanese barons. All beat her for her backwardness: for military backwardness, for cultural backwardness, for political backwardness, for industrial backwardness, for agrarian backwardness.

Stalin, 1931

The result is that Russian history has been dominated by the theme of invasion. Indeed, the very notion of 'Russia' is usually taken to have begun with invasion, with the Varangian (Viking) traders and adventurers who took over much of European Russia and established themselves as overlords over the scattered slav tribes of the region by the end of the tenth century. Then, in the winter of 1236–37, the first Mongol outriders appeared, harbingers of four years of fast, merciless conquest and ushering in an era which still casts its shadow over Russia. The capital, Kiev, was burnt to the ground, and while news of the death of their Great Khan stopped the Mongols from carrying on into Western Europe, most of Russia was left at the mercy of the Mongol Empire, the Golden Horde.

The Mongols wanted tribute and manpower and thus set up puppet states to exact these for them and keep the country quiet on pain of retribution. When, for example, the citizens of Tver rose against their occupiers in 1327, the city was sacked, its prince forced to flee into exile and its great rival, Moscow, granted control over its lands. Thus, even the Mongols found themselves relying on delegation and deterrence. Russian princes held their thrones for so long as they were willing quislings, and so the ruthless, the able and the opportunistic prospered for more than two centuries in which Russia was effectively cut off from the rest of Europe. Eventually the Mongols, already in decline, were to be expelled and Russia united, but it was to be by the Muscovites, arguably the greatest quislings of them all. Nevertheless, the period of the 'Mongol Yoke' was to leave a lasting impression on Russian culture. To be vulnerable was to be prey, and defeat meant not a mannered peace treaty and the loss of some lands or dues, but the total subjugation of the nation to an alien power. It was to be a lesson reinforced time and time again, and a lesson alien to nations such as the USA and Great Britain fortunate not to have suffered invasion for centuries.

THE CHALLENGE OF EMPIRE

A third key issue is the relationship between external security and internal order, arguably at the heart of the events of the 1980s and early 1990s. The relationship between the two have been graphically shown in Russia's history. How to guarantee security given Russia's backwardness and vulnerable position? From poverty and insecurity came a common pattern of Russian history. Its rulers felt threatened from outside, by richer, more advanced neighbours along Russia's long, indefensible borders. At the same time, this was a large, hungry and unruly country. How could one ever reform it without chaos and turmoil? Thus was born a great conservatism driven by the feeling, better the devil you know, better not take chances with change, since that could sweep everything away. Russia's history is one of a single cycle dictated by this dilemma. An external danger finally convinces Russia's rulers that the dangers in reform are outweighed by the dangers in not reforming. Yet change is never an easy or a comfortable venture, and resistance soon ensures that any changes are but superficial, as timidly brutal conservatism reasserts itself, with nothing done to tackle the underlying causes of Russia's problems. Thus it was with the tsars, thus with the kommissars.

It took defeat in the Crimea in 1853–56, where modern British rifles outranged old Russian cannon and where, lacking steamships, Russia's Black Sea Fleet was fit for nothing except being scuttled to block Sevastopol harbour, to prove that economic backwardness meant technological and thus military weakness. This led to Alexander II's Emancipation of the serfs in 1861. The peasants were given their freedom, the right to own land, but this bid to reform the very basis of society was critically undermined from the start. The class of bureaucrat-aristocrats who ran the country would not stand for the destruction of their wealth and power, and kept the best land, while forcing the peasants to pay exorbitant prices for the rest. When 'Tsar-Liberator' Alexander II was assassinated, the pendulum swung back to conservatism and repression until defeat at the hands of the Japanese in 1904–05 once again brought reform on to the agenda. After a brief flirtation with constitutional monarchy and social reform, conservatism again triumphed, until the First World War brought hunger, outrage and ultimately revolution. Of course, the converse is also true. Even if it eventually 'lost' the Cold War, success in the Civil War of 1918–21 consolidated the Bolshevik regime's hold on power, while it was victory in the Great Patriotic War of 1941–45 which gave Stalin and the Party a legitimacy it had never previously enjoyed.

This is especially important in the light of the fact that the USSR and Russia's old and new were and are all multiethnic land empires, patchworks of nationalities and communities. Even in areas populated predominantly by ethnic Russians, the size of the country and the difficulties of ruling and tying it together all contributed to localism; in non-Russian regions such as Tatarstan and the North Caucasus this merely reinforces the tensions inherent in imperial rule. The USSR was the most striking, with over a hundred different 'nationalities' within this notionally federal state, from the 145 million Russians (50.8 per cent of the total) through the seventeen million Uzbeks (5.8 per cent) down to the 1,100 Yukaghir (0.00038 per cent). The USSR was divided into fifteen 'Soviet Socialist Republics' and a variety of Autonomous Regions, yet for all its notionally federal nature, Russia was the senior republic and the leadership predominantly Russian, or at least slav.

The ethnic topography of Russia reflects the way it grew and the very lack of clear boundaries discussed earlier. From the slavic heartlands of the *Rus*, its rulers pushed westwards towards Europe through conquest, slowly rolled over the indigenous peoples and khanates of the south and expanded largely unchecked into Siberia in the search for gold and 'black gold' – animal furs. In the eighteenth century, Russia even laid claim to Alaska until it sold the territory to the United States for less than $8 million.

From a security point of view, this creates three main problems.

Table 1: Soviet Nationalities

Ethnic group	Nationality	Population	%of whole	Own region
Slav	Russian	145,155,000	50.8	Russian Republic
	Ukrainian	44,186,000	15.5	Ukraine
	Belorussian	10,036,000	3.5	Belorussia
Central Asian	Uzbek	16,698,000	5.8	Uzbekistan
	Kazakh	8,136,000	2.8	Kazakhstan
	Tajik	4,215,000	1.5	Tajikistan
	Turkman	2,729,000	1.0	Turkestan
	Kirghiz	2,529,000	0.9	Kirghizia
Caucasian	Azeri	6,770,000	2.4	Azerbaijan
	Armenian	4,623,000	1.6	Armenia
	Georgian	3,981,000	1.4	Georgia
Balt	Lithuanian	3,067,000	1.1	Lithuania
	Lett	1,459,000	0.5	Latvia
	Estonian	1,027,000	0.4	Estonia
Other	Moldavian	3,352,000	1.2	Moldavia
	Jewish	1,378,000	0.5	Jewish Autonomous Region
	Other	26,402,000	9.2	

Figures from 1989 census: total population 285,743,000

Firstly, the rulers of the centre must always be especially wary of the loyalties of their subjects, and their ability to control, even understand peoples of different languages, cultures and even religions from themselves. This has numerous military implications, ranging from the need to maintain garrison forces across the empire to the problem of guaranteeing the loyalty of an army which, thanks to conscription, will be drawn also from subject peoples. While there was little evidence that non-slav soldiers were less likely to be obedient (on the whole, for example, Tajik soldiers had few qualms about fighting their ethnic cousins in Afghanistan), this was a particular concern for the late Soviet state. After all, diminishing slav birth rates and a steadily growing Central Asian population was opening up the prospect of a predominantly Asian army by the year 2000. The third and, in the long-term, most serious issue, though, is that the political boundaries rarely reflected ethnic populations. In part this was as a result of a deliberate policy of mixing nationalities such that there would always be local populations of Russians and slavs on whom the centre could rely. Stalin, in particular, was an enthusiast of such ethnic reshuffles, forcibly deporting whole populations such as the Tartars and Volga Germans because he felt they were a security risk. The danger is that this has created unstable states which may be unable to survive the collapse of the Soviet Union. As will be discussed later, even post-Soviet Russia is an amalgam of nations, and within a year of the end of the USSR was facing demands for autonomy or even independence from some of its constituent regions.

POWER AND TRADITION

> *The tsar of all the Russias is an autocratic and unlimited monarch. God himself commands that his supreme power be obeyed, out of conscience as well as fear.*

Article 1, *Fundamental Laws of the Empire*, 1892

> *The leading and guiding force of Soviet society and the nucleus of its political system, of all state organisations and public organisations, is the Communist Party of the Soviet Union.*

Article 6, *Constitution (Fundamental Law) of the USSR*, 1977

By concentrating first on such imponderables as geography and history, it becomes clear that tradition is as important as anything else in understanding power and decision-making within the Soviet Union and, to an extent, post-Soviet Russia. The Tsarist regime had, after all, been the last of the European divine right monarchies. The Tsar was God's personal representative, and his authority over Russia as much spiritual as temporal. He had absolute power, in theory, but in practice the exercise of this power was constrained by his (or, occasionally, her) relationship with the aristocracy, which combined within itself army high command, ownership of the land, dominance over the civil service and local government. The nobility depended upon the Tsar: it was his religious and cultural authority which legitimised their rule over their serfs and peasants and his army which protected them from their serfs. Yet the Tsar was just one man, and depended upon the aristocracy for all his information. He needed them to execute his wishes and had been raised with and among them; naturally he would side with them rather than the huddled 'dark masses' of rural Russia. At times, strong Tsars tried to tighten their grip upon the nobility, but ultimately to little avail.

Peter the Great's Table of Ranks of 1622 made civil servants of them all, in the hope that this would force them to serve the state more assiduously, but weaker successors allowed the nobility to turn this around and instead it became a guarantee of their predominance within the bureaucracy. In the first half of the nineteenth century, the military-minded Tsar Nicholas I sought to break the power of the aristocracy by expanding His Majesty's Own Chancellery – which reported directly to him – and putting more responsibilities upon a handful of trusted allies (to a surprising extent Baltic German aristocrats, seen as free of the corruption of their Russian counterparts) and his secret police, the Third Section. The Tsar could never, however, free himself from dependence upon his aristocracy and, in most cases, was not willing to strike at the very heart of their power: their land. As a result, then, in practical terms, power in late Imperial Russia was vested not so much in the person of the Tsar as in the relationships between different key figures, aristocratic families and, especially, bureaucratic structures, a pattern to outlive the empire.

An elected leader may have great powers, but is ultimately responsible to the electorate and the law. Russia's rulers were limited only by what they could get away with. Revolutions can change leaderships, even the whole composition of élites, but they rarely change political cultures, those shadowy traditions and understandings which define peoples' relationships with power and each other. The Bolsheviks' utopian dreams and radical ideologies were soon subverted and corrupted by deeper, characteristically Russian attitudes, prejudices and approaches. After all, the French Revolution was followed by Napoleon and the regicides of the English Civil War eventually restored the monarchy. Rapid change inevitably brings crisis and turmoil, and in these conditions social reflex brings back the old patterns of behaviour. Comfort is sought in the familiar and the leaders who rise are those able to tap into the deeper, often unconscious habits, beliefs and traditions of their people. Change is frightening.

The Old Bolsheviks, intellectuals, educated, often at home in the capitals of Western Europe, brought a vast array of new and avant-garde ideas with them: equal rights for women, radical art, 'God-Building' philosophy, the denunciation of marriage and religion, an army without hierarchical ranks. Yet from the brutal savagery of the 1918–21 Civil War which followed the 1917 'Great October Revolution', a new generation arose. Drawn from the

11

unions, the gutters and the villages, they were largely unskilled, illiterate, ill-educated. But they were men of harsh and reliable pragmatism, the sort who would get the job done regardless of costs, careless of scruples, and whose notion of Communism was a brutal parody, little more than just cutting down the rich and seizing their money. They were also men more in tune with Russian political culture than the Old Bolsheviks, who could take Marxism and remake the Orthodox faith out of it, take Leninism and reshape it into a new tsarist order. And these were Stalin's men, the generation that was ultimately to lift him to power and betray Lenin with their adulation, turning the firebrand of revolution into what to all intents and purposes was Soviet Russia's first saint. Mother Russia knew how to have the last laugh.

Put briefly, there would seem to be five key features to Russia's distinctive political culture:

1 it is strongly *authoritarian and absolutist*, with no formal limitations on the power of a ruler;
2 his (or her) authority is also *mystical*, backed by a spiritual mandate (whether God or Marxism–Leninism) which makes any dissent heresy;
3 at the same time the state is characterised by a yawning and near-unbridgeable *gap between the rulers and the ruled*, whether French-speaking aristocrats or the Party bureaucrats in their well-policed housing blocks and summer villas;
4 the people, poor, scattered, hungry, have to work together to survive, leading to *communal* social organisation;
5 and an essentially *passive and fatalistic* set of mind.

Of course, Stalin was more than just a 'Red Tsar', although parallels can always be drawn with the bloody and tyrannical Ivan the Terrible, who personally led the sack of Novgorod in 1570 in which tens of thousands were killed and the city's archbishop sewn up in a bearskin and hunted by the tsar's hounds. Nevertheless, with his passing in 1953, old Russia reasserted itself with a vengeance. When Stalin's eventual successor, Khrushchev, tried to rule in opposition to the élite, the new Soviet aristocracy, he was ousted, 'retiring on the grounds of ill health' in 1964. In Brezhnev, Khrushchev's successor as General Secretary of the Communist Party of the Soviet Union, the élite found itself a leader who was prepared to govern in its interests, to reign rather than to rule.

POWER AND THE PARTY

The Party and state apparatus represents the one and only political force in the whole country . . . . We see before our eyes what really makes up the ruling class in our society.

Dissident *Leningrad Programme*, 1970

Power in Brezhnev's USSR was vested in the Communist Party of the Soviet Union (CPSU), which had its own complex hierarchy of decision-making and executive bodies. The 'government', from the central All-Union ministries down to local councils existed largely to translate the broad policies established by the Party into specific action and apply it. Attempts have been made to explain the organisation of power within the Party by various models, from corporatism (rule by representatives of economic power blocs) through to totalitarianism (absolute rule by a rigidly hierarchical movement), but perhaps the best model is feudalism. The basis of feudalism, after all, is a social pyramid of lords and commoners, each in turn owed allegiance by his vassals below and owing obedience to his master above, bound by mutual obligations and deals. So too did Soviet government rest on networks of patrons and clients. Although the President was notionally head of state, in practice this simply meant that he spent a lot of time greeting visiting dignitaries at Moscow airport and carrying out similar honorific duties. Instead, it was the General Secretary of the Party who held the highest post in the land, yet he had nothing like the power of Lenin, Stalin, even Khrushchev. When the Soviet élite united to oust Khrushchev, it was determined not to let any other single figure have so much power again, and thus built all sorts of checks and balances into the political system. The General Secretary, for example, lost his absolute control over the all-important Cadres (personnel) Department of the Central Committee Secretariat (effectively, the Party's own civil service), and thus could not fire rivals and appoint clients with impunity.

Arguably, real power in the pre-Gorbachev era rested in the Politburo and the Defence Council. The latter was a much more specific body, the successor of Lenin's Council of Labour and Defence and Stalin's State Defence Committee. Chaired by the General Secretary, it comprised the key figures from the Politburo with security-related responsibilities, such as the Ministers of Defence and Foreign Affairs and the chairs of the Council of

Ministers and the KGB. Its role was essentially to act as an inner circle within which to decide broad security policy and the resources it required. The Politburo, on the other hand, was the 'cabinet' of the Party which brought together the key political leaders, the 'dukes' of the Soviet system. The Politburo was made up of 'full' or voting members and 'candidate' members who could speak in discussions but had no vote. The exact number of members, the proportion of full to candidate members and the roles of the grandees on the Politburo changed constantly throughout the Soviet era, reflecting the relative strength of different individuals and interests. By the later Soviet era an 'etiquette' had evolved whereby certain posts were generally represented, such as the Ministries of Defence, Interior and Foreign Affairs, the KGB, the key industrial ministries, the major republics (in particular the Ukraine) and the Party's Control Commission. Nevertheless, it is possible to observe shifts in power within the leadership by changes on the Politburo.

In April 1973, for example, three new full members joined the Politburo: KGB Chair Andropov, Foreign Minister Gromyko and Defence Minister Grechko. Different scholars have tried to place different interpretations on this watershed development, seeing it variously as proof of Brezhnev's ability to co-opt able men loyal to him rather than his rival of the moment Shelest (who was duly retired that same month), of the ascendancy of the military/security/ foreign policy alliance or of Brezhnev's mastery over that coalition. It is certainly clear that this does mark both the rise of these three related interests and their sometimes shaky but always formidable alliance. As will be discussed in Chapter 3, Brezhnev increasingly came to depend upon the KGB to hold the country together, the Foreign Ministry to keep his policy of detente alive as long as possible and the military to give him some reflected glory and legitimacy. When Brezhnev awarded himself the rank of Marshal in 1976, he was not just engaging in another of his tiresome and childish bouts of self-adulation, he was acknowledging the interests on which he had come to rely. According to one former aide to Brezhnev, from the mid-1970s the USSR came to be dominated by Andropov, Gromyko and Grechko's successor, Marshal Ustinov.

The General Secretary was, of course, a powerful figure. He still maintained control over the Secretariat – the Party's own civil service – and Brezhnev was increasingly to come to rely on this organisation. Yet in the Politburo he was the first among equals, the chairperson, whose role it was to establish some sort of consensus within this inner-élite. As a result, policy-making tended to show considerable continuity, but suffered from always being a compromise between different interests. This worked well when times were good, but meant that the Soviet leadership was hard-pressed to adjust to changing circumstances.

The Politburo met every week, and it was, in turn, notionally responsible to the Central Committee, a body which met at least once every six months and brought together a wide range of the senior members of the élite: generals, regional Party bosses, industrial managers, newspaper editors, Academicians. If the Politburo was made up of the people in Moscow who established policy, the Central Committee represented the people out in the country who would have to apply it. Generally speaking, the two worked in harmony: the Central Committee did, after all, officially elect the Politburo. When they differed, though, the Central Committee had the final say: Khrushchev, for example, was able to use his support in the Central Committee to foil an attempt to oust him from within the Politburo in 1957.

The 1970s was a decade marked by very low turnover in the upper echelons. Of the nineteen members elected in 1966, the first new Politburo of the Brezhnev era, twelve were still there in 1980. By 1981, the youngest member of the Politburo was fifty – and the average age sixty-eight years. Over time, the formal structures of power became subverted, and politics came increasingly to rely on informal channels, cosy and unminuted chats over vodka, *ad hoc* groups of grandees gathering as and when they felt it necessary. Even the Politburo meetings were characteristically prefaced by unminuted discussions between the full members in the Kremlin's Walnut Room before the General Secretary arrived. The candidate members would have to wait patiently in another antechamber while the *vlasti*, the 'mighty', struck their deals and aired their views. The actual Politburo meetings which followed could then be as short as fifteen or twenty minutes, the important business of the day having already been sewn up and needing nothing more than a symbolic blessing.

A perfect example is to be found in decision-making over Afghanistan. Here policy ended up being decided by a group of men forming round the Politburo Commission on Afghanistan. Chaired by Foreign Minister Gromyko, it included the head of the KGB, Andropov and Defence Minister Ustinov. General Ogarkov (Chief of the General Staff), First Deputy Foreign Minister Kornienko and three civil servants were also brought in, while Brezhnev and Mikhail Suslov, the Secretary for Ideology, also involved themselves in discussions. Ten men, most of whom had no knowledge of foreign policy or Afghanistan, ended up formulating policy all but on the spur of the moment. As the over-zealous pro-Soviet government in Afghanistan began to lose control over the country, several fact-finding missions were sent, of which all but one warned against military intervention.

Yet the Soviets did invade. The final decision was taken at a meeting in Brezhnev's office on 24 December 1979. All five men there were imbued with a gut conviction in the USSR's prerogatives as a superpower, as well as no little racism. Suslov was a zealot of the highest order; to him, were the Afghan government to fall, that would be a victory for world anti-Soviet forces. In this, Gromyko was prepared to support him. Brezhnev, already near-senile and aware of the whispering campaign against him, wanted to appear strong and resolute. Ustinov was supremely confident of the ability of his gleaming military machine to win a quick, neat victory. Andropov was unconvinced, but he was aiming to replace Brezhnev and could not be seen to be weak. As with a preliminary decision in early December, nothing was put to paper. Ustinov simply picked up the telephone and ordered the USSR to war.

Of course, all political systems depend to some extent upon informal channels and structures. Indeed, such flexibility is essential for their smooth operation. Yet in the Soviet context it is worth noting the extent to which, paradoxically, informalism had been institutionalised. This was to prove very important, for two main reasons: it goes some way to explaining how power operated in the USSR, and thus how decisions were made; and it helps make clear just why Gorbachev, for all his control of the formal structures, never managed to overcome resistance from within the system. Significantly, at the time of writing, institutionalised informalism is still prevalent in post-Soviet Russia.

THE INTELLECTUAL FRAMEWORK

Under Communism, man lives from the cradle to the grave in a powerful 'magnetic field' of ideological influence. He is a particle in it receiving a particular 'charge', position and orientation.

Alexander Zinoviev, *The Reality of Communism*, (London: Paladin, 1985)

Marxism is based upon the notion that there are fundamental laws to human social and economic evolution. Humanity is heading inexorably (if not directly) towards socialism – the rule of the exploited working class – and ultimately communism, a class-less world of equality, without rulers, governments or even money. This preoccupation with understanding the underlying 'rules' of history led to the Soviets adopting a highly intellectual approach to much of their world, and certainly required them to develop some notion of a foreign policy 'doctrine'. It was almost as if they were seeking for the 'rules' of international relations, in the belief that if they were to define them, then they could win the game. This is something alien to most Western states, which will probably just have some general game-plan, a broad picture of the nation's enemies, allies and interests. The Soviets instead created something far more ambitious, trying to build some intellectual construct which would provide a basic logic on which all specific policies and decisions could be based. Of course, this doctrine was formulated by men who were at the same time Communists, politicians with their own interests and the heirs of centuries of Russian history. Doctrine reflected this confused and often antagonistic pedigree, but it is clear that the pragmatism of *realpolitik* was dominant, even if it was coyly draped in a red banner of Marxist internationalism.

According to their doctrine, in Soviet eyes the world was divided on the basis of class, between proletarian and bourgeois nations. Leaving aside the vexed question as to whether so élitist and exploitative a country could be called a 'workers' state', it is clear that this provided little more intellectual framework than a school playground notion of 'them and us'. Soviet clients and allies were, by definition, either proletarian socialist states or those of an 'intermediate stage', which typically meant still developing nations freed from (Western) imperial rule. To take the most extreme example, Khrushchev – never a man to let logic interfere with bombast – claimed that the very fact that so many nations in the 1960s had not become capitalist liberal democracies was a blow against world capitalism and thus, by definition, for world socialism. Thus a nation could even be a neo-fascist military dictatorship and still be a potential ally for the USSR.

In many ways this was a mirror-image of the USA's equally black and white (red and blue?) view of a world in need of defending against the spread of world communism. Both saw themselves as leaders not just of alliances of nations but of global political movements, both arrogated to themselves the duty of fighting a political crusade against the other, both would overlook many flaws in their allies, so long as they pledged themselves to the right side. In both Moscow and Washington, it was felt that their interests could not be reconciled in any long term way. Ultimately there would have to be a suitably cathartic showdown between the two. On the other hand, though, nuclear weapons meant that direct conflict was now all but suicidal. Conflicts could instead be projected into the rest of the world, fighting by proxy in the Middle East or Southern Africa or Latin America or Asia. Or else they could become contests of foreign aid generosity or sublimated into sport. One way or the other, though, the perception was that conflict was inevitable and yet had to be controlled.

There was though a key difference between the USA and USSR. A heritage of invasion, the instabilities caused by size, by being a multiethnic empire, by the upheavals of revolution and Stalinism, all these ensured that the primary concern of the Soviet leadership was to secure its state. Ever since the fall of Constantinople to Islam in 1453 left Russia as the 'Third Rome', the last bastion of 'true' – in other words, Orthodox – Christianity, then the survival of Russia has been an ideological and spiritual necessity. The Bolsheviks merely built upon this, substituting Marxism–Leninism for Orthodoxy. To secure the cradle of socialism, Lenin signed the humiliating treaty of Brest-Litovsk with the Germans in 1918. To secure his personal empire and give him time to rebuild his shattered army, Stalin signed a non-aggression pact with Hitler in 1939. Ideology and pragmatism dictated that the prime goal of Soviet foreign policy was survival, not the pursuit of world revolution or any such ideological will-o'-the-wisps. Trotsky's advocacy of the export of world revolution, even at the expense of Russia, had been one of the reasons behind his defeat at the hands of Stalin, while when Khrushchev's sincere but naive convictions brought the USSR to confrontation with the USA over Cuba, that convinced many within the élite that he had to be removed. Similarly, the USSR was more interested in supporting the nationalist Guomindang (Kuo Min Tang) in China than Mao's communists and was quite prepared to abandon the Greek communists in 1947 so long as it seemed in the interests of the Soviet state. The USA had always the comfortable option of isolationism; Russians have never felt that they can ignore the outside world.

THREE FEARS

It is thus important to appreciate the three great fears which have driven Russian and Soviet policy. Firstly, there is the fear of being invaded from without or, more subtly, encircled, confined and thus strangled. Secondly, there is the fear of internal unrest, always linked with the threat outside, in that enemies could sponsor insurrection or external defeats trigger problems at home. Thirdly, there is the fear that Russia will lose her standing in the world, her rightful position as one of the great nations. The role of foreign policy is thus to avert these dangers. Of course, to a greater or lesser degree this could be said about all nations, but in the case of Russia and the USSR, there was far less of a distinction between foreign, defence and domestic policy than in most Western nations. The notion that, for example, the Chairman of the Joint Chiefs of Staff, the head of the FBI and Chairman of the Federal Reserve should routinely have a major say in even relatively mundane foreign policy issues would not be expected in Washington, any more than that the Secretary of State should be expected to have a position on school curriculums. In Moscow, though, their Soviet counterparts saw it as an inevitable and positively necessary aspect of their daily struggle to secure the Motherland.

To protect her from external threat, Russian and Soviet foreign policy looked to the creation of buffer states and suitable alliances. Tsar Nicholas II, for example, placed his trust in the Triple Entente with Britain and France. Stalin laid the foundations of what would be the Warsaw Pact nations of Eastern Europe, while dealing first with Hitler and then the Allies. To maintain internal good order, though, foreign policy was always expected to be subordinated to domestic needs. One reason behind Russia's foolhardy preparedness to take on the Japanese in 1904, for instance, had been Interior Minister's Plehve's support for a 'nice, victorious little war' to pacify the masses. Yet most intangible, but nonetheless important, was the concern with preserving and enhancing Russia's image and status in the world. Perhaps this was understandable in the tsars' days, when Nicholas I could set himself up as the 'Gendarme of Europe' or Nicholas II as the protector of the slavic peoples in the Balkans, but their Soviet successors had no less exalted aspirations. With all the desperate ambition of the parvenu, the Soviets from Stalin's age onwards fought to establish their credentials as a great player in the international arena. In part this was simply because such recognition carried with it a sense of legitimacy, the implication that the West accepted the USSR's right to exist. But it was also very much Russian, the pride of an imperial nation somehow crossed with the desperate bluster of the penniless fraud.

Military policy is similarly dominated by these three issues: fear of invasion, fear of unrest and fear for national prestige. The first led to huge forces, which drained the economy of resources and were geared to fight simultaneous offensive wars in both Europe and Asia. The second manifested itself in the degree to which the state used the army as a means of socialising and disciplining its peoples and, ultimately, as a tool for internal suppression. To forestall the third fear, Soviet military power became the keystone of its claim to global superpower status, visible in the parades rumbling through Red Square or expressed through the Soviet military's traditional concentration upon *maskirovka*, a term which can be translated as an amalgam of 'camouflage' and 'deception'. The Soviets were constantly aware of the importance of putting on a strong front, even to using artists in the design stages of their warships to give them a powerful and predatory look.

The activities of the security agencies were similarly subtly different from those of their Western and historical counterparts as a result of this heavy emphasis placed upon their wider value to the state. The description of the KGB as the Committee of State Security, for example, did not carry with it the implication that its role was limited to policing at home, espionage and counter-espionage abroad. Instead, the Soviets adopted a philosophy much closer to those of the early nineteenth century, that security was simply the maintenance of public order and the furtherance of the interests of the state. It thus covered a far wider range of issues than the more limited concept of 'policing' – in other words, the prevention and punishment of criminality. This view is perhaps best summarised by one writer in the early nineteenth century, quoted in Hsi-Huey Liang's *The Rise of the Modern Police and the European State System from Metternich to the Second World War* (Cambridge: CUP, 1992): 'Police is not only the branch of state power responsible for preventing harm to the state, but furthermore that part which is charged with promoting the security and welfare of the subjects in every instance where other branches of power prove ineffective'.

THE DILEMMAS

Catherine II once said Russia is a universe in its own right. We have our own habits and ways, something peculiarly Russian.

Former Defence Minister Shaposhnikov, 1993

It is thus possible to develop an understanding of Russian and Soviet security policy built up over time, layer upon layer. The imperial heritage was one of insecurity, both internal and external. As a Eurasian nation, Russia had had periodically to defend itself from a variety of predators. These nations were often more advanced, and Russia had come to rely upon the size of its nation and manpower as a surrogate for modernity. Those same assets, though, also made ruling this country a difficult proposition, and as a result Russia's tsars had also come to rely upon a close integration of state bureaucracy, land-holding aristocracy, army and political police as its instrument of governance. Many of the experiences of the Soviet leadership went only to reinforce these lessons. The enmity of the capitalist nations ensured that Russian suspicions of the outside world were heightened into near-paranoia. The pressures of Stalinist social revolution and crash industrialisation created a police state far huger and more ruthless than anything built by the tsars, but built largely upon similar principles. How could it be otherwise when so many of those shaping the new Soviet institutions had either worked within their tsarist counterparts or knew no other model upon which to base their ideas?

The nuclear bomb, though, was to bring with it a genuine revolution in military thought. Massive armies could now be destroyed by a single warhead; whole nations could be wiped from the slate of history. Of course, nuclear strategists theorised about first-strike capability, whereby a surprise launch could eliminate an enemy's nuclear forces and thus forestall any retaliation or 'salami tactics', where an aggressor advances in small steps, each with seemingly limited goals and thus unlikely to trigger armageddon and yet, taken together, conclusive. For all this, though, full-scale war between nuclear powers became almost impossible to contemplate seriously. This had significant implications for all aspects of security policy.

A less dramatic change, though, was the increasing integration of the USSR into the global community. Tsarist Russia had traded, warred and allied with other nations, but always as a semi-detached partner, even if by the late nineteenth century she had become the focus for much foreign capital investment. Yet for the USSR, nuclear superpower status and its desperate quest for legitimacy and respect saw it engaging ever more fully into international affairs. Russia had maintained diplomatic relations with forty-seven nations as of 1914; by the Gorbachev era, the Soviets had reached a total of over 140, as well as a permanent seat on the United Nations Security Council and membership of a wide range of bodies and conventions, from the Universal Postal Union to the 1968 Nuclear Non-Proliferation Treaty. The expansion of the economy was reflected in the growth in both imports and exports, with foreign trade trebling between 1965 and 1978. With this the Soviets became – quietly – a major player in that quintessence of capitalism, the international commodities and money market. Foreign tourists came to see the sights and enrich the state treasury with their hard currency. Client states such as Cuba and Vietnam were provided with military and economic aid to maintain them within the Soviet camp. Newspapers routinely covered foreign stories – however partially – and Soviet citizens began to become used to seeing appropriate footage of strikes in Britain or race riots in the USA on their TV screens. Soviet sportsmen and sportswomen, chess grand masters, musicians and writers were groomed and paraded on the world stage for the greater glory of the Motherland.

Inevitably, then, the USSR could not divorce itself from the outside world, and her security policy had to take account of this. When Arab–Israeli tensions led to war in 1973 and then the Arab oil embargo, this had a direct impact on the USSR. It drove up the price of oil on the international markets from which the USSR, as the world's largest petroleum exporter, stood only to gain. The significant increase in state export revenue at this time did much to shore up the shaky finances of Brezhnev's Soviet Union. Yet oil prices were to tumble, from $53 per barrel in 1983 to $10–12 in 1985–86. This struck at the heart of the Kremlin's treasury, which lost twenty billion rubles annually. This, in turn, played its part in the bankruptcy of the state which, in turn, forced cuts in the foreign aid and defence budgets and led to increased disaffection in the country. 'Everything', Lenin had warned, 'connects with everything else.'

Put together, then, these two developments served to introduce a new edge to foreign and security policy. Nuclear weapons made all-out war less likely, yet at the same time opened up still further the indirect confrontations of proxy war and economic and cultural competition. It might, for example, be credible for Washington to threaten war over the siting of nuclear missiles in Cuba, but hardly over the presence of Cubans in Southern Africa, or, indeed, Soviet troops in Czechoslovakia or Afghanistan. The Motherland was thus safer than ever, but her defenders and supporters were faced with an ever more complex task in advancing her interests beyond that basic security of territorial boundaries. The USSR could not afford to opt out of the international rivalry inadequately titled the 'Cold War'. Events abroad now mattered more than ever before to Russia, and in many new ways. The era of 'peaceful coexistence' could as easily be characterised as one of frenetic competition. The traditional interrelationship between foreign, military and security policy was only emphasised. The Motherland's external security, its internal order and its global standing were and are not distinct. This helps explain the tone and urgency of the debates, and how security policy thus came to touch on so many other issues and play a critical role in the introduction of reform to the system, in attempts by conservatives to block and radicals to accelerate it, and in the collapse of the USSR.

2 THE SECURITY INTERESTS

Are we witnessing the emergence of a garrison state, a nation in arms, a modern Sparta in Marxist tunics?

Roman Kolkowicz, in R. Kolkowicz and A. Korbonski,
Soldiers, Peasants and Bureaucrats (London: Allen & Unwin,
1982)

It is perhaps easy to believe why, at first glance, so many were prepared to see the USSR as a militarised state, one ruled by the military interests and the needs and imperatives of a war-fighting policy. For a start, it was a land of uniforms. Brown-coated soldiers thronged the streets, while chests everywhere were bedecked with medals, from the Order of Heroine Mother to military-sports merit badges. Every olive drab civilian lorry had an *autokolomka* designation, proof that at any time it could be requisitioned for the military. Severe teenage Young Communists guarded war memorials clutching assault rifles. Yet this was to a large extent illusory: uniformity of dress did not reflect any uniformity of politics. After all, even in what may seem the most autocratic states, policy is a product of a process which will tend to involve a range of different interest groups and concerns. Tsarist foreign, domestic and military policy reflected the interplay of factions and characters within the bureaucratic élite. Some of the so-called 'revisionist historians' have even painted a convincing picture of the Stalin era as one in which decisions were taken as often as a result of the manoeuvres and machinations of rival alliances and interests as Stalin's dictatorial whim. In the Brezhnev era, though, such 'institutional pluralism' became the very basis of politics.

A wide range of agencies and interest groups played their part in formulating Soviet defence and foreign policy. Not least, this was the result of the USSR's twin-track government, divided between Party and state bodies. Formal responsibility for foreign relations, for example, lay with the Ministry of Foreign Relations (MID –

Ministerstvo inostrannykh del), and also with the relevant departments of the Central Committee Secretariat, the Party's own civil service. The relationship between the two was hazy, especially given that the former was for much of this time run by Andrei Gromyko, also one of the most prominent figures within the Party. Then there were other interest groups with a clear claim to a say in the process. The armed forces had come to exercise considerable power within the system, granted the right to have their views heard on a wide range of issues, from official propaganda through to industrial policy. The security services, and most notably the KGB could buy a voice and influence opinion with the information they provided on the outside world and, indeed, the state of the Union. The 'metal-eaters' (Khrushchev's phrase) of the military-industrial complex, the defence industries, disposed of huge budgets and dominated the Soviet economy.

Yet the Soviet élite was by no means as compartmentalised as this may suggest. Individuals would transfer from one agency to another, as up-and-coming Party hacks transferred from an industrial ministry to the Secretariat or as military officers were attached to the MID's arms negotiations unit. Besides, the movers and shakers of this élite, the *nomenklatura*, were members of a relatively small and self-consciously distinct ruling class, and they were also influenced by wider moods and bodies of opinion within this class. Journalists, academics, professional analysts: card-carrying Communists to a man (or, very occasionally, woman), mixed with the civil servants, talked to them, wrote the newspapers they read, dated and married them, offered them patronage and lived next door to them. By osmosis, the views of this informed constituency came to play a part within the formal decision-making context.

THE PARTY'S CIVIL SERVICE

The nerve centre of Soviet politics is the Secretariat of the Central Committee . . .

J. Löwenhardt, *The Soviet Politburo* (Edinburgh: Canongate, 1982)

The Central Committee Secretariat's International Department and Socialist Nations Department had perhaps the greatest say in defining the Party's overall view on foreign policy. In theory, their role was limited to nations of 'socialist' or 'progressive' orientation: 'progressive', in the Soviet lexicon, meant actually or potentially pro-Soviet. In practice, though, the International Department, in particular, was engaged in a constant battle to usurp the role of the Foreign Ministry, notably in Western Europe, where the presence of large Communist Parties (especially in Italy, France and Spain) provided a suitable pretext for involvement.

Until his replacement in 1986, the International Department was headed by Boris Ponomarev, under whom it acquired a reputation for stolid conservatism. The Socialist Nations Department, on the other hand, had been run by Yurii Andropov for the period 1957–67. The department was then still very much in its infancy, having been dramatically remodelled as a response to worsening relations with China and the Hungarian Uprising of 1956. The perceived need for new structures to manage relations with Moscow's East European clients led to the revival of the Council of Mutual Economic Assistance (CMEA. or Comecon), formed in 1949, and the evolution of the 1955 Warsaw Treaty Organisation (Warsaw Pact) to provide military control over the region and its armies. All this meant that the Socialist Nations Department grew and evolved at a rapid rate. Andropov had been Soviet ambassador to Hungary during the uprising and subsequent invasion by Warsaw Pact troops, but during his ten years in the Secretariat he showed himself to be flexible and innovative. Hungary was encouraged to develop an independent and even liberal variant on the Soviet pattern, so long as it accepted Moscow's overall control. It is indicative that the list of foreign policy experts who worked under or with Andropov at this time reads like a list of the intellectual parents of the 'New Political Thinking' of the 1980s: commentators Aleksandr Bovin and Fedor Burlatskii, academics Oleg Bogomolov and Georgii Arbatov, *apparatchiki* Georgii Shakhnazarov and Arkadii Volskii.

The Central Committee Secretariat's departments were forever in competition with the Foreign Ministry, but had the advantages of closer subordination to the General Secretary as well as the formidable support of Mikhail Suslov, Central Committee Secretary in charge of Ideology and arguably the second most powerful man in the USSR until his death in January 1982. Thus, so long as the secretariat was managing to dominate the broad direction of Soviet foreign policy, the Ministry for Foreign Relations was confined to an executive role, carrying out that policy. On the other hand, the growing political influence of Andrei Gromyko, Foreign Minister from 1959 until 1985, also brought with it a greater independence for the MID. From the late 1970s, with both Suslov and Brezhnev seriously ill, power began to shift from Old Square (site of the Central Committee Secretariat's offices) to the MID tower on Smolensk Square. Indeed, when Ponomarev was removed from the International Department in 1986, his replacement was Anatolii Dobrynin, a career diplomat and star of the MID, who had previously served as ambassador in Washington.

THE *INSTITUTCHIKI*

Affiliated to the civil servants of the MID, yet in many ways distinct from them was a whole sphere of professional analysts, whether academics or journalists working for the more heavyweight or foreign policy-oriented publications. They had had their place in the Brezhnevian system, but they were to come to particular prominence during the Gorbachev era, representing, as they did, rival sources of information and ideas to the established interest groups of the armed forces and the like. Part of the founding principles of the Brezhnevian order, after all, had been that decision-making would no longer flow from the dictatorial whim of a single man. This, for example, had led to the almost suicidal miscalculations over the Cuban Missile Crisis of 1962 under the wilful and tempestuous Nikita Khrushchev, when the world came closer to full nuclear war than ever before or since. Instead, decisions would be reached through logical, pluralistic, bureaucratic procedures, and involve the input of expert advice and consideration. In practice, of course, this rarely happened, as witness the case of Afghanistan discussed in the previous chapter. Nevertheless, the Brezhnev era did see the academics and institutes acquire if not an especially important role, certainly the resources to expand, the mandate to consider national policy and an increasing frustration at their inability to apply their expertise.

These academic scholars and analysts, the *institutchiki* (sometimes also called *mezhdunarodniki*, 'internationalists'), came predominantly from a complex of prestigious and high-profile establishments operating under the aegis of the Soviet Academy of Sciences. Many managed to carve themselves roles as quasi-government think tanks in the 1970s, but three were to become especially important in the debates and reforms of the 1970s:

1 the Institute of World Economics and International Relations (IMEMO – Institut mirovoi ekonomiky i mezhdunarodnykh otnoshenii)
2 the Institute of the Economics of the World Socialist System (IEMSS – Institut ekonomiki mirovoi sotsialisticheskoi sistemy);
3 the USA and Canada Institute (ISShAiK – Institut SShA i Kanady also known as ISKAN).

Oleg Bogomolov, director of IEMSS from the late 1960s, had been a consultant to Yurii Andropov during the latter's tenure in the Secretariat and retained his ear when Andropov moved on to head the KGB in 1967. It was Bogomolov and his team of analysts who, in January 1980, came up with the first comprehensive and critical assessment of the invasion of Afghanistan, and who went on to develop the thesis that if Marxism–Leninism was to be spread, it would be by force of example, by building a healthy and dynamic economy and society, and not by force of arms. This was a principle which Andropov would adopt in November 1982 when he came to power and which Gorbachev was to inherit. Bogomolov, incidentally, also became a leading figure within the group which drew up the economic reform programme which Gorbachev introduced in 1987.

Writing in David Lane's edited work *Elites and Political Power in the USSR* (Aldershot: Edward Elgar, 1988), Neil Malcolm has made the point that these academic foreign affairs specialists were often held in considerable suspicion, even contempt, by their official counterparts. Yet the importance of the *institutchiki* by the 1980s was that they were far more comfortable in the new political environment created by Gorbachev. They had been encouraged – within clear but generous limits – to speculate and think freely, they had been exposed to the Western notions that were increasingly to underpin Soviet international relations theory (many, indeed, were well-travelled in the West) and they represented a body of ambitious, energetic rivals to the existing specialists of the MID, the armed forces and the KGB. Previously, for example, all issues relating to nuclear disarmament had been the exclusive preserve of the military. Even the Foreign Ministry's appropriate department was staffed by army officers on secondment. Thus they held a monopoly on the arcane sciences of nuclear armament and disarmament. The presence of an alternative source of expertise to combat the wilful disinformation of the High Command, was at first vital to Gorbachev and his allies, yet was eventually to become a serious problem. As military support for reform waned, attempts to resist what was seen as the meddling of ignorant academics was to become increasingly overt. Besides, the *institutchiki* did not prove content to remain merely useful and obedient pawns of the reformers. Many involved themselves wholeheartedly in the democratisation of the USSR and developed their own political alliances and agendas.

THE ARMED FORCES

> *Soviet military doctrine possesses a purely defensive character and is directed towards ensuring the defence of the Socialist Homeland.*
>
> *Soviet Military Encyclopedia* (1982)

If the USSR was a superpower, then this was primarily on account of its military might, and the associated heavy, arms industries. Thanks to a defence budget worth perhaps 15 per cent of gross national product (about double the share of the USA's), the USSR disposed of the world's largest armed forces, with some five million men under arms. As if this were not enough, these forces represented the mere skeleton of the Soviet Union's full military machine: the rationale behind conscripting most young men into the armed services was to create a vast pool of reservists, perhaps fifty-five million, who in time of war could be called back into service, equipped with weapons retrieved from stockpiles and loaded into lorries sequestered from the civil economy and sent straight into battle. The conscripts may have been through a relatively basic training programme, and the reservists' skills would be quite rusty, but it was a cheap way of forming an army of the size Russian and Soviet memories of invasion demanded. Besides, by building the whole system round this approach, many of its seeming negatives could be, if not turned into pluses, at least neutralised. Conscripts would be poorer marksmen than professional soldiers – so they could be armed with the admirably cheap and reliable Kalashnikov range of assault rifles, essentially glorified submachine guns meant to be hosed in the direction of the enemy while the Soviet soldier charges. Numbers would seem, in the Soviet canon, to have been a perfectly suitable surrogate for quality. Indeed, in many ways the

29

armed forces represented the whole Soviet system in miniature: hierarchical, standardised and characterised by a mix of rigid discipline and ineradicable corruption and backsliding. If within the state the Politburo collected the *vlasti*, the powerful, and the Central Committee Secretariat informed and executed their decisions, then the Collegium of the Defence Ministry brought together the fifteen or so senior military figures, and the General Staff performed the functions of the Secretariat.

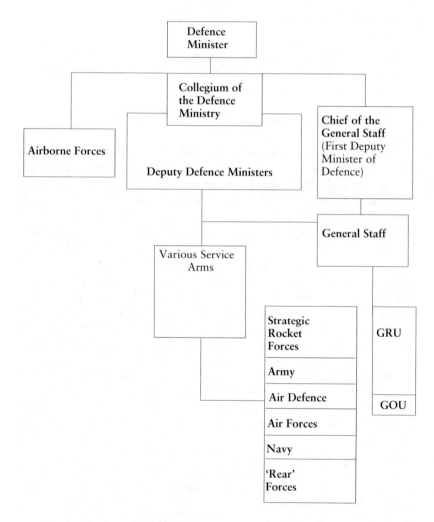

Figure 1: Military High Command

The Collegium, also called the USSR Main Military Council, was chaired by the Defence Minister and included a representative of the General Secretary as well as the Deputy Defence Ministers, who were in charge of a wide range of functions, from the Warsaw Pact Joint Forces through command of the Navy to responsibility for Logistics and Supplies. In war, this body would be replaced by a rather smaller Supreme High Command (SVGK – Stavka verkhovnogo glavnokomandovaniya, usually abbreviated to 'Stavka'). As for the General Staff, its role was to free the strategists – those commanders with the vision and responsibility to direct campaigns – from the nuts and bolts of modern war. In practice, it became an extremely powerful and important organisation, within which served many of the finest senior Soviet officers, and which also assumed responsibility for the acquisition and analysis of intelligence and the formulation of contingency plans. Overall, the Chief of the General Staff – who was automatically a First Deputy Defence Minister – was second only to the Minister. His Main Intelligence Directorate (GRU – Glavnoe razvedyvatelnoe upravlenie) was a formidable espionage and counter-espionage agency. With perhaps 5,000 headquarters staff and operatives and 100,000 officers in army commands, it had a string of successes to its name. It had been a GRU agent, Richard Sorge, who had uncovered not only the Nazi plans to invade the USSR in 1941 but also the Japanese preparations to attack Pearl Harbour. Through the GRU he also controlled 30,000 *Spetsnaz* ('Special Designation') troops, commando formations which included all-volunteer units comparable to the British SAS or US Special Forces.

Whereas the GRU was in many ways a rival to the KGB, the General Staff's Main Operations Directorate (GOU – Glavnoe operativnoe upravlenie) had no real counterpart. It was a military think tank which proved to be at the heart of many operations and military policy debates of the 1980s. An outstanding strategist, Deputy Chief of the General Staff Colonel General Valentin Varennikov headed the GOU at the time of the invasion of Afghanistan and planned the neat and effective seizure of the country in 1979. He then went on to exercise overall command of the war from 1985 until the equally well-organised withdrawal in 1989. That year he became Commander-in-Chief of the Ground Forces, a post he held until his involvement in the August Coup of 1991.

The structure of the Soviet armed forces was hierarchical, and organised by arm of service and by geographic region. The arms of

31

Figure 2: Map of Military Commands

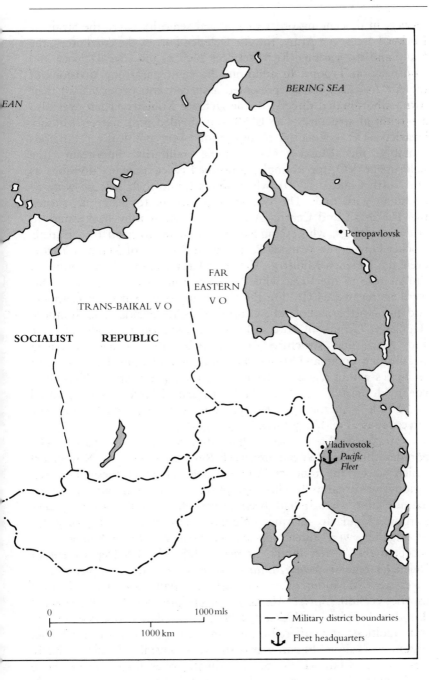

BERING SEA

EAN

Petropavlovsk

FAR
EASTERN
V O

TRANS-BAIKAL V O

SOCIALIST   REPUBLIC

Vladivostok
Pacific
Fleet

0   1000 mls
├─────────────────────────┤
0   1000 km

— — — Military district boundaries

⚓ Fleet headquarters

service, in descending order of political seniority, were the Strategic Rocket Forces, the Army, the Air Defence Forces, the Air Forces, the Navy and the various 'Rear' services such as the Civil Defence and Construction Troops. In addition, the eight paratroop divisions of the Air Assault Forces represented a special arm of service all their own, subordinated directly to the Defence Ministry. There was also a territorial structure. The USSR was divided into sixteen Military Districts (VO – Voennyi okrug). Some were politically prestigious (notably the Moscow VO), some militarily important (the Belorussian VO, for example, controlled twice as many divisions as the North Caucasus VO), while others found their role growing or declining with time. The war in Afghanistan, for example, turned the Turkestan and Central Asian VOs from shabby backwaters to critical postings, whose commanders went on to head the Strategic Rocket Forces, the Warsaw Pact and, in the case of Marshal Yazov, even the Defence Ministry. The four Fleet commands performed a similar role to the VOs, while Soviet contingents outside the USSR were aggregated as Groups: the Group of Soviet Forces in Germany and the Northern (Poland), Central (Czechoslovakia) and Southern (Hungary) Groups of Forces. To an extent, these were all defensive and peace-time structures. In wartime, the Soviets envisaged establishing command structures which would unite land, sea and air forces within regional Theatres of Military Activity (TVD – Teatr voennykh deistvii). In short, the Soviet armed forces were organised to be able – in theory – to fight any war, face attack from any direction, deal with any threat.

Of course, life is never that easy, not least in Russia. The parades through Red Square every Revolution Day (7 November) which so set the tone of Western assessments of these 'new red legions' were carefully choreographed, and carried out by picked 'parade units' which had been drilling for months for that very purpose. Similarly, alarmist Western assessments and glossy US propaganda were often appeals for greater defence budgets and accepted the 'Soviet threat' at face value. The US Department of Defence's regular *Soviet Military Power* series, for example, was so excessive that author Tom Gervasi eventually produced his own caustic version, *Soviet Military Power: annotated and corrected* (London: Sidgwick & Jackson, 1988). This military machine was far from faultless, and suffered from many of the problems of the Soviet system as a whole. Initiative was stifled as central control, originally seen as a vital means to coordinate operations across huge battlefields, became an end in itself. This was increasingly anachronistic in the fast-moving air-land battles of the late twentieth century. In Afghanistan, for example, soldiers trained to fight in large formations along carefully drilled and pre-programmed battle plans would find themselves involved in small-scale operations, cut off from their senior officers, unable to rely upon artillery barrages and air power. Until new training procedures were introduced, only élite units such as paratroopers and Spetsnaz had any real chance of fighting the war on the rebels' terms.

Along with institutional problems, the armed forces were plagued by the same collapse of discipline and social cohesion as civilian life. Conscripts and professional soldiers alike were prone to disaffection and boredom, many finding solace in drugs or, more often, the bottle. Soldiers would go to extraordinary extents to find alcohol, from draining and drinking the coolant fluids of radars to extracting the alcohol from boot polish. The MiG-25 fighter even acquired the nickname *gastronom*, 'delicatessen', since its large, nose-mounted radar required huge quantities of alcohol to cool, thus ensuring its pilots and ground crew an inexhaustible supply of moonshine. Another escape was in *dedovshchina*, a brutal code of bullying whereby new conscripts would be humiliated and exploited by longer-serving conscripts and duly humiliated the rookies when their time came. While estimates vary, whereas during the ten years of the Afghan war some 15,000 soldiers died, official statistics suggest that in the same period 62,700 soldiers died within the USSR, 75–80 per cent as a result of bullying.

CONTROLLING THE MILITARY

It is certainly not the case that the armed forces controlled the state, though. For one thing, the Party was well aware of this danger, thanks both to the lessons of Russian history (such as the abortive Kornilov putsch of 1917 or the Decemberist uprising of 1825) and Marx's warnings against 'Bonapartism', the supplantation of revolutionary power by a military dictatorship. Thus, there was a large array of agencies of political control, of which the most important were the Defence Ministry's Main Political Directorate (GlavPU – Glavnoe politicheskoe upravlenie) and the KGB's Third Directorate. GlavPU existed to fulfil two main roles: to ensure the Marxist–Leninist indoctrination of Soviet soldiers and maintain the primacy of the Party over the military. Despite its huge force of political officers, down to the *zampolity*, the political deputies attached to every unit of at least company size, the evidence suggests that it was not especially successful at either. The political commissars of the later Soviet era bore little resemblance to the hated zealots of Western Cold War fiction. Instead, they came to provide their commanders and units with a variety of necessary services, not least as hybrid chaplains and personnel officers, ministering to the lost and lonely conscripts and drunk, over-worked officers. Much of their time was involved in the day-to-day running of the units and teaching Russian to soldiers with an inadequate command of the language. Their political education classes were seen by their men rather fondly as a much-needed rest break, in which they could doze and relax before the next dose of drill or fatigues. More broadly, it is clear that GlavPU – headquartered in the same building as the Defence Ministry and staffed with career military officers – essentially saw its interests as lying with the military and, in short, 'went native'. When Brezhnev charged Marshal Ustinov with trying to persuade the armed forces to accept defence cuts in the late 1970s, for example, GlavPU chief Aleksei Epishev was outspoken in his efforts to defend the military budget rather than sell the Party line to the generals. The KGB's Third Directorate operated undercover 'special sections' (*osobye otdely*) of informants in military units. These *osobisty* were mistrusted by the professional soldiers, for obvious reasons, but it is hard to assess their true significance. The only time that they would have been of real importance, during the immediate preparations for the August Coup of 1991, the KGB was already in disarray, and thus any warnings from the special sections came to nought.

Yet the most important tool at the Party's disposal was not secret policing, but co-optation. Army officers were almost inevitably within the Party élite, and thus given a positive stake in the survival of the system. Some 90 per cent of officers were members of the CPSU, or its youth wing, the Komsomol, and the maverick 10 per cent were all university students serving short periods as junior officers as an alternative to conscription into the Other Ranks (privates and sergeants). The armed forces' incorporation into the political structure, from the local garrison commander sitting on the local Party committee all the way up to the presence of soldiers on the Politburo and Central Committee, signified not the dominance of the military but the extent to which it was just another element of the establishment. In 1981, of 470 members of the Central Committee, there were thirty-four seats for senior commanders within the Defence Ministry. As regards the Politburo, the Defence Minister was invariably a member. Marshal Grechko, Defence Minister from 1967 to 1976, became a full-voting member in 1973. His successor, Dmitrii Ustinov (1976–84) had previously headed the Central Committee Secretariat Defence Department, and did not even have to serve out any 'apprenticeship': he became a full member one month before his promotion, in obvious preparation. It was only with the rise of Gorbachev that the pattern was broken, and the Defence Minister could once again no longer expect a voting place on the Politburo.

Yet this did not show military predominance. Ustinov was a defence industrialist given a courtesy rank and promoted to the Defence Ministry as a response to the aggressively partisan politics of his predecessor, Marshal Grechko. A 'real' soldier, Grechko had resisted any reductions in the defence budget, whereas Ustinov already had a record of supporting detente and the rationalisation of arms spending. He was also given an outstanding soldier as his Chief of the General Staff, General Nikolai Ogarkov. A technical services officer, Ogarkov had a burning interest in modernising the forces and a very different outlook from the conservative tank and infantry officers who had previously dominated the high command. When he began to rock the boat with his demands for greater spending on new military technology, though, he was promptly removed to a less politically sensitive post and replaced by General Sergei Akhromeev. The military had neither veto nor casting vote. They were guaranteed but one seat on the Defence Council, and could not – as they tried – prevent the civilian leadership from signing the SALT I arms treaty and initialling SALT II. They could not prevent latest-generation combat equipment from being sent to client states in the Middle East, even though it was clear that this would expose it to capture and assessment by Israel and thus the USA. Unless it could muster political allies, it was clear that the military was a tool rather than a master.

THE SECURITY FORCES

The High Command did not even possess a monopoly of armed force. The Ministry of Internal Affairs controlled its Internal Troops (VV – Vnutrennye voiska). In theory this represented a huge force of perhaps 300,000 men, armed and trained primarily for internal security, but equipped with weapons and equipment up to and including tanks and light artillery. In practice, this force was rather less formidable, since most were actually employed as prison warders, site security guards and the like. Only about 36,000 were real 'soldiers', 'Operational Designation troops' (often abbreviated to Opnaz), the most significant unit being the MVD Dzerzhinskii Operational Designation Motor-Rifle Division, based in the outskirts of Moscow. Substantially larger than a regular army division, this unit was intended to secure the capital in times of crisis, even being equipped with its own fire engines and water cannon.

The KGB had its own uniformed services, of which the largest were the 230,000 Border Troops (PV – Pogranichnye voiska). Again, while on paper this force may look impressive, with its own ships, aircraft and light tanks, it was mainly strung out along the 67,000 km of the USSR's land and sea border. Nevertheless, the PV was a force with a certain tradition and *esprit de corps* of its own, and was, ironically, the only force which had been involved in overt hostilities between the end of the Second World War and intervention in Afghanistan (the Soviets tried not to count their interventions in Hungary in 1956 and Czechoslovakia in 1968), when they became involved in clashes along the Chinese border in 1969. Within the PV there were also certain commando-style élite units, which were also to be deployed into Afghanistan.

In addition, the KGB provided its most loyal, most effective (and, typically, most pure-bred Russian) soldiers to make up the Kremlin Guard force which protected the seat of Soviet power, certain other key government installations and 'Guard Post Number One' – Lenin's mausoleum. This was just the most prestigious element of the KGB's Special Objectives Guard (OOO – Okhrana osobykh ob"ektov), 150,000 men who protected important government centres, nuclear storage depots, KGB offices and similar critical locations across the country. Finally, the KGB also controlled a militarised but hardly military force, the Government Communications Troops (GVS – Gosudarstvennye voiska svyazi), who provided the state's secure communications lines. All told, then, by 1980, there were more than half a million uniformed paramilitaries, of whom more than half could genuinely be regarded as combat troops, albeit not fully equipped for 'high intensity' warfare.

THE SECURITY SERVICES

Sword and Shield of the Party

KGB motto

The USSR was often characterised as a police state, and certainly took a traditional Russian reliance upon coercion and censorship to an often horrifying and even counterproductive extreme. Lenin had established the *Cheka* as the Bolshevik state's first political police force, but the Stalinist order of the 1930s and 1940s had built on his *chekisty* to establish a structure which penetrated and often controlled all aspects of the state. As well as perhaps ten million dead in the prisons, slave labour camps or execution chambers of the NKVD, the system left a legacy of fear and suspicion which still endures today. After Stalin's death in 1953, the Soviet élite was unanimous in its desire to tame the secret police apparatus such that it could not be used against them, while maintaining a powerful organisation able to maintain its rule over the Soviet peoples and their newly acquired satellite states in Eastern Europe.

The first casualty was Lavrenti Beria, Stalin's final secret police chief. Despised as Stalin's bloodiest henchman, feared as the overlord of the NKVD, Beria appreciated how precarious was his position. He tried to launch a coup, yet he faced an élite united in its mistrust of him. The army prevented Beria's security forces reaching Moscow, and Beria himself was arrested in June 1953 and, fittingly enough, executed later that year. His death was a logical first step, but reducing the threat to the élite posed by the security forces involved more long-term change. The period 1953–54 was marked by a variety of organisational changes and political reforms intended to bring the security services more tightly under the control of the Party and the political élite while – and this was a crucial consideration – not weakening too much its ability to control the nation on the behalf of that élite. The bloated and all-powerful NKVD was dismembered, broken into smaller organisations with more clearly defined roles and the ability to watch and control each other. Ordinary policing became the responsibility of the Ministry of Internal Affairs (MVD – Ministerstvo vnutrennykh del) – called the Ministry for the Preservation of Public Order in the years 1962–68 – while the newly formed (March 1954) Committee of State Security (KGB – Komitet gosudarstvennoi bezopasnosti) incorporated the secret police and foreign espionage elements of the NKVD.

Chair of the Committee	
1967–82	Yuri Andropov
1982	Vitalii Fedorchuk
1982–88	Viktor Chebrikov
1988–91	Vladimir Kryuchkov
1991	Vadim Bakatin

Collegium of the KGB

(Chair, Deputy Chairs, Chiefs of certain departments, heads of local KGB organisations in one or two republics of the USSR)

First Chief Directorate	Foreign espionage
Second Chief Directorate	Counter-espionage
Third Chief Directorate	Military counter-intelligence/control of the armed forces
Fifth Chief Directorate	Controlling dissent within the USSR
Seventh Directorate	Surveillance of Soviet citizens and foreigners within the USSR
Eighth Chief Directorate	Government communications/intercepting and deciphering other nations' communications
Ninth ('Guards') Directorate	Protecting VIPs and government offices
Chief Directorate of Border Troops	Controls the PV (Border Troops)
Other, small directorates	Very specific tasks

Republican KGBs

Figure 3: Structure of the KGB

The relationship between these two organisations was never especially easy. The KGB regarded itself as a far more élite service, and looked down on its more prosaic cousin. The police officers and investigators of the MVD saw their better-paid KGB counterparts as interfering political busybodies. In his memoirs, *To Build a Castle* (New York: Viking, 1978), dissident Vladimir Bukovsky recalled that police officers would often refuse to punish political cases, not out of any sympathy for their views but simply to spite the KGB. It was also often a wider political issue. In the late 1970s and early 1980s, as Brezhnev became daily more frail and senile, KGB Chair Yurii Andropov launched an increasingly confident bid to establish himself as his successor. One weapon in Andropov's armoury was a campaign against the corruption which, during Brezhnev's reign in particular, had come to dominate the Soviet system and in which Brezhnev's friends and relatives were deeply involved. The 'Brezhnev clan' was especially strongly represented within the MVD: Nikolai Shchelokov, the minister, was a close friend, while his First Deputy, Yurii Churbanov, was Brezhnev's son-in-law. Under this self-indulgent and venal pair, the MVD had become a byword for corruption and inefficiency, as bribe-taking officials and simple criminals bought themselves immunity from the law. Shchelokov was even rumoured to have arranged the murder of Politburo member Petr Masherov when he insisted that (accurate) allegations of Brezhnev's daughter's involvement in a diamond-smuggling racket be investigated.

THE KGB AND REFORM

The Chekists [KGB officers] share the interests of all the Soviet people. And they have adopted perestroika as their own vital cause.

Viktor Chebrikov, head of the KGB, interviewed in *Pravda*, 1988

Thus, traditional rivalries between the MVD and the KGB combined with the personal enmities between the guardians of the interests of the 'Brezhnev clan' and the new political coalition Andropov was assembling. Besides, Andropov was a puritan and a zealot: he fought corruption not just to discredit his rivals, but because it offended his almost Victorian sensibilities. Above all, though, his position as the

Chair of the KGB meant that he had come to realise the dangers facing the USSR. Corruption was one of the greatest, for it was hindering attempts to modernise the economy, just as it was eating away at the Party's legitimacy. How could a Party, which preached its commitment to the workers and the evils of capitalist ruling classes, not become despised as those workers came to realise the extent to which they were being betrayed and exploited by a group of increasingly hereditary bureaucrats? In the early Brezhnev years, a combination of genuine economic reform and high export prices for Soviet gas and oil had meant that enough extra wealth was being produced for everyone. The generals could have their tanks and missiles, the Party élite their limousines and summer houses, while the ordinary Soviet citizen was bought off with the promise that life would become if not rapidly, at least steadily and reliably better. By the mid-1970s, though, this so-called 'little deal' between the state and its people had begun to break down. Oil prices fell, and with it the growth of the Soviet economy. Of all the major targets set for the 1975 Five Year Plan, not one was accomplished. This was the time for strong and vigorous leadership. Yet the various interest groups which ran the Soviet state refused to compromise, and sick, tired, lazy Brezhnev was not the man to force tough decisions upon them. So the state broke its deal with its people, and while it continued to spend on itself, failed to keep up with their expectations and needs.

Of all agencies, it was the KGB which became most keenly aware of these problems. After all, this was an organisation which had evolved substantially since Stalin's day. Andropov ran the KGB between 1967 and 1982, and in that time modernised it dramatically. From being an instrument of terror, it became a vital element within the overall structure of government and protector of the interests of the Soviet élite. Of course, it maintained the Party's political monopoly, whether ensuring the loyalty of the armed forces or dealing with dissidents and anti-Soviet nationalists. It was also the main agency involved in espionage and counter-espionage in the interests of Soviet national security. The First Chief Directorate deployed a network of perhaps a quarter of a million agents, while the Second and Fifth Main Directorates worked to defeat espionage and dissent at home, respectively. Espionage was geared not just towards state but also commercial secrets, and as Soviet technology fell increasingly behind that of the West and Japan, this became an ever-more important aspect to the KGB's work. Overall, the KGB provided what could crudely be described as a life-support system for a moribund state. Much like the armed forces, the KGB, as one of the few remaining effective and efficient organisations left in the country, began to be depended upon to fill a wide range of roles. KGB sources surveyed and analysed political, social and economic trends within the country to off-set the often inaccurate or mendacious data gathered by the State Planning agency. KGB officers fought the corruption and labour indiscipline that was strangling the Soviet economy.

As the USSR began to decay, the secret police and their Chair became, ironically, the champions of law, of progress, even of reform. Thus, when, on 10 November 1982, Brezhnev finally died – for the last time, given that he had been resuscitated after fatal heart attacks on at least two previous occasions – there was little real opposition to Andropov. Many members of the élite feared the reforms and the anti-corruption drive he would bring, but there was no credible rival and, above all, as will be discussed in the next chapter, no credible alternative platform. For Andropov stood for the perennial programme of the sophisticated conservative, to reform in order to preserve. Two days after Brezhnev's death, Andropov was appointed General Secretary of the Communist Party of the Soviet Union. He bequeathed his *chekisty* first to Fedorchuk, a hard-nosed KGB officer from the Ukraine. He, in turn, barely spent seven months in his new office before being transferred to the MVD to replace Shchelokov, removed from office and the Central Committee for 'mistakes' in his work. Shchelokov eventually committed suicide in December 1984, rather than face a public trial. Andropov did not confine himself to decapitation of the ministry: he launched a thoroughgoing purge of the corrupt and undisciplined militia and brought in 35,000 Young Communists and new recruits in a bid to clean up the MVD.

Within the KGB, Fedorchuk was succeeded by Viktor Chebrikov, a man who had worked under Andropov in Moscow for fifteen years. Chebrikov would be faced with the unenviable task of managing the KGB's own *perestroika*, to bring it in line with the demands of a new and rapidly changing USSR. The irony is that in the end the KGB bears much of the responsibility for the collapse of the Soviet Union it was pledged to defend. It supported the rise of Mikhail Gorbachev, but later thwarted his attempts at meaningful reform, and finally it brokered the 1991 coup which destroyed him and the USSR. Yet for all that, it has managed to survive armageddon. Admittedly, there were some high-profile sackings after the coup, and the KGB has been dismembered into notionally separate organisations. Yet the Foreign Intelligence Service is to all intents and purposes the old First Chief Directorate, and many of the other directorates comfortably subsumed themselves into the new Ministry of Security (in due course again renamed the Federal Counter-Intelligence Service). This ministry, after the brief reign of a reformer, in 1993 was to come under the control of Nikolai Golushko, a career political policeman from the Ukrainian KGB.

METAL-EATERS: THE MILITARY-INDUSTRIAL COMPLEX

A traditional view is that the Soviet Union did not have a military-industrial complex – it *was* one. In other words, an alliance of the industrial interests which supplied the military and their allies within the armed forces represented a political lobby which was both powerful and unified. It is easy to see how this conclusion could be drawn. The defence sector dominated the Soviet economy: military spending accounted for perhaps 15 per cent of GDP, while the defence industries not only could poach resources and talent from the rest of the economy (thanks to priority treatment in state orders and the ability to offer 20–25 per cent higher salaries), it even came to dominate many civil sectors of manufacture. Over six million Soviets worked directly for the defence industries, with another forty million jobs depending upon them. It produced not only some 10 per cent of all Soviet cars, but 60 per cent of motorcycles, half of all refrigerators and most televisions and video recorders. An aircraft plant even produced the most prized vacuum cleaner, the aptly-named *Raketa* ('rocket').

Writing again in David Lane's *Elites and Political Power in the USSR* (Aldershot: Edward Elgar, 1988), though, Julian Cooper has undermined any notion of monolithic unity. Overall control was exerted from the Security Council and through Gosplan, the State Planning Commission. Yet within the orbit of the Council of Minister's Military Industrial Commission (VPK – Voenno-promyshlennaya komissiya) came fully nine ministries with a primary military function, including the euphemistic Ministries of Medium and General Machine-Building, which built nuclear warheads and ballistic missiles, respectively. The Party's oversight was exercised through a senior Secretary of the Central Committee Secretariat and the Defence Industry Department.

In Brezhnev's years of institutional pluralism, the defence

industries were certainly stronger than the military. According to one study – William Ritter's 'Soviet defence conversion: the Votkinsk machine-building plant', *Problems of Communism* 40, 5 (1991) – the Nadiradze Design Bureau produced three unsuccessful missile designs in a row, but escaped any consequences thanks to the personal patronage of Defence Minister Ustinov, regardless of the complaints of the Strategic Rocket Forces. Yet this was a strength built largely upon two specific advantages, which would not survive into the 1980s. First of all, they held together in an alliance of convenience at a time when, for example, the various branches of the armed forces were more readily played off against each other. Even in the later 1970s, though, as defence spending began to be cut, then so too did the need to compete for funds begin to break down that alliance, as individual ministries had distinctive interests. Khrushchev, for example, had favoured a strategy built around nuclear weapons which, he felt, made conventional war obsolete, all of which was to the advantage of the missile lobby but little comfort to the ministries responsible for tanks and warships.

The defence industrialists enjoyed good informal contacts with the senior leadership. The VPK route had become an established way to the highest Party posts: Nikolai Ryzhkov, Prime Minister for the period 1985–91 had formerly been general director of the Uralmash plant, while Lev Zaikov, Moscow's Party boss during 1987–90, had been Central Committee Secretary for the Defence Industry from 1985. Perhaps most striking had been the rise of Dmitrii Ustinov to the Defence Ministry from his post as Central Committee Secretary in charge of Defence. In the late 1950s, Brezhnev had been Central Committee Secretary with responsibility for heavy and defence industry, and the contacts he secured then were to prove one of the vital factors behind to his rise to power in 1964. Brezhnev had a reputation for not forgetting his friends, notably Ustinov who, in turn, did not forgo his old allegiances when he donned the uniform of Defence Minister. L. V. Smirnov, Chair of the VPK throughout Brezhnev's time in office, had worked with Brezhnev when the latter had been Party first secretary in Dnepropetrovsk. Andrei Kirilenko, a senior member of the Politburo, who had even seemed a rival to Brezhnev in the mid-1970s, had risen from the aviation industry.

Yet Brezhnev's death was to bring an end to the ascendancy of his so-called 'Dnepropetrovsk mafia', and neither Ustinov nor Kirilenko would long survive him. Smirnov was succeeded by Yurii Maslyukov in 1985, and by 1987 almost all the senior positions within the complex had been filled by new men. With the exception of Ryzhkov, none of Gorbachev's inner team were to have any recent experience within the defence industries, and the decay of the Soviet economy was inevitably to mean further pressures upon this sector. Defence procurement had been falling since 1974, but without the protection of a Brezhnev or a Ustinov, the military industries were to face mounting criticism not just of their privileged position within the economy but also of the quality of their work. Even the military found itself newly empowered to denounce equipment it deemed inappropriate or sub-standard.

RED SPARTA?

Overall, then, it is clear that this seemingly regimented and rigidly hierarchical state was dominated by the interplay of a wide array of different groups and power blocs. The notion of, for example, the armed forces as a separate, autonomous entity divorced from active politics is something rooted more in Western theory than Soviet reality. In most Western systems, there is a distinct difference between the Defence Minister, the Defence Ministry and the armed forces. The minister is a politician, responsible to the electorate, there to take political decisions. The ministry is a civil service body, staffed by a mix of soldiers and civilians, and responsible for administering the military in accord with the minister's decisions. The soldiers are there to do the fighting and dying for their country and obey a chain of command which, until it reaches the very top, is internal to the forces. In the Soviet system, though, they could and generally would all be soldiers. The relationship of general to ministry to minister was thus much more simple, and the internal checks and balances present in the West simply did not exist. The military, the defence industries, the KGB – all were free to indulge in the usual Soviet practice of creating monopolies of skills or powers which could then be exploited for political gain. Hence, for example, Soviet military experts at arms reduction talks would often try to prevent their Western counterparts from talking freely with the civilians in the USSR's delegation, lest they find out too much about what their own military was up to! Yet this certainly did not mean any real dominance. Samuel Finer has identified a military establishment's three strengths as its organisation, its symbolic status and its monopoly of arms. In the USSR the Party had in many ways an equivalent organisation, and though the army had undoubted prestige (before Afghanistan), it had no absolute monopoly of arms.

Hence William Odom contended, in Dale Herspring and Ivan Volgyes' *Civil–Military Relations in Communist Systems* (Boulder, CO: Westview, 1978) that 'the military [was] an administrative arm of the Party, not something separate from and competing with it'. Officers were thus nothing more than bureaucrats and Party hacks in uniform who – like any large functional body, from the KGB to the Health Ministry – fought their corner, but firmly within a wider élite context. As often as not, after all, it was riven by internal competition as services and schools of opinion competed, picking up allies within and without the military. In the late 1970s, for example, the experiences of war in the Middle East sparked a debate on the continuing viability of the tank in the days of the guided missile. The infantry and helicopter forces were lobbying for an increasing share of funding at the expense of the tanks, the tankists for better tanks with more armour. Eventually the armoured lobby won, but only after both sides had lined up their allies within the defence industries, where opinion became equally polarised.

A corollary is to see the military's role in society in the same light. Its role was dictated by the Party leadership. Soldiers found themselves bringing in the harvest – over a million of them in 1983 – tending their own 'kitchen farms', building roads and, when all else failed, quelling public disorder. This was hardly the job for which most officers would have enlisted. Instead, it reflects the extent to which the military was incorporated into the overall structure of the state, far more so than in most Western nations. Russian and Soviet tradition had always been one in which the boundary between civil–military relations remained hazy. The tsarist centre had been based on the army as an institution of power, with the Russian 'service state' which effectively made all aristocrats subject to military discipline and servants of the state pre-dating Peter the Great's 'Table of Ranks' of 1622. The army was used by the tsars to administer the country, to help modernise its economy and to mould society; the Bolsheviks who succeeded them used it in the same way. There was also a very strong revolutionary tradition of close relations between army and Party. It had been for the Party that Trotsky had forged the Red Guard and then Red Army during the 1918–21 Russian Civil War, a relationship tempered during the 1941–45 Great Patriotic War, when the Party had to depend upon the army for its survival. The state even came to rely upon the military for much of its own legitimacy. By the later 1970s, victory in the Great Patriotic War and the prestige of superpower status were being played up in a bid to gloss over the growing inadequacies of the system. Brezhnev himself took to rewriting his wartime career and awarding himself ever more grossly undeserved titles and decorations in a vain attempt to transfer some of that lustre to himself. Much the same could be said of the role of the internal security agencies, notably the KGB. The whole concept of 'policing' retained its broadest sense, as not simply the enforcement of the law but the maintenance of 'good order' from whatever might threaten it, whether bank robbers or a shortage in the supply of soap, whether dissidents or noisy neighbours. Thus, the state relied upon its security agencies and, as members of the state élite, those who ran those agencies accepted their role.

The USSR was, thus, characterised not so much by a militarised society as a socialised military. Nor are Western concepts such as 'police state' especially useful, since they carry with them the implications that the security apparatus has come to dominate society and that this is an aberration, a transgression across clear boundaries. Instead, the USSR was run by a huge and entrenched bureaucracy with a common general aim – comfort, stability, survival, expansion – within which a very wide range of interests allied, competed, cooperated and interacted. It was very much an élite system, with debate conducted away from the public eye. Sometimes it was coded into seemingly arid articles in the newspapers, each of which had some institutional loyalty: *Pravda* ('Truth') for the Party, *Izvestiya* ('News') for the state bureaucracy, *Krasnaya zvezda* ('Red Star') for the military, *Trud* ('Work') for the trade unions, and so on. At other times it was simply carried out by private memo, across drinks in summer houses or behind the closed doors of Politburo sessions. Yet until the 1980s and the era of *perestroika* it was characterised by a common desire to present a united front to the outside world and the Soviet people alike and a set of common principles and interests. When that cohesion was lost to the Soviet élite, and the broad array of security-related groups in particular, the USSR was doomed.

PART TWO

'NEW THINKING' AND GORBACHEV'S USSR

3 SECURITY AND REFORM, 1979–85

1979	*December* Invasion of Afghanistan.
1980	*July* Strikes spread in Poland.
1981	*December* Martial law declared in Poland.
1982	*November* Brezhnev dies; Andropov elected to succeed him.
1983	*September* Korean Airlines KAL 007 shot down in Soviet airspace: 269 dead.
1984	*February* Andropov dies; Chernenko elected to succeed him.
	December Defence Minister Ustinov dies: Marshal Sokolov replaces him.
1985	*March* Chernenko dies; Gorbachev elected to succeed him.

Critics blame perestroika for everything, even the weakening of national security . . . . That is not true. Perestroika was brought to life by the objective need to overcome the crisis endangering national security and interests.

Eduard Shevardnadze (foreign minister 1985–90) *The Future Belongs to Freedom* (New York: The Free Press, 1991)

In 1976 Brezhnev suffered a stroke which left him clinically dead for several minutes. By the late 1970s it was clear that the vigorous young *Gensek* of 1964 was all but senile and not long to inspire the front pages of *Pravda*. Pressures for change which had been building up would soon be released and the battle to succeed Brezhnev became ever more overt; the greatest prize within the Soviet political system would soon be available for the victor. The power struggle which preceded Brezhnev's death in 1982 and culminated in the almost uncontested election of Yurii Andropov as his replacement that same day was to be dominated by both personal and factional power-politics and the perennial Russian debate: '*Chto delat?*' (What is to be Done?)

For the Soviet Union was at threat at home and abroad, such

that its very future as an integral state, let alone a global superpower, was being brought under question as the comfortable optimism of the 1970s all but disappeared. The dangers facing the Soviet leadership were perhaps most graphically illustrated by developments in two neighbouring client states: Poland and Afghanistan, the one a product of economic decay, the other a symptom of the new Cold War, and both proof positive of the extent to which nationalism could be forged into a weapon against Moscow.

THUNDER OVER THE BORDERS (1): POLAND

In 1970, Poland's Baltic ports were gripped by a wave of strikes which triggered a change of leadership and of policy. The incoming leader, Edward Gierek, gambled on borrowing heavily and importing Western technology. He hoped that this would pacify the workforce and create self-sustaining economic growth sufficient to repay the loans and provide funds for continued investment. In the short term, the initiative seemed a dramatic success. The first half of the 1970s saw the Polish economy grow more quickly than that of any other East European country, with GNP increasing at an annual rate of 6.6 per cent, compared with the regional average of 4.9 per cent. As a long-term policy, though, this was a disaster. Increased prosperity initially bought public quiescence, but at the cost of rising expectations. By the second half of the decade, the state could no longer afford to meet these expectations. Between 1975 and 1980, Poland's hard currency debt soared from $8 billion to $25 billion, while by 1976, food subsidies were absorbing fully 12 per cent of the country's GDP. The next ten years would see Poland's economy as consistently the slowest-growing in Eastern Europe.

This was serious enough, but it was the way in which economic decay bred a political challenge to the regime which most alarmed Moscow. In July 1980, increases in meat prices sparked protests, and 800,000 workers went on strike in Lublin. Agitation spread across the country, and 80,000 workers occupied Gdansk's Lenin Shipyard, demanding free trade unions and the right to strike. The Polish Party hurriedly moved to defuse the situation, purging its leadership of hard-line elements and offering a variety of concessions, which none the less fell short of the strikers' demands. Moscow ostensibly sat back, describing the situation as a 'completely internal affair', but at the same time it prepared its usual fall-back position. In September, Warsaw Pact forces held manoeuvres, and defence ministers met in Prague in October to discuss the situation, following a meeting between Brezhnev and the Polish leadership. In November, Warsaw Pact units began concentrating along Poland's borders. December 1980 saw the Polish/GDR border closed to Western journalists, as East German and Czech reservists were called up.

These heavy-handed military preparations represented both support for and a warning to the Polish leadership. They certainly strengthened the government's hand in negotiations. In December Solidarity was induced to call off a planned strike, after an editorial in the Soviet government newspaper *Izvestiya* warned that disruption to the railways linking the USSR with her forces in East Germany would represent a threat to her security interests, and the Czech paper *Rude Pravo* explicitly drew parallels with the 'Prague Spring' of 1968, which had triggered armed intervention. In the next few months, the pressure was increased, the regular Warsaw Pact *Soyuz-81* exercises clearly preparing forces and plans for intervention. Yet there was very little the Polish government could do in the light of its economic plight. The first meat rationing since the Second World War had had to be introduced in December 1980, with more extensive rationing in April 1981. The USA offered food aid worth $70 million, but the USSR could do nothing but rattle its numerous sabres. When Polish workers went on strike in 1970, the Soviets had been able to provide a sizeable hard-currency loan to subsidise food prices. By 1981, the Soviet coffers were too bare and Poland too deeply in debt for 'fraternal assistance' on a scale sufficient to buy off the Polish people.

After a year of inconclusive negotiation, threat and chaos, on 13 December 1981 Polish President General Jaruzelski declared martial law. At the time this seemed the action of a Kremlin puppet, yet in retrospect it is clear that Jaruzelski was to a considerable extent engaged in a desperate bid to square his loyalties as a communist and a Pole. The former required him to subdue Solidarity, the latter to forestall any potential Soviet military intervention. He went on to develop a complex if often *ad hoc* policy which saw army officers and military discipline employed in a desperate attempt to revive the economy, while a mix of coercion and conciliation sought to restore central control over the country. Prices were increased by 76 per cent in 1982 which, while helping stabilise the economy, led to a 25 per cent drop in average living standards. Yet at the same time the economy began going through a process of gradual and small-scale privatisation.

The reliability of the Warsaw Treaty Organisation (WTO) was being thus being called into question, as one of the most important nations within it seemed on the verge of collapse. The Warsaw Pact, established in 1955, formalised Soviet influence over Eastern Europe, providing a security counterpart to the economic coordination of the Council of Mutual Economic Assistance. The USSR's six WTO satellites – Bulgaria, Czechoslovakia, the GDR, Hungary, Poland and Romania – together could provide over three-quarters of a million active troops for the defence of the USSR, and hundreds of kilometres of additional strategic depth: were the Soviets to have to rely on time-honoured tactics of the scorched earth withdrawal, then they would do it on someone else's turf, this time. Even if Romania had already all but seceded from active membership of the Pact, by institutionalising effective Soviet control over WTO forces and basing Soviet forces in WTO nations, then Moscow's overlordship was seemingly secured. This 'buffer' acted as an ideological insulator between the Soviet people and the corruptingly prosperous West. The nations of Eastern Europe were also vital trading partners and, in addition, providing Moscow with the other trappings of great power status: an empire, extra seats and voices at the UN, more sportsmen and sportswomen with whom to trounce the West.

The USSR's Eastern European 'outer empire' was already under severe strain, though. Czechoslovakia, never wholly pacified since the 1968 invasion, saw the rise of dissident movements, notably the Charter 77 initiative. East Germany's 'economic miracle' had all but disappeared, and the country was increasingly dependent upon its special relationship with West Germany. A severe liquidity crisis in 1981–82 forced Hungary to petition for membership of the International Monetary Fund. Symptomatic was the response to the Soviet intervention in Afghanistan. Of the governments of Eastern Europe, only the GDR responded with anything more than dutiful but unenthusiastic support. Romania, ever the maverick, pointedly refused to offer even verbal support.

From the Kremlin's point of view, events in Poland carried with them a warning of potential domestic implications. Internal economic crisis had liberated and united internal dissent and dissatisfaction. Could it not happen in the USSR, too? Opposition to the regime had begun to cohere around two forces which were meant to have been vanquished in the socialist state: religion and nationalism. In a multiethnic USSR, keenly aware of the resilience of religion throughout, but notably amongst the expanding Central Asian populations, the Soviet leadership could not but be alarmed. As for Jaruzelski, while Moscow was clearly pleased to find a Pole with the determination and ability to undertake practical measures to limit the damage, that was all he was doing: not winning, just avoiding defeat. Besides, Moscow could not help wondering how far he was a loyal agent, and how far simply a clear-sighted Polish patriot disinclined to see Soviet forces once again rolling over his nation's frontiers. This was certainly Jaruzelski's line in a keynote address he made in February 1981: 'all Poles are responsible for the fate of Poland . . . for its existence as a sovereign and independent state'. Mikhail Suslov for one had his doubts about Jaruzelski, and a letter from the Central Committee to its Polish counterpart in June 1981 floated the idea of a new leadership line-up, to exclude the General. After all, it had been Jaruzelski who had refused to order the army to open fire on strikers in 1970 and again in August 1980. What might this say about the loyalties of Moscow's proconsuls elsewhere in Eastern Europe – or even within the Union? People within the Soviet élite began to talk of the 'Polandisation' of the USSR, and the need to avert a similar fate, but under Brezhnev's dead hand there was no scope for anything but piecemeal and stopgap measures. The jamming of foreign news broadcasts, suspended in 1973, resumed in August 1980. Facing a second consecutive poor harvest, the government introduced bread rationing and appealed for a 'war on waste'. The triumphalism of 1970s began to give way to a growing note of desperation.

THUNDER OVER THE BORDERS (2): AFGHANISTAN

Soviet–Afghan relations have a long history and the peoples of our two neighbouring countries have every reason to cherish the friendship that exists between them and to value their close ties, which are based on mutual respect, equality and cooperation. The USSR . . . is helping to solve the complex problems that confront a people which has begun the construction of a new society.

Pravda, 31 December 1979

If the nightmares conjured by Poland were of political crisis breeding revolt from workers and client leaderships alike, Afghanistan carried with it fears of a specifically Central Asian danger, as well as seriously damaging the USSR's standing in the Developing World. A coup in 1978 had brought to power the People's Democratic Party of Afghanistan (PDPA). Although Moscow had some doubts as to its stability and realism, with its 'April Revolution' a *fait accompli*, and the PDPA loudly proclaiming its socialist credentials, there was little Moscow could do but recognise the new regime. Colonel General Akhromeev, one of the most perceptive military minds of his generation, dourly noted that 'if the revolution is put down, left progressive forces will sustain a crushing blow. If the revolution is successful, we will get a lasting headache'.

A backward, divided nation, where clan and tribe have always been more important that the government in Kabul, Afghanistan proved resistant to the utopian dreams of the urban intellectuals of the PDPA. In Pushtun villages, that the new rulers were 'kummunist', was thought to be rooted in the Pashto words 'kum' (God) and 'nist' (not). By October 1978, this 'godless' regime's attempts to impose land and education reform (both of which attacked the bases of traditional power structures and Islam alike) had bred local uprisings. Meanwhile, the PDPA was tearing itself apart in faction-fighting between its Khalq ('Masses') and Parcham ('Banner') wings. The Soviets counselled unity, and advised a more gradual approach, but all to no avail. In March 1979, a revolt in the city of Herat left some 5,000 dead – including a hundred Soviet advisers and their families, massacred by the mob. The Soviets came to realise that the situation in Afghanistan was getting out of hand and that in practical terms there was very little they could do to bring their ever more erratic Afghan allies under control. By the end of the year, desertions had more than halved the size of the Afghan army and the majority of the country was outside effective government control. As for the PDPA, once Khalq had marginalised Parcham, its leaders turned on each other. In September, Prime Minister Amin assassinated Taraki, Chair of the Revolutionary Council. Hopes in Moscow that the more moderate Taraki could rein in the ambitious and brutal Amin seemed doomed.

The decision to intervene, as discussed in the previous chapter, had become almost inevitable, and when it came, the Soviets carried out the occupation with textbook efficiency. Paratroopers, a commando force of GRU Spetsnaz and a KGB special forces unit codenamed Zenit ('Zenith') seized Kabul and killed Amin on the night of 27 December 1979. Four mechanised divisions rolled across the border and occupied key centres and roads, while Soviet advisers attached to key Afghan units immobilised them under a variety of pretexts, from removing batteries from tanks for 'maintenance' to calling in ammunition for 'stock checks'. With only seventy combat casualties, the Soviets had seized a country. Unfortunately, they had not pacified it.

Early Soviet hopes that all they had to do was replace Amin with a more flexible and reliable leader, enforce a new alliance between Khalq and Parcham and over-awe the rebels with a show of force proved illusory. Anti-government forces could draw upon Islamic zeal, traditional resistance to central government and a cultural passion for a good brawl, while divisions within the PDPA proved impossible to solve. The Soviets were drawn into ten years of brutal guerrilla war, although not a war that they ever lost. In all, the Soviets suffered some 15,000 casualties: about as many soldiers died back in the USSR every two years from bullying, illness and accident. Total forces deployed in Afghanistan peaked at around 150,000 troops, out of a total strength of approximately five million. This is, in itself, in contrast with Vietnam, where the USA deployed up to almost half a million troops at once and suffered over 56,000 casualties. There were attempts to win the war by military means alone, notably during Chernenko's tenure, marked by a series of major ground assaults and the indiscriminate use of mass bombing of rebel bases and refugee camps. Yet Moscow was never prepared to pay the economic and political price for probable victory: sending in many more troops, for example, or sanctioning cross-border raids into Pakistan to prevent the rebels from basing themselves there with impunity.

Nevertheless, the experience of Afghanistan in the early 1980s brought home and illustrated for the Soviet élite three uncomfortable truths. First of all, that superpower status is expensive, unreliable and needs regularly to be defended. Secondly, that client states can prove rather harder to control than superpowers might like to think. One reason why Moscow felt it had to intervene in Afghanistan had been to protect its political investment, but it was also to bring the PDPA to heel. Poland and Afghanistan both showed the Soviet leadership the extent to which its control over its satellites was far less complete than it had assumed, and could only be guaranteed so long as Moscow could either impose it or buy it with aid, legitimacy and support. Just as the fat, lazy Brezhnev years had seen local Party bosses within the Union become ever more independent and corrupt, so too were national leaderships within the Soviet bloc ever more eager to see how far they could use their relationship with Moscow to their own advantages. Finally, that the USSR was isolated and facing a new Cold War, one being played to new rules and with new military, political and economic resources – which the Soviet Union sorely lacked.

THE SECOND COLD WAR

From the middle 1970s the world witnessed the onset of a Second Cold War . . . comparable, in its essentials, to the First Cold War of 1946–1953.

Fred Halliday, *The Making of the Second Cold War* (London: Verso, 1983)

For some, the Soviet intervention in Afghanistan marked the end of detente and the start of the new Cold War. American President Jimmy Carter, for example, claimed that it had 'made a more dramatic change in my opinion of what the Soviets' ultimate goals are than anything they've done in the previous time I have been in office'. Yet this is largely self-justification: detente had always been a very artificial process and it was already on the wane. Indeed, part of the reason why the Soviets felt military intervention was indicated was that they saw relations with the USA were already becoming more tense. The detente of the 1970s had been, above all, the product of simple, cold-blooded pragmatism. Humbled by defeat in Vietnam, the USA sought an honourable retreat from a global role. The Soviets, facing pressures of their own, thought that Western investment and technology could help revitalise their economy. Behind the facade of amity and concord, both retained the arrogance of superpower and sought actively to extend their influence within the Developing World. By the late 1970s and early 1980s, though, the USA was shedding its 'Vietnam syndrome', and the fall of Iran to Islamic extremists would both ensure the election of ultra-conservative Ronald Reagan and convince the US that it had to engage actively in the world. In 1979 Margaret Thatcher had been elected in Britain and Helmut Kohl in West Germany: the future seemed to belong to the political right.

Such was the internal 'logic' of superpower suspicion and competition, that both powers became locked in an escalating cycle of move and counter. In response to the dangers posed by atomic weapons, for example, the Soviets poured vast resources into strategic defences, from anti-ballistic missile systems to a whole underground city of armoured bomb shelters beneath Moscow. The US Defense Department even estimated that more was spent on defensive than offensive strategic forces in the period 1965–85. This became seen in the West as evidence of a strategy to prepare for nuclear war, of a desire to undermine the West's own capability to deter the Soviets. The result was a new drive to develop ways of penetrating such defences, from MIRV technology (whereby a missile would carry several independent warheads to make it harder for them all to be destroyed in the air) to ever more accurate and speedy missiles which could strike before defences could be prepared or blast open bomb shelters and armoured missile silos.

Intermediate range ballistic missiles (IRBMs) provide another example of this vicious circle. The Soviets had relied on SS-4 and SS-5 missiles since 1958 and 1961, respectively, as their standard IRBMs, but as these were becoming increasingly dated, in 1977 they introduced a new, more capable weapon: the SS-20. Given that Polaris A-3 missiles, mounted in US submarines, were known to have the capability of quickly and accurately wiping out the SS-4 and SS-5 forces, the Soviets saw this as a perfectly reasonable response. To NATO, though, the SS-20 was a brand new threat, and it deployed advanced Cruise and Pershing II IRBMs in Europe. Pershings could reach Soviet territory in ten minutes' flight, and to Moscow it was they which represented a genuinely new threat in Europe, once again triggering an urge to catch up. Between their inception in 1981 to the Soviet decision to walk out of the talks in 1983, the Intermediate-Range Nuclear Forces (INF) negotiations failed to come to any sensible common ground between the two positions. Both sides were accumulating larger and more expensive arsenals of ever more sophisticated weapons, and yet guaranteed security seemed no closer.

This pattern was repeated across the board, with a single common theme: the Soviet leadership increasingly felt insecure and under threat. Perhaps this was unrealistic. Even if, for example, the USSR could not guarantee the annihilation of North America, merely the likely destruction of the key cities and strategic targets, there is no evidence that the US government felt tempted to launch a first strike. It is also likely that the Soviets' optimism of the early 1970s had itself been ill-founded, rooted in exaggerated and padded reports of production, self-delusory fudging of statistics and a simplistic preparedness to see every Western reversal, from the Suez débâcle to the fall of South Vietnam, as a victory for the USSR. Certainly Soviet military strength in the 1960s and early 1970s cannot simply be measured by raw totals of tanks and soldiers. In his book *The Liberators* (London: Hamish Hamilton, 1981), pseudonymous defector 'Viktor Suvorov' paints a picture of an army so riddled with inefficiency, alcoholism, cronyism and red-tape that even the subjugation of peaceable and disorganised Czechoslovakia in 1968 depended largely on bluff and luck.

Nevertheless, the Soviet leadership believed itself newly vulnerable and also felt increasingly boxed in by crises and events, lacking the freedom of manoeuvre it had once enjoyed. Intervention in Afghanistan and the imposition of martial law in Poland were last-ditch measures to avert the collapse of pro-Soviet regimes, and in both cases the initiative had come as much from local interests as Moscow. Nevertheless, the former led to the boycott of the Moscow Olympics and great loss of face within the Non-Aligned Movement, while the USA used the latter to justify economic sanctions which endangered the construction of a gas pipeline to Europe, upon which the Soviet regime had come to place great hopes for the regeneration of the economy. At the same time, the USSR had become the world's leading importer of grain where once it had exported it. The link between foreign politics and the internal security and good order of the state thus became explicit and of growing concern to Moscow.

A 'CRITICAL ABSENCE OF WILL'

After all, the single determining factor behind the events of the 1980s was a crisis of will on the part of the Soviet élite, a massive erosion of their belief in their mission, their security, their very future. In this they should have remembered Lenin's view that when the ruling élite of a system suffers such a 'critical absence of will', then a state is ripe for revolution. In his own way Andropov did realise this, and for him, like all sophisticated conservatives before him, from Nicholas I to Bismarck, the answer was to forestall revolution by reform: but a controlled, incremental reform.

Andropov had been preparing himself for his bid for the leadership. In January 1982 he launched a new campaign against corruption, but one which went further than previous such initiatives. For the first time, he widened the scope of his campaigns to include ever more important members of the élite itself. A diamond theft in December 1981 was traced to Boris Buryatia, 'Boris the Gypsy', a noted black-marketeer and the lover of Brezhnev's daughter, Galina. She, in turn, was married to Yurii Churbanov, First Deputy Interior Minister and under the protection of Interior Minister Shchelokov and Semen Tsvigun, Brezhnev's brother-in-law and Andropov's deputy at the KGB. Tsvigun, in other words, was Brezhnev's ally at the KGB: there to secure Brezhnev's interests. While the details are still uncertain, it is clear that Andropov used the scandal to confront the inconvenient (and corrupt) Tsvigun. In choosing suicide over demotion, Tsvigun set a pattern other corrupt members of the Brezhnev circle were to adopt.

It might thus sound surprising that when Mikhail Suslov died later that month, it may have been Brezhnev who suggested that Andropov was the ideal candidate for the promotion to succeed him as Central Committee Secretary responsible for Ideology. This post was, after all, second only to the General Secretary. There may have been some hope either of buying Andropov off or, more likely, severing his links with the KGB. Either way, the gamble failed, as Andropov installed a trusted deputy in his place and was thus in an ideal position to marshal his forces for the final offensive. Having already undermined and frightened his rivals, Andropov turned instead to wooing support for his own policy platform. He argued that change was necessary in order to avoid revolution or collapse in the future and, as former Chair of the KGB, he could base his case on a deep knowledge of the problems of the USSR and the extent to which it was falling behind technologically and economically. The armed forces were prepared to listen to him: even before Ronald Reagan announced his flamboyant 'Star Wars' Strategic Defense Initiative (SDI), to counter Soviet nuclear forces by a variety of lasers, missiles and the like, the Stavka had been worrying about the military implications of a widening technology gap.

After all, the USSR was generally felt to have achieved 'strategic parity' with the United States in around 1970. Crudely put, this meant having enough nuclear missiles sufficiently well hidden in ocean-cruising submarines or sufficiently armoured in concrete and steel silos to be able to absorb a surprise attack and still devastate the aggressor, such as to make any thought of victory meaningless. It had been a goal of centuries of Russian history to secure the Motherland against any aggressors, whether marauding Mongols from the east or Napoleon's Grande Armée from the West. With the signing of the first SALT (Strategic Arms Limitations Talks) agreement in May 1972, and its implied acceptance of equality, the USSR seemed finally to have achieved security. Military parity is an ever-moving target, though. At the very time that new developments in technology were spawning new generations of weapons, the political context of any future conflict was becoming more confused. The security of the USSR's western border was beginning to look less certain in the light of strains within the Warsaw Pact. So too was the eastern border a growing source of worry. China, once the 'little brother' of the socialist family, had shrugged off Moscow's influence in 1960. In 1979 it had reopened diplomatic relations with the USA (although President Nixon had visited in 1972), a year in which it also fought a border war with Vietnam, the main Soviet ally in the region. Moscow thus began to fear encirclement, as China, Western Europe and the USA threatened the USSR from all sides and on all fronts: military, economic, ideological and cultural.

ELECTING ANDROPOV

Yurii Vladimirovich has behind him multi-faceted activities in the spheres of domestic and foreign policy and ideology . . . He put no small effort into strengthening the socialist community and into ensuring the security of our state.

Konstantin Chernenko, in his speech nominated Andropov as
General Secretary, 1982

Even if delivered through gritted teeth, Chernenko's speech underlines the extent to which Andropov's power base was built upon the security interests. The KGB had been refashioned by Andropov largely in his own image, and its support for him was guaranteed. The military saw in him the only candidate with the programme and the ability to pilot the economic regeneration they demanded. When Konstantin Chernenko, Brezhnev's faithful friend and ally was suggested as an alternative candidate for the General Secretaryship, he found his populist 'man of the people' rhetoric and back-slapping cheeriness cut little ice. Defence Minister Ustinov is reported to have replied with the ominous warning 'it will not be understood by the army'. The third member of the security troika, Foreign Minister Andrei Gromyko, similarly swung his considerable moral authority and political weight behind Andropov. For all his negative image as the stolid 'Mr Niet', forever vetoing motions at the UN Security Council, Gromyko was an intelligent and sophisticated political operator. Besides, he had the uncomfortable evidence on his desk, in the form of a report to the CPSU's Central Committee in January 1980, prepared by a team of academics under Oleg Bogomolov, director of the Institute of the Economics of the World Socialist System. It represented a devastating critique of the failings of Soviet foreign policy:

> The anti-Soviet front of countries encircling the USSR from West to East has substantially grown in numbers and solidity. Detente has been blocked . . . . Economic and technological pressure against the Soviet Union has sharply grown [while events] have destroyed the preconditions for a possible normalisation of Soviet–Chinese relations . . . . Yugoslavia, Romania and North Korea have started increasingly to distance themselves from and mistrust Soviet policy.

To this was added the economic and sociological surveys which were to culminate in the 1983 'Novosibirsk Report', widely seen as one of the most comprehensive indictments of the failings of the old order. Even the official economic figures told a tale of decline. The Ninth Five Year Plan (FYP), 1971–75, was recorded as resulting in 5.6 per cent growth; the Tenth FYP 1976–80, however, saw this fall to 3.8 per cent, while the Eleventh FYP, 1981–85, was heading for 2.5 per cent. Yet these were just the public figures: anyone within the élite had access to rather more accurate data, which were pointing to zero growth by 1982. This meant that there were no new resources available to take part in the new microchip revolution. It also meant, as discussed in the previous chapter, effective reductions in spending on the social sector, with the consequent problems, from alcoholism to dissent. Talk of 'Polandisation' was not without foundation.

The problems facing the élite were, of course, wholly of its own making. It had taken a country which, for all its natural resources, was economically hobbled by its size, the costs of exploiting many of those assets and its political culture, and had made it a military and industrial superpower. This had come at a cost of throwing all resources at short-term targets, with no thought for the long term. The result had been a system lacking the internal dynamism of the market economies and riddled with incipient problems. Many of the factories of the 1980s were still full of plant looted from Germany after 1945; many of the ideas and attitudes of the employees of those factories were little changed from those of the peasants and workers under the tsar. Just as key interest groups within the leadership were accommodated, so too were the people, their political quiescence bought with the promise of more food in the shops, better consumer goods, laxer labour discipline. Despite the continuing barrage of gaudy propaganda posters and leaden rhetoric, the rule of the Party became legitimised not by Lenin's dream of a classless society, nor even the living god-like image of Stalin, but TV, sausage and vodka. For a while, it worked, but this social contract depended on the leaders keeping their side of the bargain. When the government had to start to reintroduce food rationing, when wages began to decline in real terms because there was nothing in the shops to buy and everyone had to pay inflated black market prices, then the people were unlikely to remain compliant.

The members of the élite were aware of this, thanks to their secret reports and internal discussions. As Gorbachev himself noted, in his book *Perestroika* (London: Collins, 1987), 'the country began to lose momentum. Economic failure became more frequent. Difficulties began to accumulate and deteriorate.' Thus, they faced a four-pronged attack on their confidence and unity. They began to fear for the survival of their state and its place in the world. Second, they began to squabble amongst themselves for slices of a diminishing pie. Third, they began to face new challenges, from nationalism, through political dissent to the simple disenchantment that leads to suicide and alcoholism within the workforce. Fourth, and perhaps most corrosive of all, some even began to question the very way the state was being run, the direction it had set itself.

Thus it is important to stress just how diverse was the coalition which Andropov assembled to support both his personal bid for the General Secretaryship and his political platform of measured, controlled reform. It embraced young radicals and the dying grandees of the old order, ambitious generals and earnest agronomists, KGB officers and newspaper editors. The common denominator was security, taken in its widest terms. They saw some sort of reform as a vital, if possibly uncomfortable means to securing the future of the Soviet system, Soviet superpower and Soviet élite. As a result, security and foreign policy was to prove an especially sensitive area for Gorbachev when he inherited Andropov's power base and mandate, since it lay at the heart of the coalition. The disintegration of this coalition in the late 1980s was to prove directly linked to the collapse of the conservative–reformist consensus Andropov had brokered.

ANDROPOV: REFORMING TO PRESERVE

Overall, comrades, there are many pressing problems in the economy, and I certainly have no ready recipes to solve them. But it is up to all of us – the Central Committee of the Party – to find the answers . . . . Slogans alone will not start the process.

> Yurii Andropov, in his first major policy address as General
> Secretary, 1982

Tsar Nicholas I had defined the task before him as simply 'holding everything together', but he was, in fact, far more clear-sighted than this suggests. His reign had seen concerted efforts to rein in a self-indulgent and inefficient bureaucracy, the rationalisation of police powers (in part as an extension of this drive for centralisation), and serious study of the problems facing Russia and possible solutions to avert a potential crisis. When Tsar Alexander II emancipated the serfs in 1861, he did so on the basis of plans drawn up under Nicholas, and he would probably have been more successful had he not watered down these initial drafts. For all its brevity – he was to die in February 1984, only fifteen months after assuming office – Andropov's role was in many ways similar. Like Nicholas, he felt that the only hope of averting cataclysm was a mix of measured reform and vigorous policing. The power of an entrenched and often obstructive or short-sighted bureaucracy had to be directed towards change, especially geared towards the security of the state taken in the widest possible terms: not just military and diplomatic, but also political, economic and social.

In part this breadth of perception reflects the range of allies and contacts he had assembled during his time as a politician, a diplomat, at the Central Committee Secretariat's International Department and from the KGB. The *institutchiki* were strongly represented: Oleg Bogomolov of the IEMSS and Georgii Arbatov, founder and director of ISKAN were two long-time and heavyweight allies, while Aleksandr Yakovlev, later to be a key adviser in Gorbachev's team, was appointed by Andropov to head IMEMO in

1983. Besides which, where Nicholas had his Baltic Germans, Andropov could call on his *chekisty*, his network of allies and experts from the KGB and the security apparatus: Vitalii Fedorchuk and Viktor Chebrikov from the KGB, Eduard Shevardnadze, former Georgian Interior Minister and then the republic's Party boss. More broadly, he moved quickly to bring a new generation of puritans into the centre, men who had distinguished themselves by their opposition to the more flagrant excesses of the *ancien régime*, such as Egor Ligachev, the Siberian Party First Secretary under whose patronage Novosibirsk had become a focus for accurate and objective academic analysis, including the aforementioned 'Novosibirsk report'. Andropov was far from infallible – he promoted the corrupt and toadying Geidar Aliev, taken in by fabricated reports of his campaigns to clean up corruption in Azerbaijan – but the importance of his term in office for the Soviet Union and the evolution of its security policy must not be underestimated.

Andropov certainly set out to renovate the political agenda, introducing a new pragmatism into efforts to renew detente. He had few outright successes, though, largely because he was hemmed in by problems beyond his control or which would have required an investment in time and political capital that he could not afford. Summer 1983 saw some improvement in US–Soviet relations, with agreements at the European Conference on Security and Cooperation in Madrid and trade and cultural exchanges. Any optimism, though, crashed in September when a Korean Airlines jumbo jet was shot down by Soviet fighters over Soviet airspace, when a mistaken setting on an autopilot was presumed to be deliberate espionage. As a result, Andropov was forced to rely almost exclusively on classic KGB tactics, building and playing up European anti-nuclear and anti-American passions in a forlorn (and often counterproductive) bid to forestall the deployment of US Cruise and Pershing II IRBMs. Andropov's overtures to China, which even implied that the border could be revised to China's advantage, made some, but limited, headway. As a symbolic gesture, two border posts were reopened to traffic, while a day after Andropov's death, Moscow and Beijing signed a $1.2 billion trade deal. Little real improvement was possible, though, so long as Soviet forces remained in Mongolia and, especially, Afghanistan.

Nevertheless, Andropov did bring new ideas on to the agenda. Bogomolov's ideas on the importance of the USSR winning allies and friends by force of example rather than arms were aired in official pronouncements, given a new political weight by the obvious need to cut excessive defence and foreign aid budgets. These ideas were bequeathed to the 'Andropov coalition'. For the masses, Andropov's era was a time of mass arrests of absentees from work and a new drive against alcoholism, characterised by some as a revived 'neo-Stalinism'. Yet discipline was also being imposed on the élite and their corrupt agents. Within two years, 55,000 militiamen – more than a tenth of the entire police force – were dismissed for incompetence or corruption. Railways minister Ivan Pavlovskii was sacked and Yurii Sokolov, manager of the prestigious *Gastronom No. 1* food store in Moscow was arrested on charges of embezzlement, both in November. Next month, Shchelokov was replaced as Interior Minister by Fedorchuk; in June 1983 both he and the monstrously corrupt former Party boss of the Krasnodar region, Sergei Medunov, were expelled from the Central Committee.

Purge brought opportunity for Andropov's protégés. Fedorchuk took over the MVD, and Chebrikov the KGB. Shevardnadze came onto the Politburo, along with Egor Ligachev, who moved to Moscow as Central Committee Secretary for Party Organisation. Nikolai Ryzhkov, a former manager from the defence industries, was also appointed to the Secretariat. Most importantly, Mikhail Gorbachev, the relatively young (fifty-year-old) Central Committee Secretary for Agriculture, and a man who owed his rapid rise in part to Andropov's patronage, was given overall responsibility for the economy. He soon rose to become his master's right hand and *de facto* leader of the 'Andropov coalition'. When Andropov died in February 1984, his attempt to have Gorbachev nominated as successor foundered upon Gorbachev's relative inexperience, and instead the General Secretaryship went to the equally frail Konstantin Chernenko, Brezhnev's old friend. For the old conservatives he was a safe pair of hands; for the reformists he was a sick pair of lungs. His brief term in office – he lasted thirteen months – saw a brief pause in reform, but no real retreat.

CHERNENKO: THE CARELESS CARETAKER

Kostya [Chernenko] *will be more manageable than Misha* [Gorbachev].

Comment passed between Defence Minister Ustinov and
Prime Minister Tikhonov

Chernenko was nothing more than an interim appointment. Ustinov and Gromyko had had their doubts as to whether Gorbachev was yet experienced enough for the job, and had not yet decided whether he was 'sound'. Their doubts led to a compromise being brokered even before Andropov's death and quite possibly without his knowledge: the ailing Chernenko would succeed him, but would accept the irreversibility of reform and that Gorbachev was his deputy. The result was that the period up to Chernenko's death from emphysema in March 1985, was one of confused and contradictory policies, yet marked by the germination of many of the seeds planted by Andropov. It had been Andropov, for example, who had first begun to bring some *glasnost'*, generally (if not wholly accurately) translated as 'openness' to Soviet politics in general and foreign policy in particular. This was not out of any democratic spirit, but because he realised that he could use that openness both as a weapon to isolate political rivals and as a means to generate some debate from which he could gather useful ideas and additional information. It was only after his death, during Chernenko's reign, that a newspaper published an article accepting not only that there was serious fighting in Afghanistan, but that Soviet soldiers were being wounded and maimed and yet failed by the state on their return home. This triggered a whole series of letters and articles in the press, as *glasnost'* became used to highlight local authorities which were failing to meet the standards the centre set and exert pressure upon them.

By instinct, Chernenko was a nationalist, a populist, a heavy-handed Party boss of the old school. He presided over a dramatic escalation of the war in Afghanistan, with massive and brutal air raids and ground attacks. Despite early hints of flexibility, he introduced a much more confrontational note into arms negotiations with the USA, compounding the snub with a boycott of the Los Angeles Olympics. Andropov's overtures to China were replaced by an almost wantonly confrontational line, calling off Deputy Premier Arkhipov's planned visit to Beijing and issuing a strong statement in support of Vietnam over Sino-Vietnamese border clashes.

A dying man, he looked for immediate gains over long-term policy, seeking short cuts to history. Resources were diverted from investment in technology and industry into social programmes and food subsidies, while the main engine driving his foreign policy seems to have been the desire to protect his domestic position. This could have proved disastrous were Chernenko not limited by two factors: Party discipline and political weakness. On the one hand, Chernenko was a dutiful Party man, and allowed himself to be guided by the Central Committee Secretariat's bureaucracy. Perhaps more important, he was beholden to Gromyko, Ustinov and the 'Andropov coalition'. Gorbachev prevented Chernenko from returning the name Stalingrad to Volgograd and ensured that the anti-corruption initiative was not reversed. Disgraced former Interior Minister Shchelokov followed Tsvigun's example, committing suicide in December 1984. More substantially, his line on the need for investment in long-term development stood in opposition to Chernenko's short-termism and received robust support from the military, including Colonel General Volkogonov from the Main Political Directorate and, most overtly, Chief of the General Staff Nikolai Ogarkov.

GORBACHEV: REFORMING TO SECURE

Comrades, this man has a nice smile, but teeth of iron.

Gromyko, in his speech nominating Gorbachev as General Secretary, 1985

The death of Ustinov in December 1984 and his replacement by the politically far weaker Marshal Sergei Sokolov left Gromyko as the dominant patriarch of the Soviet leadership. Foreign affairs thus became of central importance, and Gorbachev's success in demonstrating his ability to operate on an international scene proved critical in securing his support on Chernenko's death. He had used the period well to establish his foreign policy credentials, with a successful trip to Britain in 1984 building on the attention he had received when he visited Canada in 1983. Gorbachev's election to the General Secretaryship on Chernenko's passing was by no means inevitable. It depended largely on the 'Andropov coalition' and, in particular, the security interests. His main rival was Viktor Grishin, Party First Secretary of Moscow. Grishin's power base was made up less of supporters of his as opponents of Gorbachev, his team and his programme. Sick and dying old Andropov, after all, had still been able to purge Shchelokov, Tsvigun and Pavlovskii; how much more dangerous would a relatively young Gorbachev prove? Grishin was supported by Romanov, Party boss of Leningrad city.

Romanov's drive for efficiency had appealed to Andropov but he also had ambitions of his own. Thus he supported the older Grishin, with an eye to becoming his heir apparent.

Gorbachev had some formidable allies, though. The KGB provided him with information (and leaked stories about Romanov's disorderly revels) as well as a certain legitimacy. The military saw him as the only viable candidate, in part won over by Gromyko. The choice, after all, was stark: between timorous conservatism and cosy nostalgia on the one hand, and the uncertainties of change on the other. What was at stake was the security, the very future of the Soviet state and superpower. Gorbachev was elected on the barest of margins. Of nine voting members of the Politburo, one was absent, four supported Gorbachev and four Grishin, with Gromyko's the casting vote. Gorbachev was ultimately to fail in his venture to reform yet preserve. But in his ambitions and his concerns, he was articulating the views of the security and foreign policy interests: that change was inevitable, and that it needed to be managed rather than ignored. Which changes, though? There neither Gorbachev nor his backers had any blueprint.

The choice was depressingly simple: between oblivion and uncertainty.

Senior member of the Secretariat, looking back in 1991

4 A NEW WAY: COLD WAR TO 'COMMON HOME', 1985–88

1985   *March* Gorbachev elected General Secretary.

April Launch of programme of *perestroika* (restructuring).

July Eduard Shevardnadze becomes Foreign Minister.

November Geneva summit.

1986   *January* Gorbachev proposes complete elimination of nuclear weapons by the year 2000.

February/March XXVII Party Congress: Gorbachev launches the concept of 'reasonable sufficiency'.

April Chernobyl' disaster.

July Gorbachev's Vladivostok speech.

October Reykjavik summit.

November Gorbachev's 'Delhi declaration' affirms his commitment to a nuclear-free world.

1987   *January* Central Committee plenum meeting: Gorbachev accuses the Party of resisting reform.

May New Warsaw Pact military doctrine announced. Matthias Rust's landing in Red Square opens the way for a purge of the High Command: Defence Minister Sokolov replaced by Yazov.

July Soviets table proposed new START treaty at Geneva.

December Gorbachev visits Washington: INF treaty signed.

1988   *February* Agreement on withdrawal from Afghanistan announced (talks concluded in April). Struggle for Nagorno-Karabakh begins.

March Gorbachev renounces the 'Brezhnev Doctrine'.

May Moscow summit.

The organic ties between each state's foreign and domestic policies become particularly close and practically meaningful at crucial moments. A change in domestic policy inevitably leads to changes in the attitude to international issues.

Mikhail Gorbachev, *Perestroika* (London: Collins, 1987)

The foreign policy revolution which marked the Gorbachev era has rightly been characterised as 'a diplomacy of decline'. Appreciating – in part, at least – the weakness of the Soviet position, Gorbachev set out, with characteristic shrewdness, to make a virtue out of a necessity. If the Soviet economy could no longer support the costs of superpower status, if the Soviet military machine needed to be downscaled, then so be it: but let this be done in such a way as to reflect to the credit of the USSR. Let it be seen as a gracious initiative, not an inevitable retreat. Let it also be twinned with efforts to reduce the potential external threats facing the Soviet Union, so that retreat does not carry with it vulnerability. There was more to the 'New Political Thinking' (NPM – *Novoe politicheskoe myshlenie*) than pure pragmatism, to be sure. It allowed a whole new debate to flourish as to the Soviet Union's rightful place in the world, the dangers and problems of the superpower system and how foreign policy should be formulated. It also drew upon the lessons of detente, as analysts and politicians sought to create a more genuine and thus lasting accord. Yet the primary engine of NPM was economic decline and the ensuing crisis in the legitimacy of the Soviet state. In reforming foreign and security policy, Gorbachev hoped to find answers to these problems, and thus lay the foundations for a far more stable and, implicitly, powerful Soviet superpower of the future.

GORBACHEV IN POWER

Gorbachev's early foreign and security policy was in many ways a flashier and more dynamic version of Andropov's. From his mentor he had inherited a mixed collection of advisers and allies, from academic *institutchiki* through Gromyko's MID to the KGB. He also inherited a basic line, that of developing fruitful relations with the West, of reducing counterproductive international tensions and of spreading the gospel of Marxism–Leninism and Soviet influence not by expensive military and political adventures of the 'cheque book diplomacy' of the 1970s, but by restoring to the USSR the economic dynamism and political legitimacy which would again make it an example worth imitating. Yet where Andropov was an old and weak man concerned with domestic politics and trapped by misfortune, Gorbachev, the beneficiary of Andropov's careful coalition-building, was relatively young and vigorous, and keen to demonstrate his ability to operate on a world stage; moreover, he was lucky.

Gorbachev's first priority was to consolidate his grip upon security and foreign policy. Here came his first lucky break, in that the death of Defence Minister Ustinov in December 1984 provided him with room for manoeuvre. Ustinov was replaced by Marshal Sergei Sokolov, described by Dale Herspring in his book, *The Soviet High Command* (Princeton: Princeton UP, 1990), as 'a bureaucrat's bureaucrat' and it is highly likely that Gorbachev, by this stage heir apparent, had a part in his appointment. What is certain is that it was Gorbachev who ensured that, unlike Ustinov, Sokolov was made only a non-voting, candidate member of the Politburo. This was a clear affirmation of Gorbachev's view that it was time for civilian authority over the military to be asserted. In May 1985 this went one stage further, as a number of senior officers were induced to retire, including Marshal Tolubko, commander of the Strategic Rocket Forces, Admiral Sergei Gorshkov and General Epishev, head of the Main Political Directorate. Not only were these all long-serving soldiers with political power bases of their own, they had also been engaged in outspoken lobbying for more funds for their services (notably Tolubko and Gorshkov) and were seen as hardliners (particularly Gorshkov and Epishev). As such, they had represented obstacles to Gorbachev's leadership and their departure was a measure of his eagerness to introduce new ideas.

For he then revealed his true political acumen when, on 1 July, he elevated Gromyko from the MID to the Presidency (formally, the title was still Chair of the Presidium of the Supreme Soviet) and replaced him with Eduard Shevardnadze. The move was as unexpected as it was inspired. It was Gromyko who had proposed Gorbachev to the General Secretaryship, tipping the balance for reform. Gorbachev was thus beholden to him, but Gromyko was a product of the old order (he had been Foreign Minister for fully twenty-eight years), and Gorbachev needed someone who was able to think in new ways and who, moreover, could be relied upon to execute his own policies. By making him head of state, Gorbachev could at once honour Gromyko and disempower him. Shevardnadze, by contrast, was a Georgian, with no foreign policy experience and a background as a tough anti-corruption campaigner and reliable Party boss. His reputation was as a charming, flexible yet tough man, and he grew into his job with astonishing speed. He had also been a friend of Gorbachev's since the 1950s, and the latter rightly saw him as a man upon whom he could rely.

Gorbachev could then move quickly to set his stamp upon

Soviet foreign policy. Even before 'honouring' Gromyko, he had made sure that much of the April 1985 plenary meeting of the Central Committee had been devoted to security affairs. After this meeting, he announced a unilateral moratorium on the development of new intermediate-range missiles and nuclear tests which, though of little military significance, was an early harbinger of his style of diplomacy – a headline-grabbing offer which forced the other side to match it or lose face. Behind the scenes, the meeting also approved a serious initiative to extricate the USSR from its military involvement in Afghanistan. Gorbachev went on in November 1985 to meet US President Ronald Reagan in Geneva, and this meeting illustrated the extent to which his ideas were still developing. The first such superpower summit in nearly a decade, it showed Gorbachev's preference for and his mastery of this sort of person-to-person statesmanship, beginning a relationship with the USA's leaders which was to last up to his downfall. He had little that was new to offer, for he had not yet really mastered his new brief, nor come up with a new line. In particular, Reagan was still enthused by 'Star Wars' (SDI), and Gorbachev could only repeat his rather hollow offer not to deploy a Soviet equivalent – as if the USSR had had the capability – in return for a halt to the US programme. For all this, though, both leaders were prepared to concede grounds for optimism; for Gorbachev there were now 'opportunities for progress', while Reagan saw 'useful preliminary results'.

He also began working on a variety of other fronts. Having secured the Central Committee's blessing, he began serious efforts to disentangle the USSR from its involvement in Afghanistan, what he would call 'this bleeding wound' at the 27th Party Congress in February 1986. From China to West Germany, he began to rebuild the bridges Chernenko had so clumsily destroyed. Even conventional military forces began to be audited with a view to reductions. It would be easy to see this purely as an array of specific policies reacting to particular problems and crises, but there was some common concept binding it together, so that it does make sense to use the umbrella term 'New Political Thinking'.

THE FOUNDATIONS OF 'NEW THINKING'

*. . . the best way of dealing with an enemy is to turn him into
a friend or, at worst, an ordinary neighbour. In our*

> *interdependent world, subject to nuclear, ecological and many*
> *other threats, such an approach becomes not just desirable but*
> *necessary, a prerequisite for survival and development.*
>
> Gorbachev ally Georgii Shakhnazarov in the Party's journal,
> *Kommunist*, 1989

Gorbachev certainly did not create NPM out of thin air. There was already a rich debate taking place beneath the surface of Soviet political life, to which he could turn for ideas and alternatives. This was, after all, part of his political genius: his ability to take existing ideas and build for them platforms and opportunities. Thus, his personal role was to empower the reformists: he took their abstract and academic discussions and made them relevant to the Soviet élite. First, he sold New Political Thinking to his own backers, then he went out to sell it to the outside world.

To a considerable extent, the bases of NPM were familiar staples of Western international relations theory: interdependence, globalism, post-industrialism. In other words, they were rooted in a growing awareness that the concept of a world riven by the class divide was not just unhelpful, but actively dangerous. Instead, foreign and security policies should look towards finding common ground and common interest. Peace became not just the absence of war, but a state of mutual advantage and cooperation. The similarities between Soviet and Western theory should not come as a surprise. As discussed previously, the USSR, for all its utopian rhetoric, operated in most ways like any other nation: inextricably linked within the global economic system, tied into the complete range of international organisations, with interests and problems familiar to every global player. In addition, the academics and analysts who had been prosecuting this debate came themselves from an increasingly Westward-looking background. Through the Brezhnev era, these *institutchiki* acquired opportunities to study Western concepts, meet Western diplomats, journalists and analysts and even travel, as diplomats, fact-finders or academics.

Yet there was also a specifically Soviet flavour to the debate. It reflected the USSR's distinctive problems, concerns and position, those distinctive challenges discussed in Chapter 1. Gorbachev, for example, also needed to square the Eurasian circle, and come to terms with the USSR's position as both a European empire and an Asian land power. The debate also reflected its particular context, being carried out by a country in the midst of economic crisis and political transition. As a result, it was dominated by the need to restore some legitimacy to the regime, which first and foremost meant getting food and goods into the shops at prices Soviet citizens could afford. It had finally been realised that the most pressing threat to Soviet national security was not to be found in the missile silos of Dakota or along the Chinese border, but in the food queues in Minsk and the empty refrigerators in Kiev. Hence, the particular attention which would soon be paid to the notion of *konversiya* ('conversion'), the process of redirecting defence spending and industries to civilian use. The profound political changes of the era also meant that the debate was in part a struggle for power and authority, as representatives of the old order fought both each other and ambitious outsiders to define the future of the USSR.

The Soviets were particularly concerned to integrate the outside world into their reform programme. Gorbachev needed guarantees that the demilitarisation of the Soviet state and the retreat from a forward, global policy would be met by measures to maintain the security of the regime in Moscow, whether by matching arms cuts or through renewed trading links. On the one hand this was because, given the precarious nature of his leadership position, he could not afford excessively to worry the Old Guard. Gorbachev was acutely conscious of the fact that his election had been very closely fought, and that much of what he preached went against the grain for most of the élite. If they supported him at this time, it was grudgingly, as the lesser of various evils. All that could change very quickly if he seemed to be giving too much ground to the West.

It also reflected a very real wariness about the West in general and the USA in particular. For all his willingness to see the West as partners rather than rivals, even Gorbachev was not without this caution. After all, in Soviet eyes US policy in particular seemed often hostile or too erratic to take at face value. Before the Second World War, the USA had been the largest Western exporter to the USSR, and during the war had provided generous Lend-Lease assistance. Moscow had felt, though, that the Western allies were over-tardy in launching their 'second front' in Europe, content to see the Soviets and Germans bleed each other dry, and over-hasty in atom-bombing Japan to surrender in order to forestall Soviet advances into China. After the war, Lend-Lease was promptly cut and, according to the Soviet version of events, economic war launched against the West's erstwhile ally. The 1947 Truman Doctrine envisaged the 'containment' of the USSR, while Marshall Aid for Europe was seen by Moscow as a bid to colonise the continent with capitalism at the very time when the 1949 Export Control Act was dramatically restricting sales to the USSR and East Europe. The USA had been prepared to grant the USSR Most Favoured Nation trading status in 1935, the year after Sergei Kirov's engineered assassination and the subsequent purge of the Party had given Stalin absolute power, yet in 1951 Congress revoked it.

When viewed from Moscow, post-war relations with the USA had demonstrated one thing only: that the USA's goodwill alone was no guarantee. Hence Gorbachev's passion for both bilateral talks and propaganda. If the former were to persuade governments to enter into mutually beneficial relations with the USSR, the latter was to create the public opinion in Europe and the United States that would force those governments to develop and honour them. In this, Gorbachev believed both that he could offer enough concessions to buy major assistance from the West and that in democracies, the public is interested enough in foreign policy to support the diversion of scarce resources in time of economic recession to aiding the USSR rather than reinvestment at home. In both cases he was wrong – a mistake which was to lead directly to his downfall.

ARMS REDUCTIONS

In the heady days of the mid- to late-1980s, though, everything still seemed possible, if only Gorbachev could consolidate his grip on security and foreign policy and convince the West of his good intentions. He inherited a terrible position, with talks on INF (Intermediate Nuclear Forces) in Europe stalled and the START strategic weapons talks still-born. Paradoxically, though, this proved an asset: matters could only improve, and Gorbachev's relatively moderate early overtures could seem disproportionately encouraging. That was, after all, the point. Gorbachev knew he had to achieve some rapid successes, both for domestic political reasons and to create some new momentum in improving relations with the West.

The joint statement issued following the 1985 Geneva summit had outlined various broad initiatives, from major reductions in stockpiles of nuclear weapons to guarantees to prevent the militarisation of space. These had, however, been general and rather hollow hopes of future agreement rather than a serious basis for negotiation. Gorbachev set out to build such a basis. In January 1986 he announced a dramatic reversal of Soviet policy, with a plan for global de-nuclearisation. As its first stage, it effectively accepted US proposals for the reduction of intermediate range missiles in Europe, President Reagan's 'Zero Option', with an idealistic plan envisaging the elimination of all nuclear weapons by the end of millennium. In October Reagan and Gorbachev met again, in Reykjavik. There Gorbachev offered a new deal, whereby in return for a US commitment to limit SDI research to laboratories for the next ten years, the USSR would accept a dramatic reduction of both medium- and long-range nuclear forces. He was even prepared to fudge long-standing Soviet demands that British and French nuclear forces be included with US totals.

The Soviets were convinced it was a deal Reagan – both a genuine convert to de-nuclearisation and an aging President in danger of becoming a 'lame duck' – could not refuse. Indeed, he very nearly accepted, and had largely to be talked out of it by more hawkish aides, who insisted he stand firm on SDI. Nevertheless, Gorbachev could scarcely be said to have left empty-handed. He had displayed a brilliant mastery of both summitry and global public relations. He had laid the foundations for the INF treaty, which would be signed in December 1987. He had also managed to convince most foreign observers that he was serious about revolutionising the context of superpower relations, and not merely offering old policies packaged in new ways. This was a rather mixed asset. There were those in the West – and the USA, in particular – for whom it was proof positive of the vulnerability of the Soviet system. The goal should, they argued, not be to help the USSR survive but to redouble the pressure to ensure that it fell. While this wing was never dominant, it did manage to ensure that Gorbachev never received the unequivocal and generous support he would later have needed to succeed and survive.

GORBACHEV AND THE MILITARY

Western hesitancy also caused Gorbachev problems back in the USSR. Arms cuts made sense within the context of the broad renovation of the Soviet system, but they had never explicitly been part of the policy platform on which Gorbachev had been elected. Indeed, Gorbachev had had to go out of his way to play down his reformism in his early years. When the French newspaper *L'Humanité* suggested in early 1986 that he was launching 'a new revolution', Gorbachev's reply had been a hurried and categorical 'certainly not'. In military terms, though, that was what he was bringing. He was changing the old rules of political–military relations by disregarding military considerations altogether, although – as will be discussed below – the High Command itself was revising its approach to war. Perhaps the main distinction was really a rather simple and essentially philosophical one. A basic tenet of NPM was that war – and nuclear war in particular – would be avoided by political and not military means. The corollary was that political considerations would and should always take precedence, even when they seemed to create military vulnerability and even when they infringed upon the military's own perception of its role, rights and place in society. Put simply, it was no longer so necessary to build up military security, because good foreign relations would ensure that major wars never happened in the first place.

As a result, it is striking how the period sees Gorbachev's relations with the military, always more correct than cordial, beginning to sour. Whereas the foreign policy apparatus and the security organs still cleaved to Gorbachev, the military began to become increasingly divided over its response to reform. Gorbachev certainly moved to assert his control over the armed forces as far as he could. Not only was Defence Minister Sokolov denied a full, voting seat on the Politburo but the strength of the military in the Party's Central Committee shrank steadily. The Central Committee formed in 1986 numbered twenty-four soldiers amongst its 477 full and non-voting members, compared with the thirty-four soldier members of 1981. For all this, though, the military retained its ability to flout Gorbachev's will. In July 1986, for example, Gorbachev announced the withdrawal of six regiments from Afghanistan. It was an essentially symbolic gesture, accounting for only some 7,000 out of over 100,000 troops there, but it was intended both as propaganda and as a token of a genuine willingness to seek some new understanding over an eventual total withdrawal. Within a few months, though, at least 5,000 fresh troops had been brought back into Afghanistan, under the cover of the replacement of conscripts whose national service was almost over. Gorbachev was branded a fraud, and his initiative came to nothing, yet he could not afford an open confrontation with the High Command. Again, the fragile nature of his political position prevented him from challenging his critics.

It was, of all people, a well-meaning but mildly disturbed young German called Matthias Rust who gave Gorbachev a chance to strike at the military Old Guard. On the evening of 28 May 1987 – ironically enough, Border Guards' Day – he flew a Cessna light aircraft through 700 km of the USSR's notionally secure air space and then landed on Red Square in front of bemused militiamen and intrigued Western tourists. On one level, this was more embarrassing than serious. While conceivably such a plane could have carried a bomb, in practice air defences are geared for genuine attack, and after the Korean Airlines debacle of 1983 no local commander was willing to shoot the Cessna down on his own authority. Nevertheless, it was indicative of the rusty chain of command and culture of complacency within the armed forces, and provided Gorbachev with a perfect excuse to act.

Sokolov, already seriously ill with heart disease, was retired and Air Defence Forces Commander General Koldunov sacked in disgrace. To replace Sokolov, Gorbachev made a point of bypassing the obvious candidates and appointed Colonel General Dmitrii Yazov. Yazov's career had been built on two bases, personnel issues and the eastern military districts (VOs). Between 1977 and 1979, he had been Deputy Commander of the Far Eastern VO, moving to command the Central Asian VO in 1980 and then the Far Eastern VO in 1984. The significance of this is two-fold. First of all, these regions had been involved in supporting the Soviet war effort in Afghanistan, providing supplies, training facilities and rear-area bases. As a result, from being fairly low priority regions, these VOs had acquired a new political profile, while their commanders became increasingly involved in training and personnel issues. Thus it is not surprising that when Yazov was transferred to a Defence Ministry post in Moscow in early 1987, it was with a special responsibility for such affairs. Secondly, the 'Easterners' represented a loose alliance of military officers who had served and lived together and were to prove one of the main factions within the high command in the later Gorbachev era. Yazov was certainly to bring as many of his fellow 'Easterners' into the ministry as he could: in 1989 his former Chief of Staff at the Far Eastern VO, Mikhail Moiseev, was to become Chief of the General Staff, while Yazov's successor in charge of the Central Asian VO, Petr Lushev, became Commander-in-Chief of Warsaw Pact Joint Forces and Yazov's predecessor at the Far Eastern VO, Ivan Tret'yak, replaced Koldunov in charge of the Air Defence Forces.

By appointing Yazov, Gorbachev hoped to elevate a figure able to sell *perestroika* to the military and, if necessary, impose it. Yazov had certainly been making the right noises. Back in July 1986, the army newspaper *Krasnaya zvezda* had reported a meeting of Party activists in the Far Eastern VO where he had criticised 'old thinking' in the military and in January 1987 the paper had published a glowing tribute to his work as a model reformist commander. In addition, Yazov was more interested in management than strategy, which would – Gorbachev must have hoped – render him more prepared to administer than pilot change. The fact that he was a relative outsider must also have inclined Gorbachev to assume that the colourless and none-too-bright Yazov would never become too strongly entrenched in the Defence Ministry and thus always be beholden to the General Secretary. He was right in that Yazov, while bringing quite a few of his old allies into the Stavka, never developed any independent power base. But that weakness was also to mean that he quite soon became 'house-trained' and lost any real value to Gorbachev. The fact is that senior Soviet officers had risen through a system which was not only increasingly hereditary and élitist but marked by a culture which allowed even less room for mavericks than most military institutions. Short of elevating a very junior officer or imposing a civilian Defence Minister, both of which would have created a very serious political row, Gorbachev's options were very limited. He probably played the best card available to him.

Gorbachev was not going to rely solely on Yazov, though, and used the opportunity to launch a much more concerted and surprisingly strong attack on the armed forces in general, as inefficient, unresponsive to the need for change and unprepared to play their part in the revitalisation of the USSR. At the 1987 June Central Committee Plenum meeting, he made a point of criticising the military. Boris Yeltsin, at that time the Party Secretary for Moscow and a candidate member of the Politburo, used a meeting of Party members within the Moscow Air Defence Region to note the absence 'any kind of *glasnost*' in the armed forces, 'as if you had been unaffected by the decisions of the Congress and the plenums of the Central Committee'.

HUMANISING POLICY: 'COMMON HOMES'

Thus, after Rust's flight, the context of civil–military relations changed. Yazov would not remain a loyal ally and would, in due course, be one of the plotters behind the 1991 August Coup. But he represented a new sort of Soviet general-bureaucrat, whose concern would be to manage change within the USSR to his and the military's fullest advantage, not return to the 1970s status quo. The generation of Soviet commanders who had held senior command posts during the Great Patriotic War was never to return. More to the point, though, the military could no longer be regarded as part of the reform coalition, and Gorbachev was increasingly to have to work in opposition to it.

Hitherto, while the political leadership had insisted upon overall primacy, the military had been allowed to retain its monopoly of specialist knowledge and thus considerable autonomy within those broad guidelines. If Gorbachev was to begin to encroach upon that autonomy by seeking outsiders' views, by over-ruling military advice and by revamping security policy, then he would need three things: new military principles to underpin his policies, the public and political groundswell to sanction them and people able and willing to carry them out. For the first, he developed the principles of 'reasonable sufficiency' and the 'common homes', for the second he turned to *glasnost'*. His abiding and ultimately fatal problem was always in finding the last. The Khrushchev and Brezhnev eras had already seen a shift in attitudes towards war, from the Clausewitzian days of the pre-nuclear age when war had seemed a logical, sometimes necessary extension of politics, to a post-nuclear appreciation that total war could too easily become apocalypse. Nevertheless, this was still essentially a negative view, and despite lip-service towards detente and arms reductions, rested on the theory of deterrence, of a balance of terror. The Soviet budget, though, could no longer afford to keep up in the arms race.

In classic Soviet style, Lenin was reinterpreted to lend ideological legitimacy to *realpolitik*: in his worthy (if rather tedious) flagship book *Perestroika*, Gorbachev claims that 'more than once he [Lenin] spoke about the priority of interests common to all humanity over class interests'. This was blatant revisionism, though, of Lenin's stark picture of a world divided along lines of class, and was bound to raise the hackles of the purists. Egor Ligachev, the principled puritan whom Andropov had promoted into the Central Committee Secretariat and who had acquired a significant foreign policy role within the Supreme Soviet, was one such skeptic. A flexible conservative rather than in any sense a radical, he had been prepared to see a rationalisation of arms expenditure and foreign commitments (he had, for example, no qualms about a negotiated withdrawal from Afghanistan), but not such wholesale alteration of the Marxist–Leninist bases of politics. Until his demotion in late

1988, he would continue to assert that all foreign policy needs must be grounded upon an ideological world-view, that it was perfectly acceptable to strike deals with the West, but that talk of 'partnership' should not blind the USSR to the fact that ultimately the West was its rival. To Gorbachev, this was just Brezhnev-era paranoia all over again, and Ligachev received short shrift when he tried to peddle his ideas at Politburo meetings.

At first, Gorbachev seemed especially interested in the United Nations as a possible structure through which to guarantee the USSR's security. In August 1987 he proposed a UN Security Council summit on disarmament and development, and a month later outlined a vision of a comprehensive global approach founded upon the UN Charter. He soon came to realise that the UN was just too passive and bureaucratic to adopt such a role. This was hardly very important, though, because Gorbachev had found a fertile new image for his notions of global and regional interdependence.

> . . . *the Pacific, our common home.*
>
> Mikhail Gorbachev, speaking in Vladivostok, 1986
>
> . . . *the sub-arctic, our common home.*
>
> – Mikhail Gorbachev, speaking in Murmansk, 1987
>
> . . . *the 'common European home' . . . a certain integral whole.*
>
> Mikhail Gorbachev, speaking in Prague, 1987
>
> *All that remained was for him to go to Ulan-Bator [capital of Mongolia] and talk of 'Asia, our common home'!*
>
> Richard Sakwa, *Gorbachev and his Reforms* (Hemel Hempstead: Phillip Allen, 1990)

Richard Sakwa was being a little mischievous, but it is certainly striking how Gorbachev was prepared to place the USSR in a regional as much as global context. This was for three main reasons. Relations with the USA were improving steadily, but too slowly. Gorbachev wanted to speed the thaw by removing specific bones of contention. He was also looking beyond the crude East–West divide, to developing 'good neighbourly relations' on a nation-by-nation basis. Hence his overtures to China, his flexibility over Afghanistan and his charm offensive in Europe. It was also meant to justify his more peaceable military doctrine. Whereas before the USSR had felt that it had to maintain forces capable of deterring or defeating any attack, on a global theatre, with new regional accord then forces needed only to be the bare minimum to make any military threat uneconomical. The aim was not to win any war, but just to make it too expensive for any enemy to start one.

'REASONABLE SUFFICIENCY' AND 'DEFENSIVE DEFENCE'

[The USSR needs] a military potential that gives a country reliable security and protection from attack – but excludes the waging of aggressive operations by that country.

Vadim Zagladin of the Central Committee Secretariat
International Department, 1986

Arguably it was this policy of 'reasonable sufficiency' (*razumnaya dostatochnost'*) which finally destroyed the alliance between the Gorbachevian reformists and the military. While arms cuts had simply meant making do with fewer weapons or a slightly different mix of forces, this shift in basic military doctrine had fundamental implications for the Soviet armed forces, and would require a total rethink of their structure and role. At first, the military had supported such 'military *perestroika*'. Indeed, in the late 1970s and early 1980s they had themselves been carrying out a rigorous reassessment of their traditional approach to war, reaching two broad conclusions. Firstly, that nuclear war was not a winnable proposition. Of course, this is what Gorbachev said, but the difference is that as a result they thought not that there was unlikely to be any future major war, but that it would remain a conventional – non-nuclear – affair. Secondly, that new 'emerging technologies' (advanced computers, remote-sensing equipment, 'smart' homing missiles, etc.) would revolutionise war, making simple size of forces far less important than their quality, their training and the speed with which they could be mobilised, transported and concentrated on the battlefield.

The powerful and farsighted Marshal Nikolai Ogarkov, Chief of the General Staff (1977–84), elaborated this view in his two key books, *Vsegda v gotovnosti k zashchite otechestva* (*Always Ready to Defend the Fatherland*, Moscow: Voenizdat, 1982) and *Istoriya uchit bditel'nosti* (*History Teaches Vigilance*, Moscow: Voenizdat, 1985). In them, he made it clear that he felt the security of the USSR would be based most firmly upon a dynamic and modern economy, hence general support for the principle of *perestroika*. Yet at the same time, he demanded more resources for the military to develop and buy new technology weapons of its own. Ogarkov's line – which had become Defence Ministry orthodoxy by 1985 – was not only characterised by this priority given to modernisation, but also by the renewed interest being devoted to how to win a conventional war in a high-technology age. The answer, the military believed, was in deep battle: ideally moving first, with forces based near the enemy which would strike far behind the enemy lines to shatter their cohesion and morale, or else responding to an enemy attack with an instant, retaliatory offensive. In other words, the war should be fought on the enemy's territory, so that he would not dare use nuclear weapons on Soviet forces and that the Soviets would always retain the initiative.

Gorbachev was offering the long-term technological pay-off the military demanded, but his policy was based on averting rather than winning wars. It was also predicated upon gaining the support, trade and assistance of the West, for which he was prepared to pull forces away from NATO's borders and limit the USSR's capability of launching such a lighting strike. Instead, he was to put his weight behind the notion of 'defensive defence', of organising forces so that they could defend the USSR but that no one could think them able to launch an offensive. This meant building more defensive weapons (anti-tank missiles, for example, rather than tanks), devising defensive strategies and creating defensive force structures. Thus arose a fundamental problem for the military: it had devised what it felt was a war-winning strategy based on offensive forces such as tank armies and paratroopers. It had enshrined them within its basic theoretical texts and was equipping itself with appropriate weapons and equipment. But it had also helped elect a General Secretary whose political strategy ruled that strategy out.

The generals hoped to be able to ignore Gorbachev or bring him round to their way of thinking. They echoed his rhetoric while trying to continue their own kind of reform. In May 1987 the Warsaw Pact's Political Consultative Committee, its notional governing body, announced that it was adopting a defensive military doctrine, but to a great extent this consisted of little more than tacking some pious statements and discredited initiatives on to the Pact's previous doctrine paper. Writing in a booklet called *On Guard for Socialism and Peace* (Moscow: Voenizdat, 1987), Yazov made it clear that he saw no basic contradiction between a defensive doctrine and maintaining large offensive forces. From the Great Patriotic War, he raised the example of the battle of Kursk in 1943, where a German attack had been broken by tank-heavy forces which promptly rolled into the offensive. From a military point of view, his view made perfect sense. The USSR had a proven and credible military doctrine and for decades had been training, arming, structuring and planning for just such a 'forward defence'. What Yazov failed to appreciate was the extent to which the political context had changed, and how far military doctrine was now being driven by the politicians.

Thus, the military set out to defeat or hinder these unwelcome and, in its view, dangerous notions. The generals could not afford to be seen in open opposition. The Party retained a strong institutional fear of any signs of 'Bonapartism', the military take-over of a revolutionary regime, and this would have given Gorbachev the opportunity to sack them. Nor, though, could Gorbachev push them too far. First of all, it was actually very difficult for him to find out if and when the military was flouting his policy line. Even then, he needed the generals. With his thin majority in the Party leadership, he could not afford openly to alienate such a powerful political bloc. Besides, who would he find to replace them? He could hardly sack the entire Stavka. From this time until the August Coup of 1991 (and, indeed, beyond), reformists and conservatives were locked in a largely hidden struggle to reshape military doctrine. Neither side managed to win, and the result – as in so many other aspects of *perestroika* – was a debilitating stalemate, until 1993 when, arguably, the military finally had its way.

The new line also alarmed the military-industrial complex, which feared falling orders and demands for totally different systems to fight new types of war. At the same time, it began to sever many of the links between the military and the KGB. After all, Gorbachev's doctrine of avoiding rather than fighting wars put a premium upon the intelligence services, which were now expected to provide early warning as a substitute for massive forces. The armed forces had used *glasnost'* to exonerate themselves from their disastrous showing in the first year of the Second World War, by showing how it had been Stalin's miscalculations which had left them unprepared and ill-equipped for the Nazi attack in 1941. The KGB neatly co-opted this line: what, after all, had been Stalin's mistake? Not to believe his spies when they warned him of the coming attack. Had he used his intelligence effectively, the war need not have been decided by sheer force of numbers. *Perestroika* and arms cuts meant that reliable and timely intelligence was needed as never before. Thus, the 'security lobby' was divided. The armed forces and their suppliers were hostile; the KGB was ambivalent; the Foreign Ministry positive. *Glasnost'*, Gorbachev's policy of openness and debate, would open these divisions and shift the balance of power within the decision-making process. The military had built for itself a near monopoly of 'official' experts on defence issues and was unprepared to accept the basic tenets of Gorbachev's NPM. So Gorbachev would create his own experts: this was the time in which the *institutchiki* would come into their own.

GLASNOST' AND THE MODERN SECURITY STATE

The nuclear disaster at Chernobyl' in April 1986 had illustrated the limits of Gorbachev's early and rather conservative approach to *glasnost'* as simply a more sophisticated use of propaganda. It was eighteen days after the explosion before the authorities began to admit the scale of the problem, and even then the truth came so slowly and grudgingly that most people chose to believe the grapevine. Gorbachev's national and international prestige suffered, but he did learn his lesson. After Chernobyl', he accepted that *glasnost'* needed not just to be a tactic but a whole new approach, creating a culture of far greater freedom of information and debate. This would inevitably be a slow and patchy process – it was July 1988 before the Politburo would adopt a resolution on the need for an 'information society' – but it carried with it serious implications for the security debate. Even at this stage it was clear that the armed forces were far less able than many other groups to recognise and learn the new rules of the political game. Nor were they particularly prepared to try. As far as they were concerned, Gorbachev and his reformers were breaking unwritten bargains and thus did not deserve their full candour and support.

On the other hand, the KGB was to enter into the spirit of *glasnost'* with hearty and engaging cynicism. Just as their master

Andropov had, on the eve of his election, created for himself an image in the West of a genial liberal, whose tastes ran to Jack Daniels whisky and Jacqueline Suzanne novels, the KGB worked hard on its media profile. In November 1987 it outlined a plan for Politburo approval which in due course led to a wide range of initiatives, from reorganisation to the holding of a 'Miss KGB' competition. In 1988 Chebrikov was promoted away from the KGB and replaced by Vladimir Kryuchkov. As head of the First Chief Directorate since 1974, Kryuchkov's reputation was less as a repressive secret police chief and more as a canny spymaster, an image the KGB did much to foster. Increasingly, the KGB sought to play up the less political aspects of its work, from fighting organised crime to catching foreign spies. Certainly until mid 1989, the KGB still enjoyed the confidence of the leadership, and won both partial immunity from *glasnost'* – very little critical coverage on it appeared in the press up to this time – and from any significant reorganisation or reform.

Within the Ministry of Internal Affairs (MVD), Gorbachev began by faithfully following Andropov's lead, imposing renewed discipline. The problem the reformists faced regarding the MVD was merely the problem they faced with the whole USSR in miniature: that it is far easier to destroy the old system than create a new one. They were able to purge the corrupt and incompetent, yet where to find new recruits? After all, the appeal of the militiaman's job had always been based substantially upon the opportunities it offered for petty graft. Official crime rates were not rising: from 2,083,501 crimes in 1985, the total actually fell over the next two years, to 1,798,549 in 1987. Yet *glasnost'* brought with it a new awareness of the criminality of the USSR, which sometimes verged on the hysterical. The state's first response was instinctive, and reflected the mixed impulses of the early reform era. On the one hand, violent crime deserved a violent response. On the other, though, it had to be appropriate, since the state might now have to account for its actions. These contradictory impulses were reflected in the formation of OMON, Otryady militsii osobennogo naznacheniya (Special Purpose Militia Detachments), paramilitary units trained and equipped to deal with riots, armed crimes and similarly serious public order offences. These were men with the guns and powers to deliver a devastating response to serious crime, but they were also recruited for their experience and maturity (the average age of the Moscow OMON on formation was thirty-three) such that it would also be a measured one.

Certainly on the surface, the early Gorbachev years saw a steady 'Westernisation' of the security apparatus, with greater openness, a new approach to criminality (seeing it as a social problem rather than anti-state dissidence or lingering vestiges of capitalism) and an adoption of many of the methods and structures developed by the West. This must, however, be kept in context. There were two reasons why the security apparatus seemed more prepared to embrace reform. First of all, because they felt confident and secure enough to use and, if necessary, abuse the new freedoms for their own advantages. At the same time, though, many of their leaders were sophisticated and flexible enough to realise that reform could potentially work to their advantage. Whereas the military found it hard to come to terms with the notion that wars were to be avoided rather than won, and by political consensus rather than armed might, the security services had always held the view that it was better to forestall than punish dissent and social disorder. The question became one of means to the end, and it was not until *perestroika* and *glasnost'* came to be seen as greater dangers than stagnation and cynicism that these agencies would begin to distance themselves from Gorbachev.

GORBACHEV THE PEACEMAKER

The four decades of the nuclear arms race have left mankind literally staring the problem of survival in the face [while] . . . even with all its diversity and contradictions, the world of today is becoming increasingly interrelated, interdependent and largely integral.

Mikhail Gorbachev, in *Pravda*, 1987

Gorbachev's early years in power were, therefore, years full of political growth, activity and apparent success. In terms of international diplomacy, Gorbachev quickly established himself as a superb operator. He criss-crossed the globe in the pursuit of his foreign policy objectives, from Geneva (1985) to Warsaw (1986), from Reykjavik (1986) to Czechoslovakia (1987). He even made a triumphal visit to a 'Gorbymaniac' USA in 1987, and in the course of his travels not only developed personal political relationships with foreign leaders from his old friend Margaret Thatcher to his new friend Ronald Reagan and West Germany's Helmut Kohl, but moved rapidly to consolidate his position at home. Allies or presumed allies moved into key government posts: Shevardnadze at the Foreign Ministry, Yazov at the Defence Ministry, Chebrikov in the KGB, Ligachev and Yakovlev in the central apparatus. The Soviet approach to security and foreign policy evolved with him. From strident stereotyping, Soviet propaganda became increasingly subtle and intelligent. Again, the temptation is to call it 'Western', as the Kremlin's acquired its own mediagenic 'spin doctors' and commentators. Even the US Defense Department's annual *Soviet Military Power* brochure faced an ever more confident challenge from the Soviets' own version, *Whence the Threat to Peace?* With the techniques, so too did the policies develop. Whereas Brezhnev's detente had simply been a breathing space, a pause in competition, the new line looked to create mutually beneficial interdependencies, such that different systems could coexist and potential conflicts be averted, and the arms race could be not just halted but reversed. This way the USSR could launch a *konversiya* of its whole system, and regain both its economic dynamism and political legitimacy.

Gorbachev was, after all, that most dangerous and inspirational of figures, a believer. For all the careerism and corruption of the late Soviet state, he believed both in the USSR as a great, global power and Marxism–Leninism as a millenarian ideology. He believed that were the Soviet people to be granted greater freedom and trusted with more information, they would work for the benefit of the state and realise the virtues of *real* Marxism–Leninism, as opposed to the shabby compromises of a Brezhnev or the omnivorous terror cult of a Stalin. He believed that it was possible to reform such a system's politics, economy and society all at once and to do so, moreover, without mass coercion or violence. He believed in the Party, that it could evolve its structures and programme as quickly as Gorbachev could develop his ideas.

He was wrong, but in the early years he could perhaps be excused his optimism. The Soviet people genuinely responded well to him. Russian political culture has long embraced the folk myth of the 'good tsar' who would at long last come to the people, realise what was really going on and sweep out his evil and misleading advisers and lead the people to a new, golden age. With his much publicised walk-abouts, his renewed campaign to purge and humiliate corrupt Party bosses and his open admission of the need for change, Gorbachev seemed at last to be that 'good tsar'. Of course, in the long term this was to prove disastrous, in that popular expectations reached a level Gorbachev could never match, leading to disillusion and protest. Similarly, his security and foreign policies seemed to be carrying all before them. When he signed the INF Treaty in Washington, in December 1987, this was not just a long stride forward in arms negotiations, it represented international recognition of his good faith and the need to change the bases of East/West relations. When, in April 1988, an agreement for the withdrawal of Soviet forces from Afghanistan was concluded, it did not merely signal a staunching of this 'bleeding wound', it opened the way for a new diplomatic offensive in Asia and a demilitarisation of relations with the Developing World. In this, it built on early moves, such as Ligachev's address to the Vietnamese Communist Party Congress in December 1986 at which he stressed the need to normalise relations with China.

Of course, many of these triumphs were illusory or transient. As Gorbachev became increasingly radical in his prescriptions for the USSR, then so many of his 'allies' would distance themselves from him. A harbinger of the way he would also begin to be outflanked by less cautious figures was the attack upon him by Boris Yeltsin at the Central Committee plenum meeting of October 1987, while the outbreak of fighting between Armenian and Azeri extremists over the Nagorno-Karabakh region in February 1988 was the first sign of the rising tide of violent nationalism. The West's leaders, themselves eager to reduce their defence budgets and carve their places in history, were happy to accept Gorbachev's deals on nuclear arms, but would never offer the vision, political will and material resources he would need to restructure the USSR. This was, after all, the key weakness of his plans. There were to prove insufficient internal forces supporting reform in the USSR to overcome the stagnation, economic decay and political drift of the past decades and the political culture of centuries. Unprepared and unable to use mass coercion, and without appreciable political and economic support from the West, Gorbachev was to prove unable to hold his ill-assorted coalition together. A Soviet nationalist, he was unable to understand the nationalisms of the constituent peoples of the USSR; relatively open to new ideas, he was unable to empathise with the innate conservatism of the élite; and an idealist, he was unable to retain the loyalties of the pragmatists who elected him.

PART THREE

THE FAILURE OF REFORM

5 FROM *PERESTROIKA* TO *KATASTROIKA*: THE END OF THE REFORMIST SECURITY CONSENSUS, 1988–90

1988   *February* Agreement on withdrawal from Afghanistan.

March Gorbachev renounces the 'Brezhnev Doctrine'.

May Moscow summit between Reagan and Gorbachev.

June XIX Party Conference: Gorbachev's general line of reform approved.

September 'Krasnoyarsk speech': Gorbachev outlines proposals to increase security in the Asia–Pacific region.

November Constitutional reforms, creating an elected bicameral parliament and a strong executive Presidency approved.

December Gorbachev's UN address commits the USSR to unilateral cuts of 500,000 troops.

1989   *February* Withdrawal from Afghanistan completed.

April Unilateral troop withdrawals from Hungary begin.

May Gorbachev visits Beijing.

May–June New Congress of People's Deputies holds its first session.

August *Solidarity* forms new government in Poland.

November Malta summit between Gorbachev and Bush. Berlin Wall falls. Czech government falls in 'Velvet Revolution'.

December Romanian dictator Ceauşescu toppled and killed.

1990   *January* Civil war between Azerbaijan and Armenia.

May Yeltsin elected President of Russia. Washington summit between Gorbachev and Bush.

Perestroika has failed. Gorbachev has failed. The USSR has failed.

Election leaflet, 1989

If in 1986, Gorbachev had been forced to deny that he was launching a revolution, in December 1988 he would proclaim it proudly to the whole world. At the UN General Assembly, he announced that the USSR was 'undergoing a truly revolutionary upsurge . . . bold revolutionary transformations'. While the period between Gorbachev's accession to power in 1985 and the 19th Party Conference in June/July 1988 seemed to represent the heyday of reformism, though, Gorbachev's rhetoric reflected not growing confidence but desperation. Admittedly, these had been years marked for many within and outside the USSR by the exhilaration of new ideas, new possibilities, a whole new context and vocabulary of politics. Yet reform had yet to produce much in the way of practical improvement. The INF Treaty had been signed and discussions of military doctrine were now laced with the new buzzwords, from 'reasonable sufficiency' to 'defensive defence', but policy was still largely in the hands of the generals and the defence budget was not just still huge but almost impossible accurately to measure. Despite fine talk of renovating the Soviet economy, its state only worsened: by late 1988 meat was being rationed in half the regions of the Russian Republic, while in 1989 prices rose twice as fast as wages.

Besides which, the stirring and humanistic idealism of New Political Thinking was to find itself increasingly unable to provide usable answers to the problems posed both by the unfolding events of the time. Reform was to see the end of the USSR's Eastern European empire, which made sense morally and economically, but unnerved conservative politicians, Russian nationalists and generals forced suddenly to revise the very bases of their military strategy of the past forty years. Even while grappling with the implications of the end of the Soviet empire, Gorbachev's attempt to use democracy as a weapon to break conservative resistance unleashed a new variety of nationalisms which threatened the very existence of the USSR. Gorbachev had been elected by the Soviet élite on a very narrow majority and with a very specific mandate, of reforming the existing system to ensure its future. Increasingly, though, he was to move away from this narrow perspective and come to see the corruption at the heart of the Soviet system. As he became more radical in his prescriptions, his original, Andropovian coalition began to break apart, and the more fierce and obdurate resistance to him grew.

In the winter of 1990–91, Gorbachev was to flirt briefly and dangerously with the notion of a return to the 'iron hand', the adoption of the so-called 'Chinese model' of economic liberalisation under firm political control. To a considerable extent this reflects his desperation, for the years 1988–90 were years of failure. Early in his time as General Secretary, Gorbachev had raised the image of the *tormozhenie*, a 'braking mechanism' slowing reform to the point of uselessness. Over time, it would become clear that *perestroika* was being held back by three key lacks: of a sufficient constituency for genuine, radical change within the Soviet élite; of mechanisms to implement change within a system which for so long had been designed with the express purpose of preventing it; and of new ideas able to provide an intellectual coherence to reform.

Security policy was no exception and the period saw as a result a steady radicalisation of Gorbachev's position and a frantic search for new 'quick fixes'. Not only was Gorbachev acutely aware of his tenuous political majority, but he was the product of a system which had a tradition of relying on 'big ideas' such as Khrushchev's 'Virgin Lands Scheme' (a dramatic but foolhardy scheme to cultivate hitherto useless regions) and Brezhnev's 'BAM' (a new trans-Siberian rail link, which inspired a thousand stirring agitprop posters). These grand designs have value in terms of propaganda and élite politics, but the modern world is too complex for such simple answers. The problem was that neither Gorbachev nor his inner circle proved able to create a programme for reform which managed to be both politically digestible for the élite and able to carry out the unprecedented task of renewing a system already in the final stages of decay. Instead, his general security policy came to be built on three broad themes: the conversion of defence industries to civil needs (*'konversiya'*) and a general demilitarisation of the economy; negotiated and unilateral arms cuts both to reduce the military budget and win Western aid; and, finally, Gorbachev's greatest gamble, gradual democratisation of all aspects of the state's activities, including defence and internal security.

BIG IDEAS (1): *KONVERSIYA*

Given that the Soviet economy was still to a considerable extent dominated by the defence industries, its 'civilianisation' had been a priority for the reformists from the start. Andropov had looked to importing good practice from the military-industrial complex (VPK) to the rest of the economy, and when Gorbachev appointed Lev

97

Zaikov, an industrial manager from Leningrad, as Central Committee secretary with responsibility for the military-industrial sector, in July 1985, he was clearly equally aware of its potential value. Within a year Zaikov was beginning publicly to advocate the transfer of defence industry capacity to civilian needs. In 1987 he moved on to become Party first secretary in Moscow, and was replaced by Oleg Baklanov, who had previously been Minister for General Machine-Building. This period saw a radical shake-up of the senior echelons of the VPK. In 1985 seventy-five-year-old I. Dmietrev was replaced as head of the Secretariat's Defence Industry Department by O. Belyakov, a man two decades younger. L. Smirnov, chairman of the powerful Council of Ministers Military-Industrial Commission was succeeded by Yurii Maslyukov, again twenty years his junior. E. Slavskii, the Minister for Medium Machine-Building, had actually been born in 1898, and his replacement by L. Ryabov in 1986 came as little surprise. Thus, by 1989, only two of the defence-related industries retained their Brezhnev-era ministers, and a new generation of younger, more flexible and highly educated figures had come to the fore. Having renovated the VPK, in 1988, Gorbachev used the podium of the UN General Assembly to announce the launch of a major initiative. 'Is the conversion of military production realistic?' he asked. 'We believe that it is'.

Unfortunately, *konversiya* proved not to be the expected salvation. If the experiences of Germany, Italy and Japan after the Second World War are anything to go by, the best thing that can happen to a war economy is for it to be bombed to rubble. That way reconstruction can be from scratch, and with the most modern techniques and technologies. Conversion, retooling and retraining, ironically enough, are far more difficult and expensive. One figure, often cited, is that for every ruble or dollar saved through conversion, two need to be spent, up front, in the process. In the long term, this investment may make sense – but only if the resources to fund it properly are available. Trying to make do in the absence of that initial capital ensured that *konversiya* was a disaster, both politically and economically. The military-industrial sector accounted for many of the most efficient and productive plants within the USSR's bloated industrial base, which had benefited from the VPK's priority status in the days of central planning and were thus expected to do as well in the days of self-accounting and profit-and-loss budgeting. Yet they found themselves squeezed by reform.

The defence industrialists could no longer buy the best talent because they lost their preferential salary scales: between 1985 and 1990, industrial wages within the VPK rose by 10 per cent, but the overall average rise was close to 40 per cent Most important, though, was the fact that with the defence budget falling, it was no longer in receipt of military orders on the same scale as before. In January 1989 the leadership announced plans for a major reduction in the USSR's armed forces and military spending. By the end of 1990, forces would be cut by 12 per cent and the defence budget by 14 per cent. In particular, this hit arms procurement programmes, which fell by almost 20 per cent. Nor could transfers of arms abroad pick up the slack. Like the USA, the USSR had relied heavily on the export of military equipment on long-term credits or at uneconomically low prices as a way of buying influence, especially in the Developing World. Gorbachev's axe was also to fall on these funds and according to the Stockholm International Peace Research Institute, exports fell by over a third in the period 1989–90 alone. While this saved the Soviet state money, it all added to the pressures bearing down upon the defence industries. Finally, the gradual liberalisation of pricing meant that suppliers began raising raw material and component prices for defence industry plants.

Meanwhile the defence industries were not free to develop themselves as businesses by, for example, exporting their wares or sacking workers or reinvestment. The irony is that at the very time when the reformists were preaching a decentralisation of management, the importance of the VPK to the reform programme meant that they made sure they retained a firm grip upon it and thus strangled real initiative. Central planning proved to be alive and well and telling the VPK to produce consumer goods; orders would often be issued without regard for the availability of funds or raw materials. Effective reorientation of an industry is a long-term process, and involves an investment of time and money: assessing and developing new markets, building and buying new equipment, training the workforce in new methods.

Moscow granted the defence industries neither, and thus they were forced to produce whatever they could manage quickly and on the cheap, rather than whatever made sense or whatever might find a viable market. In one Tupolev aircraft factory, highly-trained aerospace engineers found themselves being told to build bicycles, for example, while the Kharkov tank plant started producing a wide range of tank-like fire engines, emergency cranes and road-levellers. There was no real demand for them, and they were far more expensive to run than most of their rival designs, but from the plant management's point of view at least they were easy to build and kept Moscow quiet. Besides which, arms production has traditionally carried with it generous profit margins – civil production has one anywhere between two and six times thinner. In a capitalist economy, the result would be bankruptcies and unemployment, yet Gorbachev could hardly survive such a devastation of the VPK, and thus the state had to step in to subsidise these ailing factories. Conversion, far from saving the state money, began costing it more and more, just to avoid its economic consequences.

As a result, *konversiya* was also a political disaster. The figures at first seemed impressive: in 1990 alone, half a million workers were reassigned to civil purposes, while the share of civilian goods in the total output of the VPK rose to 50 per cent. Moving from the front page of *Izvestiya* to the shops, though, there appeared to be nothing to show, as such efforts coincided with a general decline in Soviet industry. By the end of 1989 only 15 per cent of new products being produced met international standards, while by 1990 the VPK was still under-fulfilling its conversion plans by 20 per cent. By appearing to promise a quick and easy solution to deep-rooted economic problems, it played its part in the rise of unrealistic aspirations amongst the Soviet people. When these failed to be met, Gorbachev's popular legitimacy began its disastrous slide. In 1989 Oleg Baklanov had warned against seeing 'conversion as a kind of horn of plenty, capable of immediately producing an economic miracle', but as the government failed to develop a viable economic reform programme, conversion increasingly began to be presented in just such a light. More directly, though, it alienated many of the technologically-proficient, hard-working and ambitious workers and industrial managers who had previously supported *perestroika*, their prestige and salaries equally effectively undermined by *konversiya*. It was perhaps understandable why one of the eight leaders of the 1991 August Coup proved to be that very same Oleg Baklanov.

BIG IDEAS (2): DEFENCE CUTS

Are the Americans willing to do nothing to help us? Are we the ones who have to make all the moves? We take these huge steps and all we hear from Washington is, 'More! More! You must do more!'

Eduard Shevardnadze to his aides, 1989; cited in M. Beschloss and S. Talbott, *At the Highest Levels* (London: Little, Brown, 1993)

Conversion needed not only to be matched with cuts in the size of the Soviet military machine, but illustrated the USSR's desperate need for foreign aid, trade and investment to provide the resources for *perestroika* to work. If *konversiya* was a desperate bid to find a quick answer for the economy, Gorbachev found himself having to turn to arms cuts as the only option he had left to play in foreign politics. He played this card rather more effectively – his strengths were always as diplomat rather than economist – but ultimately it was not enough. Indeed, it finally turned the High Command against him, turning passive resistance into active subversion.

Whereas the rise of conversion had been as a response to the failure of Gorbachev's other economic initiatives such as cooperatives and profit-and-loss accounting, his radicalisation over the armed forces and international relations was a reaction to the 'human' *tormozhenie* at work. With the exception of the tortured reassessments of the role of the Party in the dying years of *perestroika*, perhaps the most open and bitterly fought debate of the *glasnost'* era was over the future of the military and its doctrine. At the very least, this illustrated several key elements of the development of policy at this time: how Gorbachev was moving away from alliance with the military; the extent to which this was generating internal bureaucratic resistance; and just how far the *institutchiki* were beginning to drive the debate. The High Command had been prepared to accept the rhetoric of 'defensive defence' since 1987, yet this had led to little real innovation in military thinking. After all, Soviet military doctrine had always claimed to be defensive. The USSR's huge tank formations and paratrooper forces were presented as reflecting nothing more than a determination to fight a 'forward defence'; in other words, not retreating into Soviet territory as had happened in the Second World War when the Western USSR had been devastated, but delivering a convincing counter-attack to any assault. It had certainly not resulted in any particular willingness on the part of the military to accept budget cuts.

Gorbachev had hoped that in appointing a relative outsider such as Yazov, without any real power base in Moscow, his new Defence Minister would prove rather more tractable. As it was, Yazov soon became house-trained by his ministry. Yazov and, in particular, Chief of the General Staff Akhromeev were prepared to accept the need for economic regeneration, even at the cost of some budget stringency. Yet this could not be at the expense of military security. Akhromeev's solution was to immerse himself in arms treaty negotiations, seeking to ensure that Soviet cuts were met by comparable Western reductions. Even in 1987, he had written that 'The security of each state is directly dependent upon the security of all. It can only be achieved by limiting and reducing armaments and by strengthening confidence-building measures and international cooperation between nations'. Akhromeev proved a formidable negotiator at summits from Reykjavik (1986) to Moscow (1988) and was instrumental in the successful conclusions of the INF talks. Whereas Akhromeev's was an essentially active and optimistic position, Yazov's was far more negative. According to the then Foreign Minister, Shevardnadze, Yazov consistently misled the leadership on a series of issues, especially when he felt it might otherwise be tempted to make further concessions to the USA. One example was the large radar at Krasnoyarsk, in Siberia, built to detect incoming US missiles. This was a clear violation of the 1972 ABM Treaty, a fact of which Washington was well aware thanks to its satellite surveillance. The Kremlin, on the other hand, was misinformed that it was a satellite monitoring station and thus exempted from the treaty. According to one account, in 1988 the army even began building 'show military settlements' to impress visiting government officials. In particular, Yazov became increasingly outspoken in his rejection of 'defensive defence', of 'reasonable sufficiency' and their corollary, that peace was best served by diplomacy than counter-attack:

> *The defensive military doctrine of the Warsaw Pact, which is calculated exclusively on repulsing a military threat, does not at all mean that our actions will be of passive character . . . In case of aggression, our armed forces, together with fraternal socialist armies, will defend socialist achievements with all resolution.*

General Dmitrii Yazov, 1987

The failures of limited reform and conservative resistance it brought made Gorbachev increasingly aware of the need for more dramatic and far-reaching changes, and with it a more confrontational line with the military. At first, he retained some measure of distance by merely allowing (or encouraging) academics and commentators to express their views on the need for military reform. This was typical Gorbachev: letting others develop various ideas from which he could select those he felt most useful and appropriate. In September 1988, for example, the journal *XX vek i mir* (*Twentieth Century and Peace*) broached the notion of a radical reform of the structure of the armed forces. It argued that rather than being based on a large body of conscripts with a professional corps of officers and specialists, the army should be divided between local territorial militias, equipped and trained for defence, and a small, all-professional, mobile central force. Equally characteristic were Gorbachev's moves to consolidate the reformists' grip upon foreign and security policy. Not only did Shevardnadze continue to receive Gorbachev's full backing at this stage, but Evgenii Primakov, Yakovlev's successor as director of IMEMO, was brought into the Politburo as a candidate member in September 1989.

This reflected the renewed emphasis Gorbachev placed upon his personal diplomacy and his campaign to woo the world. In May 1988 he hosted a summit with Reagan in Moscow, which furthered their own 'special relationship', and Gorbachev's 'Krasnoyarsk speech' in September was a powerful appeal for nuclear arms cuts, and contained an offer to give up Cam Ranh Bay naval base in Vietnam if the USA renounced the use of naval facilities in the Philippines. In December he met the Chinese Foreign Minister and prepared the ground for a visit to Beijing next year, the first by a Soviet leader for thirty years. For all this, though, Gorbachev's diplomacy had still to go beyond encouraging words and cheering crowds.

In part this was as a result of resistance from within the military. There was a need for a bold gesture to force change upon the military, and again it was characteristic of Gorbachev that he chose to make it in the form of a public announcement, effectively challenging his rivals to submit or openly defy him. In December 1988 he made the move which perhaps permanently soured his relations with the military. Speaking at the United Nations, he suddenly announced that the Soviet armed forces would undertake a unilateral reduction of half a million men, of whom about half would come from units based in Eastern Europe. The reaction within the High Command was one of horror. Ironically, the decision cost Gorbachev his closest real ally, the 'honourable general' Akhromeev, while fickle Yazov stayed on. The highly-respected Chief of the General Staff, a man prepared to accept certain defence cuts in the name of modernisation, felt he could not stomach the position in which he had been placed. Akhromeev retired, with dignity, on the grounds of ill-health, although he remained a military adviser to Gorbachev. The move also alienated yet further the VPK, since it meant that many orders for military equipment were cancelled with only three or six months' notice, throwing production schedules into chaos. The Tupolev aircraft design bureau, for example, lost fully half its 1990 orders.

Akhromeev's replacement, Colonel General Mikhail Moiseev, was selected for his close links to Yazov (he had been Yazov's deputy and then successor at the Far Eastern Military District), and soon established himself as more of a hawk either than his minister or his predecessor. While paying lip-service to *perestroika* and arms reduction, he set himself against any dramatic reform of the military. In particular, he took the offensive in countering demands from civilian politicians, journalists and academics for an end to conscription and the formation of a smaller professional army, or one based upon territorial militias. He proved an articulate champion of the old methods. Rather more able to play the public relations game than most generals, he did everything he could to ensure that the word *naemnaya* ('mercenary') was used to describe a professional army, rather than *profesional'naya* or *dobrovol'naya* ('volunteer'). He also tried to fight the reformists on their own ground, claiming that a mixed conscript–volunteer army was some five to eight times cheaper than an all-professional force. He was being more than slightly cavalier with the truth, in that many of the costs associated with the old structure were not represented in the defence budget, being borne by other agencies or simply taken in the form of direct transfers of resources. Besides, a more skilled volunteer army need not be as large as one primarily made up of recalcitrant and ill-trained conscripts. For all this, though, Moiseev did have a point. The Soviet armed forces were already about one-third volunteer, and a conscript is relatively cheap (Soviet soldiers on national service generally only received the equivalent of few dollars 'pocket money' per month instead of proper salaries). National service also ensures that there is always a large pool of recently-trained reservists who can be called back into the ranks in time of war. Given the size of the USSR, its history and the range of potential threats facing it, the High Command felt that this point was absolutely vital.

The resistance of Moiseev and his colleagues, though, was also based on a variety of other, less objective grounds. A smaller army needs fewer generals. In a bureaucratic system, the power and standing of any interest group is measured by the size of its budget. Furthermore, these were professional military men, who had been raised to tales of martial glory and become accustomed to the serried ranks of beribbonned soldiers goose-stepping through Red Square. If they had also been as convincingly gulled as to the state of the army as politicians had been about the real state of the nation (and anecdotes abound of bases being spruced up for inspection, even to the extent of whole clifflines being painted grey to improve the scenery) then it is not surprising that they felt pride in their services. To hear academics and journalists tell them how they should do their job, and take away so much of the majesty and grandeur of the Soviet armed forces understandably angered and embittered them. Consider, after all, the roll-call of Gorbachev's security concessions, even before the collapse of the Warsaw Pact: the cancellation of new weapons programmes, withdrawal from Afghanistan (a war the High Command felt could have been won had sufficient resources been assigned to it), unilateral cuts in forces in Europe and along the Chinese border (with promises of more to come), dramatic reductions in the military budget. And for what?

> *For what did we make these sacrifices? So that Western politicians can tell their people they have 'won', so that our own leaders can be hailed as saints by our enemies, and so that the achievements of the Soviet people and soldiers can be thrown away in months.*

Army officer at an election meeting, 1989

BIG IDEAS (3): DEMOCRATISATION

> *The existing bureaucratic machine cannot be incorporated into restructuring (perestroika). It can be broken up and eliminated, but not restructured.*

Economist Vasilii Selyunin, 1988

Moiseev's trench-by-trench defence of the old ways was characteristic of the whole bureaucratic apparatus. Factory managers and administrators had made a mockery of Gorbachev's hopes for a gradual, bottom-up revival of the economy through small-scale private enterprise and a decentralisation of decision-making. Local Party structures had been purged, reviled and entreated, but refused in the main to adjust to Gorbachev's idealistic notion of 'socialist democracy'. *Glasnost'* had bred at first a powerful current of opinion in favour of change within the country in general and the intelligentsia in particular, but hopes of harnessing this to *perestroika* were dashed upon the rocky conservatism of the local élites. Thus Gorbachev turned to his biggest idea yet, *demokratizatsiya*. This was 'democratisation' with a distinctively Soviet twist, in that Gorbachev tried to build for the Party a guaranteed role within this semi-democratic system. To him, this was his last chance to force the Party bureaucracy to change its way rather than to replace it. In practice, though, it was to destroy the USSR.

Gorbachev's growing awareness of the need to change the fundamental distribution of power within the USSR and involve the masses in politics was an evolutionary process. The Andropovian Gorbachev of 1985–86 subordinated all political issues to economic modernisation, although by the 27th Party Congress in 1986 he was beginning to talk of 'socialist democracy'. From this he moved to endorsing internal elections in which more than one candidate could stand – previously very rare in the USSR – although there was still no thought of diluting the 'leading role' of the Party. In June 1988, though, at the 19th Party Conference, Gorbachev went further than ever before, proposing multi-party elections to a new parliament, the Congress of Peoples' Deputies (SND – S"ezd narodnykh deputatov), which would have a real legislative role and not just be a rubber stamp body like the old Supreme Soviet. The SND would elect from within its number a smaller parliament, which would become the new Supreme Soviet, and which would sit year-round. This Supreme Soviet would also elect a President of the USSR, who would be a genuine, executive leader rather than merely a titular head of state. This was certainly not democracy as applied in the West, in that many seats on the SND were reserved for candidates appointed by bodies such as the Young Communist League, there were no organised parties other than the Communist Party, and Gorbachev was clearly going to be elected President, but it did represent a genuine political revolution.

Elections to the SND were held in March 1989, and at its first session, in May, Gorbachev was duly sworn in as President. The consequences were three-fold. Aspirant politicians eager to break into public life and old-style Party hacks desperate to hold on to their positions both found themselves in the unaccustomed position of having to campaign for election. Gorbachev still retained a level of personal popularity, but *perestroika* was no vote-winner. Instead, many looked to win popular support by championing local interests, representing themselves as best able to wrest concessions from Moscow or challenge its interference. Secondly, for those bureaucrat-politicians not able to play this new game, the whole affair was an outrage, which undermined the role and authority of the Party, and they would no longer trust Gorbachev. Thirdly, it meant that decisions would henceforth have to be debated and even made openly, and by a new generation of public figures, including dissidents such as Andrei Sakharov as well as Boris Yeltsin, Gorbachev's ally turned enemy. *Glasnost'* would thus have to be far more comprehensive and complete than ever before, and the notional servants of the state would need to be prepared to accept the legitimacy of the new legislators. At the first session of the Congress of Peoples' Deputies, Olympic weightlifter Yurii Vlasov accused the KGB of crimes 'unknown in the history of humanity', Andrei Sakharov clashed with veterans of the war over his assessment of the intervention in Afghanistan as a 'brutal invasion' and Colonel General Rodionov, the military commander in Georgia whose troops had killed twenty protesters while dispersing a demonstration, was forced to justify his actions to irate parliamentarians. It was clear that *demokratizatsiya* would have serious implications for foreign and security policy.

This period thus saw the press – with official sanction – making rather more realistic assessments of Soviet military intervention in Hungary in 1956 and Czechoslovakia in 1968. This was clearly a deliberate exercise to prepare the ground for a possible retreat from Eastern Europe, but, as ever, it acquired its own momentum. From the 1939 Hitler–Stalin Pact to the Cuban Missile Crisis, no aspect of past security policy escaped the new *glasnost'*. This was by no means simply recovering a history too long distorted; it also had direct, contemporary political relevance, in that past blunders were used to prove the case for taking decision-making out of the secret meetings and into parliament and public debate. With democracy, the argument went, there could have been no Afghan war, no Cuban Missile Crisis. The *institutchiki* also supported this line for obvious reasons, in that it gave them a new role as independent experts and shapers of policy. Indeed, many were direct beneficiaries of democratisation: Oleg Bogomolov of IEMSS, sociologist Tat'yana Zaslavskaya and political commentator Fedor Burlatskii were all elected.

Two parliamentary committees were established with a security role, the Commission for Defence and State Security and that for International Affairs, envisaged as bodies both to generate debate and scrutinise legislation submitted to parliament. They were attacked and undermined from the first, though. This was a problem facing the Commission for Defence and State Security, in particular. For the radicals, it was too heavily dominated by serving officers, KGB staff, defence industrialists and the like: nineteen out of forty-three members, including three senior KGB officers, a marshal, a general and an admiral. Its chair, Vladimir Lapygin, was himself a designer of missile guidance systems. The conservatives were generally suspicious, while the Defence Ministry – an organisation which, after all, was still trying to keep military maps dating back to the eighteenth century classified – was not prepared to cooperate with it in any meaningful way. Thus these commissions were forced back upon their own resources, but they never gained the support, information or professionalism they needed to have a genuine and positive role. Les Aspin, chair of the analogous US House committee, estimated that the Commission for Defence and State Security would have needed a staff of a hundred experts; it actually had a budget for only ten.

LOSING CONTROL

The key problem with the new parliamentary structure was thus that while it could cause problems for the government, it proved unable to present rival solutions, in part because of the simple inexperience of its members of parliamentarianism. Western nations with decades of experience with modern democracy hardly have a flawless record. Without traditions and parties – beyond the Communist Party – to instill discipline, without a clear constitutional role, in the midst of political and economic crisis and torn between radicals (who believed the current system illegitimate because it was not democratic enough) and conservatives (who believed it illegitimate because it was too democratic), it is pointless to try to assign blame. It is nonetheless clear that the new system failed to work, and in doing so divided and dismayed Gorbachev's allies and strengthened the hand of his enemies. The Foreign Ministry (MID), which at first welcomed the new structures, found itself increasingly frustrated in its attempt to find common ground with parliament. Compare, for example, the tone of the prologues of two surveys of its activities, presented to the Supreme Soviet in 1989 and 1991, respectively. The first proudly described itself as

both a revival of and a break with tradition. It is a break with
the tradition under which foreign policy decisions were taken in
a narrow circle . . . [but] a revival of the tradition of Lenin's
day, when the People's Commissariat for Foreign Affairs
presented annual reports to the Congress of Soviet.

Yet by 1991 the ministry was bewailing that

the USSR Supreme Soviet not only did not request such detailed
surveys and their publication, but, ultimately, did not react at all
to the ministry's surveys. If our legislators, elected organs,
executive authorities and society do not have a basis of
information and knowledge, it is hard to expect them to take
informed, considered and rational decisions. They improvise
solutions that are unprofessional and amateur.

This was more than just the gripes of a group of bureaucrats not
being given the respect they thought they deserved. The MID had
led the way in opening itself up to democratisation, and felt that it
had in return received nothing but complaints and partisan
interference, whether from conservatives angered by its 'defeatism'
or radicals looking to score political points. A perfect example of the
essentially negative role of parliament was to be found in the
nomination debates to Prime Minister Ryzhkov's new Council of
Ministers. About a third of his nominations were rejected – most
only to be replaced by almost identical clones from within the Party
and state bureaucracy. Marshal Yazov was rightly savaged, as the
defence minister under whom more soldiers died from illness and
disease than in the entire Afghan war. Yet there was no credible
alternative acceptable to the Defence Ministry and radicals alike, so
he was duly – if grudgingly – approved. Did this impress upon
Yazov the need to serve and please his new democratic masters? Of
course not: it merely heightened his and his ministry's feeling of
being under siege from hostile and opportunistic amateurs, those
whom conservative general Al'bert Makashov described as 'our
learned peacocks'. So long as the generals – and many others within
the government – felt that the parliamentarians were more interested
in their media profiles and channelling resources to their
constituencies, they could tell themselves that they were being
downright patriotic in undermining and ignoring them. This is a
conflict encountered in any democratic system, but usually it is
tempered by a clear division between civil and military

responsibilities, one not present in the USSR, and a consensus on the legitimacy of the elected representatives.

The burden of 'democratising defence' increasingly fell to Gorbachev's beleaguered team of reformists at the top and individual rebels and whistle-blowers at the bottom. It was Gorbachev who first announced to the Congress of People's Deputies the 1989 Soviet defence budget which, at seventy-seven billion rubles, was some 15 per cent of the state budget, or four times figures previously admitted, while Ryzhkov provided details of foreign aid and debt and the cost of the war in Afghanistan. Even so, there were those who felt that even these figures were too low: Major Lopatin, a member of the Commission on Defence and State Security, claimed that the real military budget was 120 billion rubles, while the Defence Ministry later admitted that the official figures excluded many associated expenses, such as on pre-draft combat training in schools and universities. The commission was only given a detailed break-down of the budget in 1990 – several months after the figures had been released to the UN – and when, in 1991, it finally got down to debating it, no Defence Ministry experts were apparently available to testify before the commission. Georgii Arbatov, director of the US and Canada Institute, went so far as to claim that the commission only heard of some strategic modernisation programmes from US Defense Secretary Cheney. Generally it was clear that where possible, the military establishment would pursue its own policies and forge alliances with political forces hostile to the direction of reforms.

The massacre of demonstrators in April 1989, for example, had taken place while Gorbachev had been abroad. Colonel General Rodionov, an outstanding military figure, was made into a scapegoat for obeying his brutal orders forcibly to disperse the protesters. Those orders came from a cabal of disgruntled former supporters of reform, including Yazov and Egor Ligachev, who used Gorbachev's absence to make a statement of their position. This way they played Gorbachev at his own game. He had a majority within the senior Party circles, but an often fragile and grudging one. When he chose to turn issues into votes of confidence, such as when he walked out of a Central Committee meeting in April 1991, his opponents were forced to back down, lacking a viable alternative candidate or programme on which they could all agree. Yet by the same token, Gorbachev did not have such a solid political mandate that he could afford to seem too confrontational towards his conservative opponents. Besides, by nature a centrist, he tended to back away from outright collision and, moreover, remained to the last convinced of his ability ultimately to convert or outmanoeuvre his rivals. In his over-confidence there was more than a little of the Khrushchev, who, just before the political coup which ousted him, told his colleagues 'What are you cooking up against me, friends? Look, if anything happens, I will throw you around like puppy dogs'.

PERESTRELKA: NATIONALISM AND THE END OF EMPIRE

The only weapons Gorbachev had at his disposal were *glasnost'* and appointment, using either the truth or the shadowy power of the General Secretary's office to undermine his opponents. These were not enough. This is, after all, the underlying theme of the final years of the USSR: of a pervasive collapse in the leadership's ability to lead and to govern, thanks largely to the increasing disunity of the Soviet élite. Other forces swept in to fill the void, largely nationalism, localism and the demagoguery of a new breed of politicians. This was the era in which, as punsters had it, *perestroika* gave way to *perestrelka* – cross-fire. Implicit within Gorbachev's drive for decentralisation and freedom of expression had been a new latitude for local interests. He had tried to prevent this from ever generating local nationalism within the multiethnic Soviet state, but this proved impossible.

The Baltic states of Latvia, Lithuania and Estonia, the last to be incorporated into the USSR, were the first to assert themselves, followed by the fractious Caucasian republics. Baltic nationalism had really begun to take open form in the summer of 1987, and local Party leaderships from the first tried to accommodate this. At the 19th Party Conference in 1989, they had argued strongly for regional economic autonomy, while 1989 saw all three republics establishing their own laws on citizenship. Opinions polarised, Russian nationals in the Baltic adopting an essentially conservative and defensive stance, while the Balts themselves became ever more radical, outdistancing the local Parties which themselves became split between 'Muscovites' and 'autonomists'. In the Caucasus, by contrast, matters were far less civil. When a long-running feud between Armenia and Azerbaijan over the region of Nagorno-Karabakh looked to be on the verge of full-scale war,

Soviet paratroopers had to be deployed in the streets of the Azeri capital Baku to restore Moscow's control. In Georgia, mass protests in Tbilisi were attacked by troops, an action which led to the resignation of the Party First Secretary. Everywhere, ethnic minorities began asserting their rights, sometimes with disastrous consequences. In the Ferghana Valley in Uzbekistan, a demonstration by Mesketian Turks in June 1989 was attacked by Uzbeks, leading to well over a hundred deaths. Some 9,000 MVD troops had to be dispatched to restore order, and this perfectly illustrates the role in which the central authorities were placed, able purely to react after events and with force. *Glasnost'* had allowed new ideologies and nationalisms to spread, while Gorbachev could no longer hire and fire as easily in the days of democratisation. His control over Party appointments, while still considerable, was increasingly useless when it was leaders such as Boris Yeltsin in Russia and Zviad Gamsakhurdia in Georgia who were becoming dominant. Gorbachev's new generation of rivals were not, after all, appointed Party bureaucrats but elected politicians.

Yet if the 'inner empire' was shaking, the 'outer empire' was falling apart. The year 1989 saw revolutions in East/Central Europe, as a series of popular uprisings and élite coups brought down the puppet regimes of the Warsaw Pact with the Kremlin's acquiesence or even encouragement. From the first, Gorbachev had made it clear both that Soviet relations with its satellites of East/Central Europe would be based purely in terms of its national interest, and that the days of the 'Brezhnev Doctrine' (the use of military intervention to safeguard Soviet domination) were over. In September 1988 a reorganisation of the Central Committee Secretariat downgraded the importance of the section dealing with Warsaw Pact Communist Parties, while in a declaration in October 1989, Moscow stated that 'there can be no justification for any use of force: whether by one military-political alliance against another or within such alliances'. Gorbachev's notions of *glasnost'* and *demokratizatsiya* legitimised attempts by radicals and reformists to bring change to their regimes. More important, though, were the practical aspects of Gorbachev's policies. For a start, he began to reduce the level of Soviet commitment to its Warsaw Pact allies, both economic and political. Given that all these countries were facing economic crises of greater or lesser proportions, this freed all sorts of pent-up pressures for change. Faced with the option of intervening to protect the 'outer empire', sitting back and seeing what happened or engaging more positively, Gorbachev opted for a mix of the last two.

Gorbachev said a very crucial thing, that a leadership that isolates itself from its people will no longer enjoy the right to exist . . . . [and that] it was up to each Communist Party to find a way to renew itself . . . . That gave us a lot of courage.

East German reformist communist Kurt Mayer, 1990

Thus, Gorbachev let some revolutions happen, such as in Hungary and Poland. Others, he probably helped along their way. Gorbachev's public snub of Honecker when visiting Berlin in October 1989 contributed to the East German President's downfall and thus to the reunification of Germany. As early as 1987, the KGB had established a secret programme to nudge the GDR towards an acceptance of reform, although neither Gorbachev nor his spies had though this would lead to the outright collapse of East Germany. In Romania, the brutal and erratic Ceauşescu regime was toppled by a combination of popular uprising and military coup, and some observers have pointed to links between the senior army commanders involved and the authorities in Moscow. The Soviets certainly moved immediately to support the post-Ceauşescu regime with diplomatic recognition and a promise of emergency fuel deliveries. In Czechoslovakia, the KGB was probably involved in an attempt in November to provoke a minor crisis sufficient to lead to the installation of a reform communist government, although in practice the result was a far more dramatic shift in power. To an extent, this was simply inevitable. The 'outer empire' of East/Central Europe had been an artificial construct, built on the foundations of Soviet military power and buttressed by economic support. In their absence, there was little these nations' dispirited élites could do but follow the example of so many of their Soviet counterparts and reinvent themselves as born-again nationalists. In this, it must be said, many were quite successful. In Bulgaria and Romania, the new regimes were essentially 'reform communist', even if they were forced to share power. For everyone concerned, change and decay could not be prevented, only managed. Even the conservatives in Moscow, for all their expressions of dismay, realised this:

Nowadays the supporters of violent methods in politics cannot justify the Tbilisi action even before their own parliament. Coping with the whole of Eastern Europe has been beyond them for a long time now, and they are perfectly aware of this.

Commentary in newspaper *Komsomol'skaya pravda*, 1990

THE RETREAT FROM GLOBALISM

If Moscow could no longer support its clients in East/Central Europe, then the fate of its 'outermost empire' across the globe was at least as gloomy. Issuing a decree on foreign aid in July 1990, Gorbachev admitted what had already become clear to all, that further economic assistance and cooperation 'shall be carried out on the principles of mutual advantage', with the aid budget dependent upon 'our country's actual resources'. During the 1986–90 Five Year Plan period, the USSR exported 56.7 billion rubles-worth of weapons, of which 8.5 billion were transferred free of charge. Yet even those notionally exported for money earned the USSR little revenue. India bought the most Soviet equipment, accounting for 15 per cent of the 1980–91 total, yet could not pay for it and owed Moscow just under ten billion rubles by 1989. The total foreign debt to the USSR in 1989 was around 86 billion rubles, largely as a result of the transfer of weapons and raw materials as a means of buying influence. Nearly 90 per cent of all debts owed by African nations, for example, were for military assistance. Moscow could no longer afford to indulge its clients so generously, both for economic reasons and because it hindered attempts to find common cause with the West and China. Besides, budgetary pressures forced Moscow to come to terms with the fact that – like most empires – the centre had been deluding itself over the amount of real control its rubles and tanks were buying. For all its use of Soviet weapons, India jealously guarded its neutral position, while Castro felt little need to moderate his criticisms of *perestroika*, just because Moscow paid over the odds for his sugar.

The aid budget was cut from 12.5 billion rubles in 1989 to 9.3 billion in 1990 – next year it was to fall to 0.4 billion. The economy of Cuba, the USSR's largest debtor, had been kept alive by cheap Soviet oil and artificially high sugar prices. In 1990 Moscow reduced its oil supplies to Cuba such that the island had a 20 per cent shortfall in its fuel needs, and in 1991 Soviet–Cuban trade switched to a hard currency basis. The Cubans were furious, but there was little they could do as their economy slid into crisis. The most visible expression of this retreat from empire was, clearly, Afghanistan. Gorbachev had long sought to staunch the flow of men and money heading towards this impoverished and turbulent neighbour, but had faced resistance from the Kabul regime (which needed its Soviet protector) and extremist and mercenary rebel groups (who opposed any compromises either on principle or because the presence of Soviet troops guaranteed them both popular support and foreign financial aid). There was also the need to convince doubters in Moscow, who felt any withdrawal would be a loss of face and a High Command which quite appreciated a half million square kilometres of live-ammunition exercise ground on which to train its officers and test its equipment. As it was, a general commitment to negotiating an equable settlement had been made at the 27th Party Congress in 1986, but even so, Aleksandr Yakovlev later revealed that it took four years to overcome passive resistance in the Politburo to any withdrawal. Nevertheless, in April 1988 the negotiations in Geneva were concluded and a deal struck. In effect, it represented little more than an agreement for the USSR to withdraw its troops in return for a US commitment not to continue to support the rebels, leaving them free to take on Kabul on their own, but it meant that Gorbachev could bring the boys home.

On 15 February 1989, in a carefully televised spectacle that showed how much the Soviets had learned about the art of media manipulation, Colonel General Boris Gromov, commander of the Soviet Limited Contingent of Troops in Afghanistan, walked over the Friendship Bridge on the Soviet–Afghan border, the last Soviet soldier (officially) back from the war. The war in Afghanistan did not stop – as of writing, the country is still torn apart by fighting which shows no sign of ending – but at least the Kabul regime had been buttressed enough that it would last a decent interval. There would be no embarrassing sudden collapse as of South Vietnam, no Soviet diplomats being hurriedly lifted by helicopter from embassy roofs. Indeed, Kabul's communist regime would outlive Moscow's.

If the Cold War had projected the internal pressures and paranoia of Washington and Moscow on to the rest of the world, so too were the insecurities and chaos of the dying Soviet Union projected elsewhere. The rising communities of the USSR were often characterised not by their common identity as their common enemies and rivalries, witnessed by the wars which were to rage across Eurasia in the 1990s. East/Central Europe once again regained a measure of freedom, but often this proved the freedom to starve, to strike, to persecute your neighbours, divide your country and re-elect Party hacks with a shrewd line in nationalist rhetoric. Released from the delicate pressures of neutrality, Yugoslavia exploded, while the dominant images of the 'New World Order' were not peace-building and general prosperity but burning skies above the Gulf and huddled refugees from Bosnia to Cambodia.

CONFLICT BETWEEN THE SECURITY INTERESTS

After all, this chaos and fragmentation applies as easily to the Soviet élite. The security interests lost their common identity of purpose and then even lost their internal cohesion. This was to have direct influence on foreign and security policy and also to the launch and failure of the 1991 coup. Again, consider Gorbachev's two remaining weapons, *glasnost'* and the power of appointment. He could encourage the media to highlight the failings of those resisting him, but by then he could no longer control *glasnost'*. He and his reforms came under equally fierce scrutiny, while in those days of media freedom, his rivals were equally free to use public debate against him.

The Defence Ministry's publications, notably the daily newspaper *Krasnaya zvezda* (*Red Star*), became critical of Gorbachev's policies, while commentators and authors closely affiliated to the military lobby also joined the fray. Two of the most forceful were Karem Rash and Aleksandr Prokhanov. The ministry's *Voenno-istoricheskii zhurnal* (*Military History Journal*) ran a series of Rash's articles in 1989 in which he praised the army as 'the backbone and sacred institution of a thousand years of statehood' and called on it to intervene to save the Motherland from what he called 'feminisation' and decline. This was doubly significant: that the Defence Ministry was prepared to let such a rabid and almost fascistic anti-reformer loose in its flagship history journal, and that the focus of the argument was shifting. No longer were the armed forces 'selling' themselves as a bastion of Marxism–Leninism; instead, they were invoking the security and glory of the Russian state. After years of loyal military subordination to the Party, the pressures of *perestroika* were beginning to break the bonds between the two.

Prokhanov's later writings show that the conservatives were conscious of the need to come up with some mission that could survive the fall of the Party. In 1990 he wrote an article entitled 'Dostatochnaya oborona' ('Sufficient Defence') in a conservative journal which effectively admitted that the Party was doomed and set out a new basis for the army's legitimacy, one framed very much in traditional Russian terms, as the saviour of the nation:

In essence, the army must fulfil that mission once fulfilled by the monasteries in times of invasion and expansion. In the barracks there will be shelter from death and from the mêlée, from devastation and from famine . . . . In conditions of civil chaos, only the army will have the strength to protect [the people], to preserve the seed corn of future progress, to defend the values and sanctums, so that when the troubles pass, they can be returned to life.

Heady stuff, and all too easy to discount as overheated political rhetoric, were not the High Command itself showing signs of looking once again to its pre-revolutionary roots. Rash's articles were recommended reading for officer cadets; all military journals and newspapers began covering the tsarist era far more comprehensively and positively; in 1990, a new draft officer-training programme introduced a course on the Imperial military at the expense of one on Marxism-Leninism. Meanwhile, the Defence Ministry began using *glasnost'* to assert its role as customer in its relations with the military-industrial complex. In May 1990, for example, *Krasnaya zvezda* ran a piece on the new Tu-160 'Blackjack' nuclear bomber which savaged the design firm for producing an aircraft that was badly conceived, inadequately tested and downright unsafe. For so long forced to make do with the equipment the defence industrialists wanted to build for them, the soldiers were going to use their new freedom of speech to change that.

Thus, the armed forces were distancing themselves from their former allies. But so too were other lobbies. The KGB had already begun to drift away from the military. Aware that it was facing a growing tide of criticism and anxious that *glasnost'* would mean that its past atrocities would come under ever sharper scrutiny, it also looked to create a new role for itself in dealing with crime. In May 1990, KGB Chair Kryuchkov met a group of liberal politicians to express concern at public distrust of the KGB. He chose to emphasise the extent to which his organisation was involved in fighting corruption and terrorism, claiming that this engaged fully 80 per cent of its personnel. Although both KGB and Interior Ministry (MVD) spoke of the prospects for cooperation, this was clearly a bid by the KGB both to clean up its image and also take over the MVD's role fighting crime. The ground was set for a bureaucratic 'turf war' which would outlast the USSR and see traditional mistrust and jealousies between the two organisations flare into open political conflict.

To an extent this was reflected in the fate of Vadim Bakatin. In 1989 Gorbachev appointed Bakatin, an energetic and respected reformist, Minister of the Interior. A close ally of Gorbachev's and a member of the Central Committee since 1986, Bakatin had a clear political mandate to modernise the MVD. By November 1990 Bakatin, reviled unfairly as a failure, was to be replaced by Boris Pugo, a hardline former KGB general. The reasons for this were three. First of all, events proved beyond the ability of any one man to control. Crime rates kept growing as a result of economic hardship and social collapse, and any reforms he introduced would inevitably take time to have an effect. The public and parliamentarians, though, wanted results now. Secondly, he was having to deal with greater problems with fewer resources given the crisis in state finances; increases in his budgets were more than swallowed up by inflation and growing demands upon the police. Finally, he faced considerable opposition from within the MVD.

In 1990, Bakatin adopted the so-called 'Tol'yatti model' of policing, based on an experimental programme in the city of that name, which involved setting up 'municipal militias' responsible to local authorities, keeping only investigation and coordination functions at the higher level. The idea was that not only would this create forces more responsive to local needs, but that a decentralised police structure could not then be used in the future by conservative opponents of reform. In both he was ultimately successful, in that his initiatives began the fragmentation of the police force which ensured that it could not be used in the coup of August 1991. At the time, though, many within the central MVD bureaucracy in Moscow could not forgive him for reducing their powers, and without the support of his own deputies, he was unable to ride out conservative opposition to his policies.

CONFLICT WITHIN THE SECURITY INTERESTS

The military and the defence industries were thus no longer working in such cosy harmony. The KGB was trying to preserve itself, at the expense of the armed forces and the MVD if necessary. The Foreign Ministry was hoping to use democratisation to shake off the grip of the Central Committee Secretariat. At the same time, the bureaucratic empires of the Soviet system were being torn apart from within. For some, the changes under way offered new opportunities, for others they merely presented problems. Within the military-industrial complex, some managers eagerly embraced marketisation, convinced they could only gain. Others stood four-square against anything which could end their pampered security. Merely leafing through the May 1988 issue of the *Voenno-istoricheskii zhurnal* throws up the debate and division even within the High Command. Colonel General Lobov – who later became Chief of the General Staff – broke with military orthodoxy by claiming that traditions of fighting a 'defensive' war by offensive means was a byproduct of Stalinism and 'an abandonment of the propositions of Leninist military doctrine'. A Colonel Ul'yanov, by contrast, looked to pre-war Marshals Frunze and Tukhachevskii for historical legitimacy, and portrayed 'offensive defence' as both ideologically sound and, in an age of missiles, helicopters and submarines, inevitable.

The voting patterns of military parliamentarians reveals this widening divide within the armed forces. Of the votes cast by senior officers at the first sessions of the Congress of People's Deputies, only 16 per cent supported measures backed by the democratic bloc. For middle-ranking officers, though, the figure was 63 per cent, rising to 73 per cent for junior officers. Seventeen middle- and junior-ranking officer-parliamentarians submitted a radical programme for military reform to the Defence Ministry in December 1989, which envisaged a much smaller army made up solely of volunteers and increased accountability to parliament. The Defence Ministry promptly buried the proposal in red tape, and in April 1990 the group's leading light, Major Lopatin, was expelled from the Party on trumped up charges as a result of pressure from the ministry.

Even the KGB began to show open signs of division. Individual mavericks began speaking out about abuses of power by the Party or the KGB, while in 1989 Major General Oleg Kalugin, a former chief of counter-intelligence, proposed more concrete reform of the security apparatus. As he warned: 'What should the people do when they witness the crumbling of the stereotypes to which they have grown accustomed? The result is either demoralisation or resistance to change. The latter inevitably grows into a certain political philosophy – a conservative philosophy.' Kalugin was disciplined and forced to retire, going on to become an outspoken parliamentarian. Yet he was by no means alone, as would be made clear during the August Coup. While to some, Gorbachev's evident inability to control his armed forces and security apparatus made him vulnerable to a coup, the failure of that coup shows that the fragmentation of opinion applied as much to his conservative rivals as to the reformists.

In 1987 *Time* magazine made Gorbachev its Man of the Year. In 1988 it was *Der Spiegel*'s turn, while British independent television declared him Statesman of the Decade in 1989. Opinion polls in Britain registered his popularity as higher than the British Prime Minister's, and his visits to Germany, the USA and even China were greeted with euphoric 'Gorbymania'. In May 1990, though, Gorbachev's election to the Soviet Presidency would be countered by Boris Yeltsin's election to the Presidency of the Russian Federation, and Moscow riven by disputes between Soviet and Russian authorities. At the 28th Party Congress in July, Gorbachev managed to amend Party rules to reduce the chances of a constitutional coup against him, but Yeltsin walked out of the hall and of the Party. Outside the USSR's borders, the security environment was changing almost beyond recognition. Forces were withdrawing from East/Central Europe, and the reunification of Germany in October was seen by many within the élite as a repudiation of everything for which twenty million had died during the Great Patriotic War. The entire context of internal security was also changing, as the Kremlin found itself contending with whole peoples and national leaderships. So long as this was confined to minor border republics such as Armenia and Estonia, this was a problem; once it spread to mighty Russia, the heart of the USSR, then the whole Union itself was in danger.

6 CONFRONTATION, COUP, COLLAPSE, 1990–91

1990   *May* Boris Yeltsin elected President of Russia.

   September Coup scare.

   October Germany reunited.

   November Second CSCE summit in Paris: CFE treaty signed.

   December Boris Pugo becomes Interior Minister. Shevardnadze resigns as Foreign Minister.

1991   *January* Troops attack pro-independence protesters in the Baltic states: fifteen killed in Lithuania, four in Latvia.

   February Warsaw Pact Foreign Ministers agree to dismantle the alliance by the end of March 1992.

   March Massive pro-Yeltsin demonstration in Moscow.

   April '9+1' talks between Gorbachev and republican leaders start.

   June CSCE foreign ministers meet in Berlin: Cold War officially over.

   July Warsaw Pact formally dissolved.

   August 'August Coup' ends in failure.

   December Russian, Belarussian and Ukrainian governments proclaim the formation of the Commonwealth of Independent States – USSR declared dead.

The 'philosophy of new thinking' and 'the primacy of universal human values over class values' have developed, in fact, into a disregard for the interests of the socialist state and the satisfaction of the imperialist oligarchies' ambitions . . . . Today the Soviet Union is weaker than ever.

Conservative commentator Aleksandr Prokhanov, 1990

Although Prokhanov was a nationalist extremist who never let the truth get in the way of a dramatic phrase, it was possible to see his point. According to one opinion poll, by mid-1990 only 1.5 per cent of Soviet citizens were prepared to profess hope for the future or give a positive answer to the question 'what has *perestroika* done for us?' A more free and critical press may be a fine thing, but is it really worth the empty shelves and larders? Democratisation may be a prize to be treasured, but how many have to die in Transcaucasia in the wars it brings? Germany had been reunited, the Warsaw Pact being run down, the 'socialist brothers' around the world losing their subsidies, but for what? Gorbachev had been elected to save and strengthen the USSR, not to sell it off, and by personal inclination he wanted to protect Union and Party alike. He had gambled on democratisation in 1989 and lost. After the 28th Party Congress in July 1990, he conceded that 'the USSR is rapidly becoming a second-rate power', and later that year he would come close to using force to regain some of the centre's authority. In the event he showed himself to have the clarity of vision and weakness of stomach to back out of his alliance with the hardliners and choose yet another option, reaching out to the newly elected republican leaders to create a new federal basis for the USSR. In such an accommodation with the democratic governments of the republics Gorbachev might still conceivably have saved the Union and *perestroika*, but it was to be too late. Dashing the authoritarians' hopes of martial law, he forced them to launch their clumsy and half-hearted coup, which shattered the Union beyond repair.

IN PRAISE OF COERCION

Developments in the USSR have reached a critical phase and the fate of the Soviet fatherland is at stake.

Anonymous KGB officers in an appeal circulated in 1990

Whereas in early 1990 direct attacks upon the policies of *perestroika* were confined to such anonymous denunciations and a small circle of extreme reactionary generals and bureaucrats, by mid-year, many within the Party and military were prepared openly to question Gorbachev's leadership. At a Politburo meeting in September, for example, KGB Chair Kryuchkov warned him against forming any coalition with the democrats that did not take the interests of the secret police and Party bureaucracy into account. To some extent Gorbachev's 'tilt to the right' in late 1990 was a product of this growing chorus of threats and warning from the authoritarian wing of the Party. Yet it is important to appreciate just how someone who had dedicated his time as General Secretary to the liberalisation, democratisation and, in effect, Westernisation of the USSR could also be tempted to return the country to a state of enforced discipline for positive reasons. For a start, Gorbachev was a product of a system and a political culture which had always seen modernisation associated with authoritarianism. Peter the Great had opened his 'window on the West', but only by suppressing internal opposition and sacrificing the lives of thousands of serfs in the building of his capital of St Petersburg. When Russia began to industrialise in the late nineteenth century, it was on the back of the state's exploitation of the peasants – 'let us starve, but let us export', Finance Minister Vyshnegradskii had said, even though it is rarely the finance ministers who go hungry in this world – and the repression of their attempts to resist. Stalin's regime, for all its bloody brutality, had established the USSR as a global superpower. In a way hard for Westerners to understand – especially Britons and North Americans, who have avoided recent invasion – the Russians still equate weakness with invasion, and development with a strong and demanding state.

Part of Gorbachev's greatness is that he was able to fight against this political culture, but there were times when traditional Russian solutions must have appealed. This is particularly true when one considers the role of Andropov in his political evolution. Andropov possessed a frightening clarity of vision, a very intellectual approach, prepared to see violence and repression as a perfectly viable method, albeit one often counterproductive or irrelevant. Like Feliks Dzerzhinskii, founder of the Soviet secret police, he derived no pleasure from coercion, but nor would he ever shrink from it were he to deem it necessary. Indeed, conservatives and authoritarians at the 28th Party Congress in July 1990 frequently tried to appeal to Gorbachev in the name of Andropov.

Gorbachev was especially susceptible to the temptations of the iron fist because of the circumstances in which he found himself in the winter of 1990. This was a year in which GNP fell by about 2 per cent, exports shrank by 12 per cent, industrial performance worsened and the real rate of inflation hit perhaps 10 per cent. Nationalists were dominant in the Baltic states and Transcaucasia, and Armenia had just declared itself independent. The Russian government itself was increasingly assertive in its relationship with the Soviet leadership. The spring call-up had seen over a quarter of draftees refuse to serve their time as soldiers. Facing such problems, Gorbachev came to realise just how impotent he had become. *Demokratizatsiya* had not given him a mandate and a means to introducing quicker and more effective reform, but elevated a whole new generation of political opponents, while destroying much of the unity, purpose and morale of the Party. Like Tsar Nicholas I in the nineteenth century and Yurii Andropov in the twentieth, he looked for reliable, disciplined and effective institutions through which he might rule, and the only ones available seemed to be the armed forces and security services.

It is also important to stress just how far Russia's political culture conditioned not just élite but also mass responses. The authoritarians played two cards most heavily in their bid to convince Gorbachev that he should adopt their methods: the growing lawlessness and disorder of the Union and a nationalist appeal to preserve the strength and prestige of the Soviet superpower. One reason why these themes were so effective was because they also appealed to a significant proportion of the population. Optimistic Western press coverage of pro-democracy rallies in Moscow and interviews with articulate, English-speaking radicals have done much to create a false impression of opinions in the factories and farms, especially outside Moscow and Leningrad (St Petersburg). A survey in 1990, for example, found over a third of Soviet citizens advocating the death penalty for homosexuals, and more than a fifth thought that hippies also needed killing. In another poll, the statement 'national power is more important than open government' received the approval of over half the sample. In 1993 a quarter of Russians voting in national elections supported Vladimir Zhirinovskii, a nationalist advocating Russian expansion through Turkey, Finland and Poland. Thus, we should be struck by the fact that Gorbachev held back from using force and secret police methods so long and so resolutely more than that at one time he was tempted to see them as a solution to his and Russia's problems.

THE INTERNATIONAL DIMENSION

The international scene certainly did not offer many reasons to continue to avoid authoritarian methods. From Gorbachev's point of view, he had offered up three great prizes to the West: ending Soviet resistance to the reunification of Germany; agreeing to scale down dramatically forces in Europe; and winding up Moscow's East/Central European system. In return, he had made it clear that he needed political and economic aid. The West accepted his tribute, and then, in the eyes of many reformists, betrayed him.

Having worked hard to improve relations with West Germany while distancing himself from the Honecker regime in the East, at the end of January 1990 Gorbachev had effectively acknowledged that reunification was inevitable. In July 1990 he even accepted that the united Germany would be a member of NATO. To an extent, German reunification in October 1990 played its part in convincing the Soviet leadership of the need for progress in European conventional arms talks. Better, after all, ensure that the new Germany establish a rather more moderate army than simply add its new Eastern resources in building ever more formidable forces. In November, the 2nd Conference on Security and Cooperation in Europe (CSCE) met in Paris and the Conventional Forces in Europe (CFE) treaty was signed. CFE committed the Soviets to withdrawing forces from East/Central Europe and the destruction of some 23,000 items of equipment, from tanks to missile launchers. In this context, it was almost inevitable that the Warsaw Pact would not long survive and even before its formal dissolution in February 1991 had become moribund.

In the long term, perhaps, all these concessions and moves were inevitable as the USSR decayed. Yet one must not discount Gorbachev's political effort and courage in piloting this withdrawal from confrontation and this demilitarisation of European relations. Over Germany, Gorbachev had sometimes been ahead even of the views of the relatively liberal Foreign Ministry, thanks to some of his *institutchik* advisers, such as Professor Vyacheslav Dashichev of the Institute of the Economics of the World Socialist System, and Gorbachev's personal relationship with Germany's Chancellor Kohl. He certainly had had to face much criticism of this move, as nationalists and conservatives sought to play up the dangers of another Great Patriotic War (the Second World War). Speaking at a Central Committee meeting in February 1990, for example, Egor Ligachev raised the spectre of the 1938 Munich agreements which opened Hitler's way to the east, warning of

> the impending danger of the accelerated re-unification of Germany or, in fact, the swallowing up of the German

Democratic Republic. It would be unforgivably short-sighted folly not to see a Germany with a formidable economic and military potential looming on the world horizon . . . [We must] not allow a new Munich.

Perhaps most serious were those criticisms which looked instead to the impact at home of the 1989 revolutions in East/Central Europe. Their tenor and their source is perhaps best illustrated by an article by Valerii Musatov, deputy head of the Central Committee Secretariat's International Department in 1991. This Party hack had no doubts as to the dangers and – writing, significantly, in the Party's own newspaper, *Pravda* – was not afraid to spell them out:

> The turn of events in Eastern Europe had a powerful negative influence of the broadest strata of Soviet society. They encouraged attacks on the CPSU which repeated the scenario played out in Eastern Europe . . . . The very serious overall psychological impact caused by the break-away of our allies remains.

The assistance Gorbachev received from the West in return for these hard-won concessions proved minimal. In September 1990 the USSR finally recognised and opened full diplomatic relations with South Korea and Saudi Arabia, in both cases with an eye to furthering trade and winning aids and credit. Saudi Arabia did, indeed, offer a $4 billion loan, albeit largely as an inducement for the USSR to support the use of force versus Iraq at the United Nations. There are very strong grounds for suggesting that the Soviet economy was beyond the reach of any but the most dramatic aid programmes or, indeed, that by helping the existing system survive a while longer they would have forestalled genuine reform and thus been counterproductive. Nevertheless, Gorbachev's allies and his radical and conservative critics alike believed that Western aid could have helped to stabilise the economy and ease the lives of ordinary Soviet citizens.

The West seemed unprepared to make any sacrifices of its own to preserve the shoots of democracy in the USSR. If anything, the evidence seemed to suggest the opposite, that in the name of order Western governments would greet martial law with open condemnation but secret relief. In December 1981 the *Financial Times* had printed the response of a West German banker to the declaration of martial law in Poland: 'What I am saying may be a bit brutal, but I think the Polish government was no longer in a position to govern the country. I now see a chance for Poland to return to a more normal working schedule and this could be a good thing for the banks.' When a country with five million troops and 30,000 nuclear weapons becomes ungovernable, after all, it is not just the banks that have an interest in its stability. Besides, Gorbachev had the example of China before him. When tanks rolled into and over the student demonstrations in Tiananmen Square in 1989, the world echoed with protests. Yet the USA continued to grant China Most Favoured Nation trading status, and after a few token sanctions, the nations of the West were once again vying to sell it arms and technology, while Britain manoeuvred to hand over Hong Kong in as quiet and conciliatory a way as possible. As one Russian academic at a round table in early 1991 put it, 'it seems clear that the West has nothing against brutal dictators – only ineffective ones'.

THE 'WINTER ALLIANCE'

At first we loved [Gorbachev] impetuously because he was so unlike Stalin, and then we began increasingly to resent the fact that he did not act as decisively as Stalin.

Ruslan Khasbulatov, *The Struggle for Russia* (London: Routledge, 1993)

It seems to have been early in the gloomy and miserable winter of 1990 that Gorbachev began to give in to the temptations of coercion, perhaps in October. Broadly speaking, the deal was this: if Gorbachev was prepared to unleash the security forces, muzzle the media and abandon for the moment political liberalisation, then the authoritarians would enforce the sort of order on the country which would allow his economic reforms to be applied. For those who harboured doubts as to whether or not economic liberalisation could coexist with political repression, the hardliners cheerfully pointed to South Korea, Singapore, Taiwan, Pinochet's Chile and even China – all nations they would once have vilified as revisionist or fascist capitalist lackeys. It was certainly in October that elements of the General Staff's Main Operations Directorate began updating the longstanding file on *Operatsiya Metel'*, 'Operation Snowstorm', the emergency programme which had been drawn up during the Brezhnev years for dealing with massive public disorder or natural disaster.

First of all, the security forces had to be made ready. In November Gorbachev sacrificed Interior Minister Bakatin, and next month appointed in his stead Boris Pugo, who had been the head of the Latvian KGB during 1980–84. Colonel General Boris Gromov, a hero and commander of the Afghan war, was brought in as his First Deputy Minister with responsibility for the Interior Troops (VV). These security forces were also swollen by several army divisions which were transferred to the Interior Ministry (MVD). The MVD became increasingly militarised, as it was prepared for martial law. Its OMON 'Black Beret' paramilitaries grew in numbers from 8,000 in May 1991 to 10,000 by the time of the coup. The Interior Troops likewise underwent rapid expansion. This began under Bakatin, who had hoped to create a corps of dedicated, professional security troops who could deal with interethnic violence with minimal force. Having launched a new recruitment programme in 1989, which had proved to be rather unsuccessful, the MVD now looked to quicker methods of getting security troops on the streets, regardless of their training and aptitude. The conservatives looked increasingly to involving the army in internal security. Not only were whole army units brought into the VV, but joint army–police patrols began operating in major cities from January 1991. As for the KGB, while it had disbanded its infamous Fifth Directorate, responsible for suppressing dissent, in September 1989 it had set up a Directorate for the Protection of the Constitutional Order, which largely took over the roles and personnel of the Fifth. This assumed a growing role at this time, armed with a new Presidential decree empowering its officers to enter any business premises without a search warrant and led by a new generation of senior figures following a reshuffle in late 1990 and early 1991.

The authoritarians soon took to flaunting their new latitude. Three army motor-rifle (mechanised infantry) divisions, for example, originally included within the CFE talks were transferred to the Naval Infantry (marines) and thus exempted from the limits the treaty set upon forces the Soviets could retain west of the Urals. These three divisions – the 77th Guards at Arkhangel'sk, the 3rd Guards at Klaipeda and the 126th at Simferopol – were largely equipped with modern equipment and weapons and their transfer was a blatant bid to side-step the terms of the treaty. In military terms, this was noteworthy but hardly that important; in political terms, though, it was very significant. It was part of a pattern – other units were being relabelled as security or Strategic Rocket Force elements to evade the CFE process – and yet it earned the High Command no rebuke from the Kremlin.

With hindsight, the signs had been there to see. In September 1990 there had been a coup scare, when paratroopers were flown to Moscow in full combat order. Yazov lamely claimed that they had been brought in to help pick the potato harvest – live ammunition, armoured carriers and all – yet this proved simply an exercise to test deployment times and schedules and the ability of the military to overawe Yeltsin's supporters. Limits began to be placed upon *glasnost'* in general and criticism of the President or his new allies in particular. Certainly Eduard Shevardnadze realised the implications of Gorbachev's new alliance and in December resigned from his post as Foreign Minister, warning of a drift towards dictatorship. His replacement, Aleksandr Bessmertnykh, a competent grey man of the bureaucracy, was no match for the authoritarians, and Soviet foreign policy began again to drift back to Cold War rhetoric and suspicion.

Overall, the period of Gorbachev's 'winter alliance' is one marked by little of the energy and ability in foreign policy of the early years. Moscow engaged itself in an effort to avert war in the Gulf, which had no real chance of success. As for Gorbachev's April 1991 visit to Japan, this proved a lacklustre disappointment, largely because of compromises he had had to make during the period of alliance. The Japanese were eager for concessions over the disputed Kurile islands, which the USSR had seized from Japan in the Second World War. Marshal Yazov, however, had dug in his heels and insisted that the islands were a strategic necessity, and effectively left Gorbachev no room for manoeuvre. As for East/Central Europe, the alliance briefly restored the Central Committee Secretariat's International Department to its old position above the Foreign Ministry, which it characterised as having adopted a 'feeble' line on East/Central Europe. The International Department lost no time in issuing, in January, a policy document which called on the use of economic and political leverage and intimidation – it pointedly noted the extent to which the region still depended on Soviet oil and gas supplies – to ensure the protection of the USSR's security interests there, a post-Warsaw Pact 'Brezhnev Doctrine' of sorts.

THE STRATEGY OF TENSION

The coming year is a special one. On it falls the task of deciding the fate of our multinational state. For all of us, Soviet people, there is no more sacred matter than preserving and renewing a Union in which all peoples may live willingly and well . . . . It is precisely in the Union, in its preservation and renewal, that the key lies to accomplishing the great, fateful tasks that confront us in 1991.

Mikhail Gorbachev, *New Year Address*, 1 January 1991

That 'special year' began with a series of threats, incidents and provocations staged by the authoritarians and aimed at clawing back some of the gains of the nationalists and shaking their growing confidence. To some extent, these were operations designed with specific aims in mind, but they also contributed to creating an air of chaos and fear to justify the imposition of strict central control. Although the authoritarians looked approvingly at post-Tiananmen China and also Jaruzelski's Poland, in many ways the more striking parallels are with Italy in the 1970s and 1990s, when a corrupt conservative alliance of mafiosi and entrenched political groupings turned to terrorism to demonise their opposition and, if necessary, justify their own imposition of a police state. The Chilean strongman General Pinochet, the Italian 'black godfathers' and Jaruzelski's allies would all have recognised and accepted the new line:

Of course, martial law is no bowl of cherries, and to consider it a remedy for all ills would be simply naive. It is an extraordinary measure necessary to save a disintegrating state. To be more precise, it is a political shock therapy applied in cases where there is simply no other way to pull together a society which has become disorientated by rally hysteria. It is a cold shower for those hotheads who, to achieve their ambitious goals, are prepared to resort to extreme measures . . . .

Pravda, 11 March 1991

The day after Gorbachev's portentous New Year Address, that 'shock therapy' began to be applied. In Riga and Vilnius, capitals of the fractious Baltic republics of Latvia and Lithuania respectively,

OMON 'black berets' seized important Party and government buildings. Tempers and tensions rose, as pro-Moscow elements (largely drawn from Russian expatriates) and nationalists held rival protest marches. Up to this point, the events could be seen as the actions of maverick local hardliners, but Gorbachev then began demanding that the Lithuanian parliament accept the pre-eminence of the Soviet constitution. Given that this was an open challenge to the parliament and its authority, it was hardly surprising that it reacted with defiance. Four days later, OMON and KGB special forces stormed the Vilnius TV centre; one attacker and thirteen defenders died. A week later, it was the Latvian Interior Ministry's turn, besieged by OMON in response to its refusal to pay homage to Moscow: four died.

The bloodshed heightened nationalist resistance to Moscow, yet the authoritarians believed themselves successful. Of course, they had given the Balts even more reasons to hate Moscow: opinion polls in the Baltic states after the outrages would register majorities in favour of independence of 75 per cent and better. Yet the authoritarians realised that it was too late to keep the Baltic states under their control. This was hardly that important since together they only made up perhaps 2 per cent of the total Soviet population. The real audience to which the authoritarians were playing was elsewhere, back in Russia or in other republics where nationalist and separatism had not yet had a chance to entrench itself as strongly. By their open displays of force as well as random car bombings, the deployment of paratroopers 'to round up draft dodgers' and similar displays of hidden and state power, the authoritarians sought to convince the wavering that it was too soon to write off the old power of Moscow and the more determined dissidents that it would be wise to adopt a more conciliatory approach. In many ways this was an extension of a strategy used to forestall Moldavia's dash for autonomy in mid-1990 by leaning on Lithuania. It almost seems insulting to those who died in January 1991 or the brave champions of local interests against this 'new centralism', but the state was not so much resorting to its fists as merely flexing its muscles.

Up to a point, the strategy worked. In March, a nation-wide referendum was held on the need for the preservation of the Union, against a backdrop of incidents and headlines calculated to foster the impression that the only alternative was anarchy and civil war. The question was rather unsubtly loaded, but nevertheless the 76 per cent 'yes' vote suggested that there was still a lasting belief in the Union or, more likely, a fear of a post-Union future. Besides which, the authoritarians became convinced that their plans were sound and their forces reliable. In the Baltic states, the local police were divided and generally impotent, while OMON and other forces had been recruited from Russian nationals and Party loyalists and proved brutally effective in their role as the dogs Moscow could choose to muzzle or unleash at will. Meanwhile, the plans continued to be refined. After the killings in Vilnius and Riga, General Gromov supervised a wargamed exercise in Moscow to test the ability of his forces to seize the key locations in the city. The results of this exercise were then used as the basis to draw up a universal plan theoretically suitable for any city and given a further test run in Omsk in June.

So far, though, the authoritarians had been counting on Gorbachev's blessing to legitimise their state of emergency both constitutionally (he did have that power as President) and in the eyes of the outside world. Nevertheless, Gorbachev was still a reluctant partner. Over Lithuania, he had not only publicly disassociated himself from the bloodshed, but shown little sign of having the ruthlessness to follow it up with the unsubtle warnings to the other republics which had been expected. Indeed, the retirement of KGB First Deputy Chair Filipp Bobkov in February may suggest that the KGB had actually gone further than Gorbachev had expected or sanctioned. The mantle of military dictator sat uneasily upon his shoulders; a massive protest in Moscow in March caused it to slip. Called in support of Boris Yeltsin, who at the time was facing a motion of censure within the Russian parliament, it seemed to the authoritarians an ideal opportunity to test their ability to maintain public order in the capital. Gorbachev, genuinely concerned about the threat that up to half a million angry demonstrators literally a stone's (or half-brick's) throw from the Kremlin could represent, tried to ban the protest, and his allies used this pretext to muster a force of 50,000 police, Interior Troops, soldiers and KGB officers, backed with dogs, mounted officers, brand new water cannon, fire trucks and the rest of the panoply of modern riot control. From personal experience, I can attest to the fact that this medium-sized army managed to control the marchers in a professional and largely non-violent way, but what was significant were the different conclusions which the hardliners, Gorbachev and the radicals drew from the event.

To the authoritarians, this was a triumph. They had managed to assemble and coordinate the largest public order operation of the *perestroika* years, and had done so with Gorbachev's acquiescence.

They had not even had to use force. They were, they felt, ready for *Metel'* once Gorbachev gave the word. Yet it was precisely at this time that Gorbachev began to realise the dangers in his new alliance and look for ways to find allies at the far end of the political spectrum, to broaden and radicalise reform rather than control it. As at so many pivotal moments, it was up to the senior reformist Aleksandr Yakovlev to ask the central question. What if there had been violence, if someone had died? In that case, did Gorbachev feel he could control the forces that would unleash, and could he live with himself? The tale of Bloody Sunday, when panicked Tsarist troops fired on a peaceful crowd and triggered the 1905 revolution was one familiar to every good Bolshevik. As for Yeltsin and the radicals, the sight of a Moscow dominated by grey and blue uniforms did have the sobering effect intended, but the result was simply that when Gorbachev made his overtures to them, they were more receptive, more prepared to accept compromises in the interest of putting up a broad front to the authoritarians. The March protest was largely an upbeat, almost casual affair – few of the marchers realised that from that day the real battle-lines for August were being drawn.

THE UNION TREATY

> Yazov: *It takes a defence minister to head a coup. Do you think I'll make a good Pinochet?*
> Q: *I don't mean you, mister minister.*
> Yazov: *Whom could we make a coup against? Tell me if you know, and I'll think it over. I might stage a coup, in the long run. Who knows?*
>
> . . .
>
> Yazov: *I hope you won't publish this. Anyway, I'll say I've never talked to you on this topic.*

Defence Minister Yazov, in an extract from an interview with the Czech newspaper *Lidove Noviny* which was censored and then released after the coup, 1991

Thus, in late April Gorbachev launched the so-called '9+1' talks between himself and the leaders of Russia, Ukraine, Belorussia, Azerbaijan, Kazakhstan, Kirghizia, Tajikistan, Turkmenistan and

Uzbekistan. Also named the 'Novo-Ogarevo' process, after the summer-house where they met, this marked the beginning of a new attempt to find some common ground between Gorbachev's centre and the more moderate republican leaderships. The negotiations were difficult, but in August concluded with a draft for a new Union Treaty which would change the very basis of the USSR. This would turn it into a real federation, in which many powers and responsibilities would be devolved to the republics and the centre would become far more of a coordinating body, handling defence, foreign policy, communications, internal trade and other such matters. Above all, control over taxation and thus the centre's budget would increasingly pass to the republics.

Wooed and then cuckolded, the authoritarians turned their full anger on Gorbachev, orchestrating a campaign to weaken and humble him. At the April Central Committee meeting, he had to threaten to resign to force a vote in favour of continuing reform. In June, Prime Minister Pavlov sought to persuade the Supreme Soviet to give him emergency powers which would, in effect, allow him to pass decrees without Gorbachev's approval. In this he was supported by Defence Minister Yazov, Interior Minister Pugo and KGB Chair Kryuchkov, who suggested, in terms more reminiscent of Stalin's 1930s, that *perestroika* was a CIA plot. Gorbachev roundly defeated this abortive constitutional *coup d'état* with a confident performance in parliament that left Pavlov looking like a naughty schoolboy, but his failure to use the opportunity to purge his enemies has been seen by many as a critical factor in the eventual coup. To some, it suggests that Gorbachev even wanted or encouraged the coup, either to destroy his conservative rivals or scare his radical critics, but it is perhaps more appropriate to say that Gorbachev felt he could still control these men. He later admitted that by this stage he felt that the Party itself was not so much a power-base as a burden, but that, as the only remaining organisation binding the nation together, it was too powerful to let it fall unchallenged into the hands of his rivals. So too did he feel it better to know his enemies and have them still formally subordinated to him than pick an open fight with all three leaders of the ministries of coercion.

Relations between him and the authoritarians moved from political confrontation to guerrilla warfare. To an extent, this had already started: on the eve of Gorbachev's trip to Oslo to collect his Nobel Peace Prize, Soviet troops set up checkpoints around Lithuania, and OMON then launched a series of attacks against Baltic customs posts. Gorbachev found himself having to field notes of protest from Nordic nations and the European Community at the very time of Pavlov's bid to take over his powers. The conservative commander of Soviet forces in Germany began to cause difficulties over the withdrawal of his troops back to the USSR. As Gorbachev negotiated with Western leaders in London in July, OMON occupied the Vilnius telephone exchange for no obvious reason, and the night that George Bush arrived in Moscow to sign the START nuclear arms reduction treaty, unknown assailants – probably OMON or KGB troops – killed six Lithuanian customs guards.

In response, Gorbachev's renewed campaign against those he called the "hurrah patriots" also signalled a resumption of his pressure for genuine military reform. In his rebuttal to Pavlov, Gorbachev made it clear that he was now prepared to strike yet more fiercely at the heart of the military–security–industry alliance: its budget.

If I didn't keep in mind that this country's economy is not geared to human needs, is over-militarised, if I didn't try to eliminate this burden and turn it to the people's benefit, then I would be derelict in my duty and should step down.

Mikhail Gorbachev to the Supreme Soviet, June 1991

Within a week he had marked the anniversary of the Nazi invasion in 1941 with a decree loosening the Party's grip on the army and then used an address to officer cadets to call for 'thoroughgoing military reforms'. As ever, Gorbachev was looking at military reform as part and parcel of his domestic policies and international negotiations. If he was going to abandon his alliance with the authoritarians, he would have to re-establish himself as a partner for the radicals and the republican leaderships. Yet this was at a time when polls were showing that almost two-thirds of the population mistrusted him and the Union government, and so he had to give the republic leaders good reasons to listen to him. Aware of the fragility of his personal position, he needed to make himself indispensable to radicals and reactionaries alike, and hoped to enlist the help of other world leaders to do it, with aid and loans sufficient to buy him a little more time and reassert his role as the USSR's great advocate on the international scene.

In May, the last SS-20 nuclear missile was destroyed in line with the INF treaty, while Evgenii Primakov was sent to Washington to secure a $1.5 billion grain credit to guarantee bread supplies over the coming winter. He was rebuffed with a list of further concessions which the Soviet leadership would have to accept, including a commitment to becoming a fully market-based economy and further reductions on the defence budget and aid to Cuba. Within a month, Washington had relented, but with the USSR's foreign debt at the $70 billion mark, and the 1991 grain harvest 50 million tonnes down from 1990's total, this assistance proved of little more than token value. In June, the Conference on Security and Cooperation in Europe met again and the Cold War was officially deemed over. That month, Comecon was formally dissolved, next month it was the Warsaw Pact's turn. The START treaty which George Bush signed in Moscow entailed particularly sharp cuts on the Soviet side. Having always built up larger forces to offset their backwardness and inaccuracy compared with their US counterparts', the Soviets had far more to lose from the decision to establish a common ceiling of 6,000 warheads on each side.

All in all, the Soviets hurriedly made a whole serious of concessions. From Gorbachev's point of view, the pay-off would have to be at July's G7 summit of leading Western industrial nations in London. There he was certainly greeted cordially in what inevitably became called a '7+1' summit. Yet the handshakes and photo-opportunities could not disguise the fact that he returned largely empty-handed, with only the long-delayed Most Favoured Nation trading status with the USA to show for his trip. Even Gorbachev's speech accepting his Nobel Peace Prize had to be turned into a platform to appeal in vain for international support. He had handed over every card and won nothing, and the last buttress of his position had crumbled away.

THE COUP

> *Compatriots! Citizens of the Soviet Union! We are addressing you at a grave, critical hour for the destinies of the Motherland and our people. A mortal danger looms over our great Motherland. The policy of reforms, launched at Mikhail S. Gorbachev's initiative and designed as a means to ensure the country's dynamic development and the democratisation of social life has entered for several reasons a blind alley.*

From the coup leaders' address to the nation, 19 August 1991

On 23 July, various conservative newspapers carried *'Slovo k narodu'* ('A Word to the People'), an open letter from twelve hardliners calling for the creation of a 'patriotic movement' to 'save the Fatherland'. They wanted an emergency martial law regime and if necessary they thought they were prepared to impose one to avoid the concessions Gorbachev was planning to make to the republics. On 2 August, Gorbachev went on national television to announce that the '9+1' talks had borne fruit. On 20 August, Russia, Kazakhstan and Uzbekistan would sign the new Union Treaty, with the other republics following later. This came as no surprise to the hardliners, who had been bugging the meetings, including one four days earlier in which Boris Yeltsin and the Kazakh President, Nazarbaev, urged Gorbachev to purge the security apparatus, and dismiss Pugo and Kryuchkov. As Gorbachev left for his summer holiday in the Crimea, his enemies struck. Late on 18 August a delegation visited Gorbachev, uninvited and unannounced, including a representative of each of the Party bureaucracy (Oleg Shenin), military-industrial complex (Oleg Baklanov) and army (General Varennikov). At the same time, his telephones were cut off and KGB Border Troops moved into position around his summer-house. Invited to authorise martial law, he refused – told them to 'go to hell' – and became a prisoner in his own country. At 6 a.m. the next morning, Radio Moscow announced that he was ill and that Vice President Gennadii Yanaev was assuming power as acting President in the name of a State Committee for the State of Emergency in the USSR (GKChP – Gosudarstvennyi komitet chrezvychainogo polozheniya SSSR). Effectively, martial law was declared.

The *vosmerka* (pronounced 'vuzmyorka'), or 'octet' of the GKChP represented a cross-section of the Party interests threatened by reform in general and the Union Treaty in particular. The security interests were strongly represented. Gennadii Yanaev was little more than a figurehead: the real movers behind the conspiracy were KGB Chair Vladimir Kryuchkov, Interior Minister Boris Pugo, Prime Minister Valentin Pavlov and Oleg Baklanov, the First Deputy Chair of the Security Council and, in many ways, the foremost defender of the military-industrial complex. The other plotters were Defence Minister Yazov, Peasants' Union Chair Starodubtsev and Aleksandr Tizyakov, a senior industrialist. For what did they stand? (A good question, really.) They promised to return some sense of discipline, of order, of pride and of purpose to the USSR. They certainly did not want to return to the 1970s, nor even the Stalin era. Indeed, it is striking that their public

Table 2: The vosmerka of the August Coup, 1991

Gennadii Yanaev	Deputy President of the USSR
Valentin Pavlov	Prime Minister of the USSR
Vladimir Kryuchkov	Chair, KGB
Boris Pugo	Minister of the Interior
Marshal Dmitrii Yazov	Minister of Defence
Oleg Baklanov	First Deputy Chair, Security Council
Vasilii Starodubtsev	Chair, Peasants' Union
Aleksandr Tizyakov	President, Association of State Enterprises

pronouncements made so little reference to socialism or Lenin, but instead to national pride and patriotic duty. The ideology of the *vosmerka*, if it had one, was closest to 'national bolshevism', the discipline and drive of Marxism–Leninism harnessed to the mystical, militarist and nationalist idea of Russian imperial destiny. Of course, the plotters wanted to protect their personal positions and fiefdoms from Gorbachev and his new republican allies, but there is also a sense that this was not so much a final gasp of Soviet socialism but the first stirrings of a post-Soviet Russian nationalism. Ultimately, they were angry because of the damage Gorbachev had done to Russian pride and power more than that inflicted upon Marxism–Leninism.

As it was, the coup lasted just three days, and by 22 August Gorbachev would be back in Moscow and the plotters under arrest (although Boris Pugo maintained a proud MVD tradition, preferring suicide to trial). It was also characterised by inept and hurried planning (while crowd control had been carefully choreographed, for example, no one had devised a strategy for dealing with public figures and the international media) and a half-hearted defeatism which dogged the *vosmerka* from the start. Defence Minister Yazov, for example, an essentially weak-willed man dragged into the coup by his Chief of Staff, General Moiseev, and unwilling to defy such commanding (and rather frightening) figures as Pugo and Kryuchkov, refused to order his troops to open fire on civilians. Pavlov and Yanaev, by all accounts, spent most of their time drunk.

✦ THE COLLAPSE

Soldiers, countrymen, sons of Russia! I, President of Russia, elected by the will of our much-suffering nation, appeal to you at this time of tribulation for our country. A choice lies before you: either to aid and abet a group of conspirators and usurpers by obeying your criminal orders and thereby go against your own people or to defend democracy and the nation's legally elected government.

The former will embroil the country in fratricidal civil war and bloodshed; the latter will ensure peace, constitutional order and security. My dear sons! I am relying on you to make the right choice . . . . Great Russia, insulted and humiliated as she may be, calls out to you.

Boris Yeltsin's appeal to soldiers of the MVD Dzerzhinskii
Division, 21 August 1991

It is important to appreciate just why the coup failed. Crowds took to the streets in Moscow and other major cities in protest against the GKChP. These were stirring statements of popular resistance to martial law, but the uncaring lesson of history is that crowds do not prevail over soldiers prepared to use their weapons. Boris Yeltsin could stand on a tank and yell defiance to the plotters live on CNN television, but a single sniper's bullet could have ended that gesture as surely as an artillery airburst would have scattered the crowd. Instead, the mob succeeds when it is pitted against a force unwilling to resist or already convinced it will fail. This is what lay behind the Bolshevik victory in 1917, when a handful of dedicated revolutionaries could topple a government and seize the heart of Russia almost without bloodshed. This was also true in 1991, when the forces of the state proved to have so little willingness to defend their new government. History also has another lesson: that conscript armies will rarely rebel so long as their officers – and the junior officers and senior non-commissioned officers, in particular – are united and sure both of their role and the legitimacy of their orders. Had the Soviet officers corps been prepared to back the coup, it quite possibly would not have failed. One could actually make the case that what was striking was the very lack of resistance to the coup outside the politicised journalists and politicians of Moscow and a few urban crowds. Russians from three cities polled during the coup, Voronezh, Krasnoyarsk and Leningrad, showed the range of opinions.

In run-down, hungry industrial Voronezh, only half were prepared to condemn the coup, and a quarter prepared to believe that it could lead to economic improvement. In the Siberian city of

Table 3: Attitudes to the Coup, 20 August 1991

	Voronezh	Krasnoyarsk	Leningrad
Do you consider the activities of the GKChP lawful?			
No	49 %	76 %	54 %
Yes	28 %	12 %	23 %
Don't know	23 %	12 %	23 %
Will the GKChP improve or worsen the economic situation?			
Improve	24 %	9 %	16 %
Worsen	38 %	77 %	46 %
Don't know	38 %	14 %	35 %

Source: Trud, 22 August 1991

Krasnoyarsk, where workers were beginning to appreciate the power of industrial action in forcing Moscow to give them a share of the profits from their labours, martial law meant an end to this new liberty. The country was not crying out for a coup, but that is hardly the point. It was also not prepared to rule out of hand an emergency regime if it could be seen to bring economic stability. Opinion in the countryside, alas, remained unsurveyed, but the results from other polls suggest an even more reactionary and pragmatic attitude there.

The coup failed, above all, because those forces which were called upon to impose the state of emergency lacked the unity and will so to do. This was perhaps the most striking case of that 'critical absence of will' discussed in Chapter 3. Instead, the coup simply laid bare the extent to which the security apparatus had already fallen apart, divided along lines of ideology, nationality, self-interest and morality. Documents uncovered later, such as a memo dated 19 August on guidelines for a state of emergency, outlined six basic rules:

1   not to lose the initiative;
2   not to enter into discussions with the public;
3   to smash any signs of dissent instantly and decisively;
4   to deluge the country with lies and damaging information about the political opposition;
5   to use rumours of force to avoid the actual need for force; and
6   rapidly to reshuffle key organisations and structures.

Instead, the plotters were irresolute, engaged in discussions with all sorts of public figures, sometimes at cross-purposes, almost ignored the media, did little to remove waverers from their ranks, and the sole use of force, a late-night foray by personnel carriers near the parliament building in Moscow, was more a gesture which went wrong, involving as it did only a handful of vehicles and some frightened conscripts. The plotters did not even follow their own rules.

It was perhaps least surprising that the militia (police) failed to provide the coup with the support it needed. The general devolution of power within the country and Bakatin's reforms in particular reinforced the natural disinclination of locally recruited and locally housed policemen to adopt a political role. Why enforce the writ of distant Moscow on their friends, relatives and neighbours? Admittedly, some of the specially raised units followed their orders, but this tended to be confined to those which had been recruited or indoctrinated for a political role, such as the OMON riot troops in the Baltic states and the MVD Interior Army's Dzerzhinskii Division, its élite security unit based in Moscow. Those forces which had instead been exposed to the new professional ethic which Bakatin had tried to foster, such as the OMSN anti-terrorist commando force and the cadets of the Ryazan' Higher Militia Academy, either refused to obey the GKChP's orders or defected outright to defend Yeltsin. It was a force of OMSN, led by Russian Vice President Rutskoi, which eventually flew to the Crimea to escort Gorbachev back to Moscow. Similarly, when Andrei Dunaev, Russian First Deputy Interior Minister, began bringing police units to Moscow to oppose the coup, Pugo threatened to have him shot. Yet by whom?

The regular army was similarly unprepared to support the junta, sometimes out of conviction, sometimes out of simple common sense. Colonel General Viktor Samsonov, commander of the Leningrad Military District, for example, was ordered to impose martial law on the city but instead struck a deal with its mayor to keep his troops in their barracks. He had been transferred from Armenia in 1988 on suspicion of harbouring sympathies for local radicals, but since at that time the conservatives had been on the defensive they had been unable to prevent this able soldier from receiving this politically important posting. Even during the period of the 'winter alliance', Gorbachev had not been so trusting as to let the reactionaries carry out a root-and-branch reshuffle of the senior military hierarchy and thus the plotters had been forced to play the cards already dealt. Other officers may have been willing to obey their orders, but not to the extent of a bloodbath. This was especially important in the non-Russian republics, where local police forces and public opinion were much more fiercely resistant to the reimposition of Moscow's control. Overall, though, while of the

High Command only Shaposhnikov and Grachev – commanders of the air force and paratroopers, respectively – openly resisted the coup, even Yazov was a half-hearted plotter. After the first day he confided that he may have made a mistake and throughout the GKChP's brief reign he tried to prevent his soldiers from becoming involved in fighting with protesters. Eventually it would be the Defence Ministry's decision to disengage from the coup that brought it to an end. Only the Main Political Directorate seems to have had much enthusiasm: one officer, Colonel General Novozhilov, later recounted how although he was opposed to the junta, his political deputy kept distributing GKChP documents behind his back.

It was in the KGB, though, that the collapse of the authority of the centre was most striking. Perhaps this reflects the nature of secret policemen: not only have they that much more to lose if they end up on the losing side but they will often be flexible, pragmatic, even cynical individuals able to assess the odds and less bound to some abstract notion of duty and unit honour than, say, soldiers. The KGB's Alfa commando group, for example, refused orders to storm Yeltsin's parliament building, and later claimed to have done so on moral grounds. Speaking off the record, though, members of the unit have admitted that it was mainly because it would have proved a suicide mission, given that the 106th Airborne Division, which was to have cleared them a route through the crowds around parliament, could no longer be trusted. In the republics, many local KGB apparatuses had already been wooed successfully by local governments. The Georgian branch of the KGB, for example, had renamed itself the Georgian National Security Department and pledged allegiance to elected President Gamsakhurdia. Elsewhere, KGB structures were paralysed by internal struggles between 'Muscovites' and 'locals'. Some 70 per cent of regional KGB organisations refused to support the coup, most notably in Leningrad, where the city KGB disobeyed their orders to arrest the mayor and other local leaders. Even in Moscow, the KGB was divided. In May, Kryuchkov had agreed with Boris Yeltsin that a specifically Russian KGB would be set up alongside the USSR KGB, and tales from the days of the coup spoke of the almost farcical goings on within the KGB's Lubyanka headquarters, as 'Russian' and 'Soviet' KGB officers tried to eavesdrop on each others' plans and then go and have lunch together before returning to their shadow-boxing. Gorbachev's KGB bodyguards stayed loyal to him, even though their commander, General Yurii Plekhanov, was one of the delegation which placed him under arrest.

The result was not so much that the KGB was helpless, but that since Kryuchkov failed quickly to demonstrate his authority, most within it were prepared to adopt a 'wait and see' approach, unwilling to commit themselves until they had a clearer idea of the odds. This vicious circle affected the plotters standing with all branches of the state and the security forces: the longer it took the GKChP to establish its grip on the country, the weaker it appeared. The weaker it looked, the less likely it was that the wavering majority would support it, thus making it weaker still. Eventually even the very highest figures within the security structures began openly opposing the coup. The Ukrainian and Belorussian KGBs, for example, eventually came out against the plotters, while a meeting of the senior commanders within the Defence Ministry on the morning of Wednesday 21 August led to a consensus forming that Yazov would have to resign as minister and announce that the GKChP was illegal. Eventually, the plotters were not so much defeated as gave up in dismay as they realised the way the tide was flowing against them. Once the Defence Ministry's views had been communicated to the rest of the GKChP, it agreed to fly to the Crimea and seek Gorbachev's forgiveness.

Could the coup have succeeded had it been, as originally intended, a state coup? Would the authority of the President have lent legitimacy to the emergency regime and thus rallied the security forces around it, while Gorbachev's presence reassured foreign governments? Perhaps. But by this stage, such an emergency measure would have been ultimately irrelevant, its time long gone. Power had already devolved from Moscow so far that it would have taken the outright use of force to reimpose it, not just the proclamation of martial law. The problems facing the Soviet economy would take more than a crack of the whip to solve. While it has been said that the August Coup brought down the Soviet Union and the Party, it is probably fair to say that it merely proved to all that the Union and Party were already to all intents and purposes dead.

The USSR, as a subject of international law and a geopolitical reality, has ceased to exist.

Joint declaration of Russian, Ukrainian and Belorussian
Presidents, 8 December 1991

PART FOUR

THE NEW RUSSIA

7 RUSSIA'S SECURITY, 1991–93

1991   *December*   USSR dissolved: Commonwealth of Independent States established.

1992   *February*   Minsk Summit of Commonwealth of Independent States.

        May   Tashkent Summit of Commonwealth of Independent States.

        July   Second Tashkent Summit: peace-keeping accord signed.

        December   7th Russian Congress of People's Deputies sees open split between President and parliament.

1993   *January*   Moscow summit between Yeltsin and US President Bush: START-2 arms treaty signed.

        April   Vancouver summit between Yeltsin and new US President Clinton. National referendum endorses Yeltsin's leadership, but not his policies.

        September   Yeltsin dissolves parliament.

        October   Military and security troops used to enforce dissolution of parliament ('October Coup').

        November   New military doctrine approved.

        December   Parliamentary elections to new parliament sees swing to Communists and neo-fascist Liberal Democrat Party.

Great Russia is rising from her knees. We will without fail transform her into a prosperous, peace-loving, law-governed and sovereign state.

> Boris Yeltsin on his inauguration as Russia's first elected President, 1991.

To many, the end of the USSR and the return of Russian to the world community of nations marked the beginning of something new. It meant an end to the 'barracks socialism' of the Soviet Union, its imperialism masquerading as 'proletarian internationalism'. Yet it certainly did not mean a return to the old Russia of tsars and cossacks, the 'prison of nations', the 'gendarme of Europe'. No, this was a new Russia, of democratic institutions, popular legitimacy and modern – in other words, Western – in attitude. As George Bush put it on accepting the Republican candidacy in 1992:

> *The Soviet Union can only be found in history books . . . .*
> *This convention is the first at which an American president can*
> *say, 'The Cold War is over, and freedom finished first!'*

To be fair, this was campaign rhetoric rather than sober analysis, and there is also some truth here. But the new Russia can no more pretend to have inherited nothing from its Soviet parent than the USSR could be uninfluenced by the tsars' system. Russia readopted the tsar's symbol of the double-headed eagle, but if one head faced into the future, the other was still peering into the past. Particularly striking were the continuities in foreign and security policy. The period 1991–93 was one of stops and starts, the slow formation of a new political system. The creation of a 'Commonwealth of Independent States' ensured the end of Gorbachev's hopes to keep the USSR intact, and from this point the focus must shift to specifically Russian politics. The debate over Russia's military role and forces, though, demonstrated the two basic features of this period. First of all, it owed much to late Soviet thinking. Secondly, it was also blocked by the political stalemate which developed between Boris Yeltsin and his parliament, until he took the dramatic (and unconstitutional) step of dissolving it and then sending in the troops to back up his orders in September–October 1993. To do this, Yeltsin had to make sure that he had the support of the 'Power Ministries' (Defence, Internal Affairs and – as successor of the KGB – Security). Once again the Russian head of state's relations with his policemen, soldiers and secret policemen can be seen to have been a vital part of his domestic politics, just as his security policies were to be shaped as much as anything else by the needs of this alliance.

THE COMMONWEALTH OF INDEPENDENT STATES: A NEW IDENTITY?

On returning to Moscow after the coup, Gorbachev tried to revive

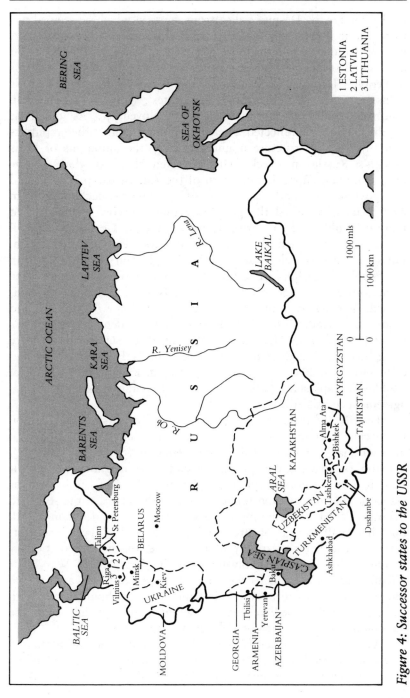

Figure 4: Successor states to the USSR

his Union Treaty. Despite a disastrous start, in which he seemed not to realise that the Party was divided and discredited beyond repair, within a couple of months there began to appear signs that he might have some success. At an emergency session of the USSR Congress of People's Deputies in September, republican leaders approved his plans for a new 'Union of Sovereign States', a plan to which seven republics would pledge themselves in November. As much as anything else, this reflected a feeling amongst some other republics that this sort of structure might help keep the ambitions of Boris Yeltsin's Russia in check. This reflected the way that, in the immediate and euphoric aftermath of the August Coup, Yeltsin and his government made a series of over-hasty declarations. In particular, they raised the possibility that Moscow might seek to redraw republican boundaries to her advantage. Gorbachev, for all his flaws, represented the only credible counterweight to Yeltsin. Boris Yeltsin was well aware of this, though, and responded with a successful campaign to establish a far looser structure, the Commonwealth of Independent States (SNG – Sodruzhestvo nezavisimykh gosudarstv). By striking deals with the Ukrainian and Belorussian leaderships, Yeltsin managed to defeat Gorbachev's initiative, and on 8 December 1991, the three slav heads of state agreed to establish the Commonwealth. On 21 December, they and eight more republics – Armenia, Azerbaijan, Kazakhstan, Kirghizia, Moldavia, Tajikistan, Turkmenia and Uzbekistan – signed a formal agreement to this effect.

The SNG had therefore been conceived by Yeltsin largely to foil Gorbachev's return to centre stage. He envisaged it as an international structure substantial enough to pacify Russia's neighbours but weak enough that he could use or ignore it at will. It was, in one memorable phrase, a 'gigantic fig leaf'. It is perhaps symbolic that it was even founded on a convenient lie: the so-called 'Minsk Accord' on founding the SNG was concluded not in Minsk but the small village of Brest. Given that it had been at Brest-Litovsk, where, by the treaty of that name, the new revolutionary regime ended Russia's involvement in the First World War (at a terribly high price paid to the Germans) the decision was made to rename the accord to avoid association with this humiliation. With such a negative pedigree it is perhaps unsurprising that the Commonwealth never really amounted to anything.

As a military structure, the SNG proved little more than a temporary caretaker of the former Soviet Union's military assets. Its notional defence minister was Marshal Evgenii Shaposhnikov, previously commander of the Soviet Air Force and one of the two senior military figures openly to have defied the GKChP. For this and his personal connections with Boris Yeltsin, he was richly rewarded, becoming USSR Defence Minister in August and then Commander-in-Chief of SNG Joint Forces in December. Although genuine in his commitment to reform – especially the profession-alisation and depoliticisation of the armed forces – he was to prove a disappointing and lightweight figure. As an airman, he was already regarded with suspicion within a military hierarchy traditionally dominated by the army. He was further to prove unable to address the intellectual implications of change. This was particularly striking in contrast with his newly appointed Chief of the General Staff, Colonel General Vladimir Lobov, who had not only risen without Yeltsin's patronage but had an established track record as a moderate reformer and a pedigree as a military intellectual second to few. In December, largely on personal grounds, Shaposhnikov dismissed Lobov, replacing him with Leningrad's Colonel General Samsonov. While Samsonov shared Lobov's general views on military reform, he was seen as a more amenable figure and, with less of a grounding as a military theoretician, posed less of an intellectual and political challenge to Shaposhnikov.

Securing his position within the SNG Joint Command would mean little unless that command had a role, though, and Shaposhnikov tried to guarantee this by insisting that it was both cheaper and more efficient to retain a common armed force for the SNG rather than letting or forcing each republic to build up its own. Individual republics' forces should, in his view, be limited to small, lightly armed units, national guards, intended mainly for security and ceremonial duties. It is fairly obvious why Shaposhnikov and the Russian government wanted to preserve unified forces. Any such joint military structure would inevitably be dominated by the Russians, given that it would be constituted from the old (Russian-dominated) USSR Defence Ministry and be commanded by an officer corps which was 80 per cent Russian. This was equally clear to everyone else, and from the first Ukraine, Azerbaijan and Moldova (formerly Moldavia) had declared their intention to establish their own national armies. Only the Central Asian states supported the Russian joint forces notion with any enthusiasm, unwilling to cover the costs of creating their own armies.

In May 1992, in Tashkent, a meeting officially held to strengthen and regularise the Commonwealth effectively declared it dead. Ukraine and the newly renamed Belarus (Belorussia) stayed away; Armenia and Azerbaijan were at war; and even the most convinced adherents on the joint forces idea accepted that each republic would henceforth create its own army. The new security accord signed at Tashkent represented little more than an agreement by the various nations to go their separate ways. The role of the SNG command would steadily wither until it was nothing more than a transitional body supervising the destruction and transfer of nuclear weapons. At a further Tashkent summit in July, SNG leaders concluded an agreement on peace-keeping within the Commonwealth, but in May Russia herself had established her own Defence Ministry. Not only was this a clear first step to disentangling Russia's forces from the Commonwealth, from that point efforts to give the SNG some credible military role were hindered by differences of opinion between Shaposhnikov and the Russian Defence Ministry.

The prospects for a Commonwealth for nations with no wealth and largely unprepared to accept that they had much in common had never been good. There had been hopes that practical considerations of mutual economic and military dependence could prevail, even that the SNG could represent some regional forum for the negotiation of new relations and the resolution of disputed issues, maybe manage the interregional trade which was still a necessity after seventy years of Soviet economic integration. The SNG, though, failed to find an independent identity in its early years. It never acquired any legitimacy, any charter, any real reason to live. Nor did Shaposhnikov ever manage either to impose his will upon the Russian Defence Ministry – in May 1993, for example, it vetoed his plans to create multinational forces – or to shake off suspicion in other republics that he was little more than Yeltsin's puppet. Having fulfilled its real purpose – forestalling Gorbachev's return – the Commonwealth slowly faded from view, unloved and unmourned, until its joint military command was effectively abolished in June 1993 and replaced by a council of member states' Defence Ministers. Shaposhnikov was offered the post of secretary of the Russian Security Council – again in the role of Yeltsin's loyal factotum – although he resigned from this job, too, in August. Ironically, the end to any military role for the SNG was probably the best thing for it in the long run. It could then become a much-needed organisation through which the leaders of post-Soviet republics could meet and, above all, reach trade, customs and cooperation agreements so that they could work together to rebuild their national economies.

THE RUSSIAN DEFENCE MINISTRY

When he established a Russian Defence Ministry in May 1992, Boris Yeltsin was faced with the dilemma of whom to appoint as minister. Various names had been raised, including Shaposhnikov, Colonel Generals Konstantin Kobets and Dmitrii Volkogonov, Galina Starovoitova and Andrei Kokoshin. Kobets had been a close ally of Yeltsin's since becoming his military adviser in March 1991, with a solid if undramatic soldierly record. By contrast Volkogonov was a wily military historian who had transformed himself from being an almost Stalinist Party hack of the Main Political Directorate in the pre-*perestroika* era to an outspoken radical, winning himself Yeltsin's ear but the contempt of many senior officers. The remaining two were both academic specialists, Starovoitova on interethnic relations, Kokoshin on arms control and defence economics. The appointment of either civilian would have been of great symbolic importance, but generated further resistance within the ministry (especially in the case of Starovoitova, as a woman).

It is a measure of the complexity of the debate that Yeltsin first made himself Defence Minister as a stopgap measure and then appointed another political lightweight, Lieutenant General Pavel Grachev. The former commander of Soviet paratroop forces, Grachev was very similar to Shaposhnikov in many ways: a young, tough and effective soldier who had resisted the August Coup junta, but also an outsider without any real political constituency beyond the paratroopers and not up to such a demanding role. Perhaps this was the idea, in that Yeltsin may have thought – ironically enough, like Gorbachev with Yazov – that such a man would be more easily controlled. As it is, though, Grachev's career as minister saw the collapse of the morale and unity of the Russian armed forces and his reputation as a brave, no-nonsense soldier became replaced by one of a dim and biddable henchman, interested only in feathering his own nest (tales abounded of his sales to himself of army property at ridiculously low prices).

Kokoshin became a First Deputy Defence Minister. A former deputy director of the USA–Canada Institute and since 1990 head of the Centre for Conversion and Privatisation of the Defence Industry, he was the archetypal *institutchik* made good. As such, he not only brought fresh ideas to the ministry but also faced the resistance of a military establishment suspicious of outsiders. It certainly led to no dilution in the generals' control over the Defence Ministry, as they closed ranks against this unwelcome outsider. Ironically enough, it had been the dismissed General Lobov who, in late 1991, had put forward different programmes for bringing the services under civilian control, either by the appointment of an outsider as the minister or creating committees to supervise the ministry from within. The civilian Kokoshin, try as he might, could not implement Lobov's ideas.

The relationship between the new High Command and its civilian masters was thus thrown into sharp relief. When Shaposhnikov first assumed control of the USSR Defence Ministry in 1991, he spoke of a radical renovation of the senior military command, of an 80 per cent turnover. The end of the USSR, the messy SNG interregnum and the rise of the Russian Defence Ministry certainly brought about considerable changes, but it is less clear how far they really affected the high command. A new generation rose to office, but in the way it is dominated by powerful 'circles' of friends or 'brotherhoods' of soldiers with shared experiences and interests, the Russian Defence Ministry looks strikingly like its Soviet forebear (just as, it could be argued, the Red Army soon came to resemble closely its tsarist predecessor).

The immediately post-coup period saw a purge of unreconstructed 'old thinkers'. The three Military District commanders who openly supported the coup – Kuz'min in the Baltic VO, Kalinin in Moscow VO and Makashov in the Volga–Urals VO – were duly replaced, while Colonel General Valentin Varennikov, the wily and incisive Commander-in-Chief of Ground Forces and an outspoken proponent of the need for martial law, was arrested. Marshal Akhromeev, although in no way implicated in the coup, committed suicide soon after, heartbroken by its implications and the disintegration of the state and Party that he had held dear and vowed to protect.

With Grachev a new 'brotherhood' came of age: the *afgantsy*, veterans of the Afghan war. Of the seven key appointments first made within the Russian Defence Ministry, five went to *afgantsy*: Defence Minister Grachev had earned his Hero of the Soviet Union medal during his five years as a paratroop commander in *Afgan*, Chief of the General Staff Colonel General Dubynin had commanded the 40th Army in Afghanistan, 1986–87, while three First Deputy Defence Ministers – Colonel Generals Gromov, Kondrat'ev and Mironov – all had Afghan experience, Gromov commanding the 40th Army, 1987–89. The average age of the new High Command was only forty-eight, but this should not be taken as proof either that the entire military structure was colonised by gung-ho paratroopers with Afghan experience, or that the new Russian Defence Ministry was not being formed under the shadow of several influential figures of the old order. For a start, several of these 'new men' had held very senior posts under the old order. Boris Gromov, indeed, had been Boris Pugo's deputy at the Interior Ministry, and the fact that he was only temporarily suspended after the coup's collapse is probably more indicative of friends in high places – possibly Vice President Rutskoi, himself an *afganets* – than total innocence.

This reflects an obvious desire within the military establishment to use the coup as an opportunity to purge political rivals, those near retirement and the incompetent, yet to salvage those who could still be of use in the future or those within the right 'brotherhoods'. A case in point is Colonel General Igor' Rodionov. In 1989 he had been heading for the top: commander of the prestigious 24th Samaro-Ulyanovsk 'Iron' Division, a Major General at the age of forty-one, commander of Soviet forces in Afghanistan and then First Deputy Commander of the high-profile Moscow Military District, before being made head of the increasingly volatile Transcaucasian VO. There he was to obey the orders which destroyed his hopes of rising to the Defence Ministry, when in April 1989 he obeyed his orders to disperse Georgian protesters by force. The political storm which broke was violent enough to see Rodionov transferred, but it is a mark of the regard in which he was held within the military that as soon as the worst of the protests died down he was not retired or given some trivial job but put in charge of the USSR's senior military school, the General Staff Academy, grooming the next generation of high-fliers. He made it a centre of thoughtful but undoubtably reactionary military and political analysis, and throughout 1991 made his support for martial law clear. After the coup, though, he managed to avoid any fall-out, and his academy in due course became the Academy of the Russian General Staff. He was even tipped by some observers to replace Dubynin as Chief of the General Staff, and although this proved a little too much to expect to pass unnoticed, he retained his role as head of Russia's foremost military think-tank.

THE RUSSIAN ARMY: A NEW BEGINNING?

Essentially, we have got to create a Russian army from scratch.

Russian Defence Minister Grachev, 1992

Grachev was hardly being honest: the continued grip of Soviet-era commanders ensured that the new Russian army was built upon many of the ideas and assumptions of the old era. The shrinkage of Moscow's domains to something like its seventeenth-century boundaries, the partition of the former Soviet armed forces and the marooning of units now under Russian control not only in East/Central Europe but also in newly independent successor states from Moldova to Tajikistan all presented the General Staff with new challenges. Yet in the absence of a clear political lead, many of the changes – from the renewed interest in the traditions of the old tsarist army to the nuts and bolts of unit organisation and tactics – simply reflected processes begun under the late Soviet era. The result was an evolution rather than dramatic change.

The best example is of the way the Russian forces began to move – albeit slowly – away from relying upon conscription to man the majority of their units. The dying years of the USSR had already seen the collapse of the system of conscription. With *glasnost'* had come accounts of the brutality and misery of army life, which, while often sensationalised, were in essence true enough. The rise of grass-roots politics and democratisation had then allowed people to express their concerns and demand changes, from the Afghan veterans who mobilised to campaign for access to medical facilities and invalidity pensions through to the 'mothers' unions' which, from around 1989, began to protest against bullying within the military. They certainly had reason for protest. *Dedovshchina* (there is no convenient translation: it means something like 'grandfatherism') had become ubiquitous, a characteristically Russian type of bullying, whereby conscripts who had served longer in the ranks banded together to abuse, exploit and molest newcomers. Along with widespread illness and disease, drug and alcohol abuse and a cavalier approach to safety regulations, it accounted for the lives of 6,000–8,000 soldiers per year, to which must be added the mounting casualties from the peacekeeping operations in Central Asia and Transcaucasia which marked the fall of the Soviet Union. At the same time that national service was looking far less attractive, so too were local authorities less able or willing to enforce it. The result was that conscription all but ceased in those regions where Soviet authority was weakest. In the autumn 1990 draft, for example, less than a tenth of the Georgian young men slated for national service bothered heeding the call, while only Kazakhstan, Kirghizia and Turkmenistan provided their full quotas of all Soviet republics.

Consequently all but the most conservative members of the Soviet high command had already begun to realise that the old model of an army officered by professionals and university students on national service, but predominantly (two-thirds) manned by conscripts was no longer viable. It was no longer supportable on economic grounds, now that the Defence Ministry was having to pay market prices to feed, clothe and arm its five million troops. It no longer made sense in military terms: new generation weapons systems were increasingly beyond the ability of the conscript to learn to use in his brief period of national service, and new tactics emphasising initiative and versatility were replacing old reliance upon the mass attack. Above all it was no longer politically feasible when so many young men were simply refusing to serve. Those who did were all too often unmotivated, nationalist (there was a fear that the army was simply training the next generation of anti-Soviet guerrillas it would later have to fight) or from the Central Asian states and thus quite possibly unable to speak Russian – the army's official language – and treated with suspicion by the Russians in Moscow.

In 1990 a new system of 'contract recruitment' was launched as a first step to shifting the balance between professionals and conscripts, offering higher salaries to those prepared to enrol for fixed terms of service. There was no notion yet of creating an all-professional army along British or US lines, but it did mean that the generals were trying to recruit more volunteers to whom to entrust key services, such as the Strategic Rocket Forces and the security troops. Indeed, debate on this issue can be traced back to 1988, and it was those military conservatives Yazov and Moiseev who had introduced this innovation as part of a three-stage reform plan. In the period 1991–94, efforts would have been concentrated on the withdrawal of forces from Mongolia and East/Central Europe; 1994–95 would have seen organisational changes at home in response to these troop movements; in the period 1996–2000, though, offensive strategic (nuclear) forces would have been halved, ground troops cut by a further 10–12 per cent and the overall strength of the military reduced to 3,000,000–3,200,000, with the ratio of professionals to conscripts rising steadily until volunteers made up the majority.

This was well short of many radicals' expectations, and was a naked bid to hold off any real reform until 1996, yet it reflected the way that the Soviet high command was beginning to appreciate that the battle to resist fundamental change had been lost, and the next one was to manage that change. Thus were liberated a connected series of ideas which were to be applied in the post-Soviet era and reflected in Russia's new military doctrine, the official notion of what sort of wars Moscow's forces would be expected to fight, why, when and, above all, how. Russia incorporated the majority of these plans into her own programme, extending the contract recruitment scheme while pledging to cut forces from 2,800,000 to 1,500,000 by the end of 1995 for many of the same reasons. In 1992 and most of 1993, though, it could not embark on major restructuring because it had yet to have approved its new military doctrine. In 1992 it issued its own draft version and quietly began implementing many of its provisions, but before this could become officially adopted there had to be some resolution of the political stalemate between parliament and President.

THE STALEMATE: SECURITY COUNCIL vs SUPREME SOVIET

Left, right, green, red, blue: just about every political force, current and faction is now seeking to influence the army. . . . I am answerable to the president, the Security Council, the Supreme Soviet and the Congress of People's Deputies.

Defence Minister Grachev, 1993

Power in Russia was vested in two institutions: the President and his government on the one hand and parliament (the Russian Congress of Peoples' Deputies and Supreme Soviet) on the other. Superficially, this resembled the US system, with its division between the executive (the President) and legislature (Congress). Relationships between legislature and executive in such systems are often problematic, but what was very different in Russia was that not only were these two institutions trying to run a country on the verge of ruin, but there was no generally agreed consensus and constitution to define their relationship. In the US case, there are clearly defined distinctions between the role of the President and the legislature and a Supreme Court to interpret and enforce the Constitution. Even in a country such as Britain with no written constitution, there are broadly accepted 'rules of the game', and other institutions – such as the House of Lords and law courts – to uphold them. Security policy thus became a battleground between rival political interests. Their priorities often had nothing to do with the issues in question, but everything to do with carving out roles in the still forming political structure.

In the eyes of the Supreme Soviet, Russia's standing parliament, it had to have oversight and control over the security services and 'power ministries'. After all, it argued, if the Soviet experience had taught anything it was that open, constitutional checks and balances were necessary to ensure that control over the army and security services did not tempt the head of state into tyranny. Of course, there was also a political subtext, a simple duel for power between the executive and the legislature. This was particularly the case for the ambitious Ruslan Khasbulatov, the Speaker of the Supreme Soviet and thus the closest thing to its leader. The result was a muddled compromise in which both presidential and parliamentary oversight was exercised alongside legal supervision from the Prosecutor-General. The President appointed the ministers and chaired the Security Council which had a major but rather shadowy role in deciding defence, foreign and security policy and upon which sat the relevant ministers. On the other hand, parliament established two Commissions, one for Defence and State Security and another for International Affairs with an eye to involving itself in foreign and security policy. As for the Prosecutor-General, his role was to ensure that the security services operated within the (admittedly very broad) terms of the 1992 Law on State Security, although in practice they proved able to snub, divert or openly defy the Prosecutor-General's office with impunity because of the struggle between parliament and President.

The problem was that the President felt that the Supreme Soviet – elected under old, Soviet-era rules – was not a truly democratic or representative body, while parliament suspected the President of autocratic ambitions. Both were trying to establish their own roles and legitimacy, and both felt that they had first to win the support of the security interests or at least undermine the other's control over them. Thus, the defence, foreign policy and security lobbies found themselves in the privileged position of being able to play both sides off against each other. In February 1992, for example, parliament passed a decree assuming the right to a say in the financing and staffing of the security services; four days later Yeltsin issued his own, claiming that the final voice was his. The result was that neither could establish proper oversight of the former KGB.

These interests could not only resist the authority of the Security Council and Supreme Soviet Commissions but they also came to play an increasingly influential role within the very structures intended to control them. The Supreme Soviet Commission on Defence and State Security was, as of 1993, still staffed predominantly by parliamentarians previously or still working for the security services, military or defence industries. Khasbulatov's senior aide on security matters was Filipp Bobkov, formerly a deputy head of the KGB, and he acted both as a matchmaker to connect Khasbulatov with various figures within the security apparatus and their protector and champion within parliament. The same process was at work with the military, both sides eager to build alliances with the high command, neither prepared to let the other assert its supremacy, and thus both conniving at giving the soldiers a free hand.

FOREIGN POLICY, 1991–93

This muddle also prevented the formulation of any clear foreign policy and thus allowed various people and groups to make it up as they went along. Perhaps the most basic division was between the so-called 'Atlanticists' and 'Eurasians'. The former wanted to see Russia join the West European community as soon as possible. The latter saw rapid Westernisation as either impossible or downright counterproductive, and instead looked to creating a role for Russia as a bridge between Europe and Asia, able to play in both regional theatres. In many ways this was a reprise of a traditional Russian debate, between 'Westernisers' and 'Slavophiles', those seeking to cast off their distinctive Russian heritage, and those glorying in it.

The philosophical argument will more fully be discussed in the next chapter; what is worth studying here is quite how the struggle between these two camps took shape and how it complicated and reflected other competitions between institutions and individuals. By identifying himself so closely with the 'Atlanticist' school, for example, Russian Foreign Minister Kozyrev linked its fortunes with his own. An intelligent man and sophisticated academic, his brusque style nonetheless won him many enemies amongst officials of the former USSR Foreign Ministry now working for its Russian counterpart, while his surprising speech at Stockholm in December 1992 did little for his credibility. There he claimed that henceforth Russia would look after her own interests, to the extent of a re-annexation of the Baltic States, only to return to announce to his startled audience that he had simply wanted to illustrate how policy might change were the radicals in Moscow to be defeated.

Kozyrev from the first had pushed for Russia's integration into regional and global institutions, with an eye to becoming what he called a 'normal' nation. In part this stemmed from a view that incorporating the nation into the community of Western, democratic nations was part of the renunciation of the Soviet past, and in part a hope – like Gorbachev's – that this would lead to Western investment and assistance. The admission of Russia – like most of the SNG nations – into the International Monetary Fund and the new European Bank of Reconstruction and Development in April 1992 reflected both these ideas. Until late 1992, Yeltsin was clearly supporting Kozyrev's liberal and 'Atlanticist' approach. Along with a number of symbolic acts – such as denouncing the Soviet invasions of Hungary and Czechoslovakia in 1956 and 1968, respectively, and handing over to South Korea tapes of radio messages during the interception and destruction of a Korean Airlines jet in 1983 – Yeltsin worked hard to develop a relationship with the USA. By October 1992, though, he was beginning to tire of the 'Atlanticist' line. Not only was it failing to produce the immediate assistance some had (unrealistically) expected, but it was providing a cause around which a wide range of his enemies and rivals could rally, from his disgruntled Vice President Rutskoi to conservative parliamentarians. That month saw the resignation of First Deputy Minister Shelov-Kovedyaev; young, liberal, Westwards- looking, he was the archetype of the new 'Kozyrev generation' at the Foreign Ministry, and his removal was merely the first concession to the 'Atlanticists' as Yeltsin's support for them waned, and power drifted from the Foreign Ministry to the President's Security Council.

For if the 'Atlanticists' were dominant within the academic and media community, as well as having the support of a large number of the younger, radical politicians in Yeltsin's entourage, the 'Eurasians' were associated with a few senior figures – such as Sergei Stankevich, the Russian State Counsellor – and many within the security services, armed forces and military-industrial complex. For a start, consider the sectional interests at work. Desperate to reassure the West of their good intentions and their commitment to what they saw as Western values, the 'Atlanticists' identified themselves with major arms cuts, a reduction in Russia's arms exports and a ban on sales to nations such as Syria and India, scaling down intelligence operations in the West and a general demilitarisation of the country. For the military, this meant yet further cuts, coupled with a policy which could cause ever greater tensions on Russia's southern and eastern borders. For the defence industrialists, yet further reductions in defence contracts, an end to state subsidies and restrictions on exports, such that massive closures would seem inevitable. In part as a result, parliament began swinging behind the 'Eurasian' bandwagon.

Over the Kurile Islands, for example, a bone of contention between Russia and Japan since 1945, Russian policy became tied in many of the same knots as had bound Gorbachev. In the interests of improving relations, the Foreign Ministry floated the idea of making some concessions during the preparations for Yeltsin's Tokyo visit of 1992. The Defence Ministry reacted with anger, General Grachev telling a press conference that Russia would not withdraw from the islands since they were a key link in the her Far Eastern defences. The General Staff went on to produce an alarmist report that all but claimed that were Russia to surrender the Kuriles to the Japanese it would end up inviting them through the gates of Moscow. Once it became clear that the high command was united against any concessions, parliament weighed in, largely in the hope of wooing the generals from Yeltsin's side and humbling his Foreign Ministry. The result was a deadlock, in which Yeltsin had no more chance of persuading the Japanese of his willingness and ability to reach a compromise over the Kuriles as had Gorbachev in 1991.

Institutional rivalry and constitutional deadlock left policy up for grabs, created and amended by whoever had the power and willingness to act. This was sometimes a ministry or senior political figure, such as Grachev laying down the law over the Kurile islands. As often, though, it was bit-part players who seized the opportunity. In the republic of Moldova, for example, the former Soviet Fourteenth Army became increasingly clearly identified with the local Russian community, which set up its own 'Dneistr Republic' and started a guerrilla war to win autonomy from the Romanian-speaking majority. There the initiative was with the local commanders, and not Moscow, and most strikingly Major General

Lebed'. As commander of the 106th Airborne Division, he had defied the coup plotters in 1991 and deployed his paratroopers in defence of Boris Yeltsin. In 1992 he was assigned to the politically sensitive 14th Army and in short order had all but made it the army of the 'Dneistr Republic', denouncing the legal Moldovan government as 'Nazis' and 'murderers'. It is clear that Lebed' had his protectors in Moscow – the same week that he was given a gentle slap on the wrist for his public stance he was also promoted to Lieutenant General – but their role was purely as guardian angels. Instead, Russian foreign policy towards Moldova was essentially being dictated by a gung-ho paratrooper with a taste for theatricals and the freedom to champion a Russian community he felt faced repression and discrimination.

THE 'OCTOBER COUP' – AND KGB, RIP?

This stalemate was damaging both to Boris Yeltsin's political position and Russia's very future. Through 1992 and 1993, the rift between president and parliament widened steadily. The 7th Russian Congress of People's Deputies in December 1992 failed to back Yeltsin's favoured candidate for the Prime Minister's post, the radical economist Egor Gaidar:

It is no longer possible to work with such a Congress. The walls of this hall blush from endless insults, from the filth that swamps the Congress owing to the sick ambitions of bankrupt politicians.

Boris Yeltsin, December 1992

The 9th Congress, in March 1993, tried unsuccessfully to impeach Yeltsin. In response he called a national referendum while privately sounding out the military and security forces on acting against parliament. The referendum backed Yeltsin but not his policies – and thus failed to break the logjam. With constitutional methods apparently useless, Yeltsin felt he could do nothing but turn to the security forces.

After all, the critical role the security apparatus had played in the August Coup had ensured that one of Yeltsin's priorities would be to ensure that the KGB and Interior Ministry (MVD) were brought under his control. Immediately after the coup Vadim Bakatin, the reformist Interior Minister whose head the KGB had demanded and received in 1990 as part of the 'winter alliance' with Gorbachev, was placed in charge of the organisation with a brief to dismantle and democratise it. While many of the KGB's facilities and personnel were transferred to (or simply taken over by) republican governments, the central rump of the service was broken into three separate services. The Inter-State Security Service, run by Bakatin, was to become some sort of post-Soviet equivalent of the USA's FBI, coordinating counter-espionage within the republics, while the Central Intelligence Service would handle foreign espionage, like the CIA. The State Border Protection Committee would assume responsibility for the KGB's quarter of a million Border Troops. Meanwhile the Russian government formed its own small Federal Security Agency and other forces, such as the Government Communications Troops and the KGB's VIP protection squads were floated off as separate organisations.

This assumed the existence of some sort of Union, though. By December 1991, this was clearly unlikely, while Yeltsin wanted to consolidate his hold on the key services. The formal dissolution of the USSR thus became the excuse for a further reshuffle. The Central Intelligence Service became the Russian Foreign Intelligence Service (SVR – Sluzhba vneshnoi razvedky), the Border Troops became the SNG State Border Troops but, most significantly, both the Federal Security Agency and Bakatin's Security Service were swallowed up by the Russian Interior Ministry to form the Ministry of Security and Internal Affairs (MBVD – Ministerstvo bezopasnosti i vnutrennykh del). The MBVD was headed by Viktor Barannikov, for whereas Bakatin was an independent-minded figure close to Gorbachev, Barannikov was generally seen as a loyal follower of Yeltsin's. This was classic Yeltsin, a move defended on the grounds of creating a more effective body to protect democracy which in practice gathered more powers in the hands of one of his allies. It also demonstrated the extent to which the process of the creation of new institutions was dominated by the struggles of organisations to build their empires. The Russian Interior Ministry (MVD) turned out to be behind the plan, seeing it as a way to take over its more glamorous security service rivals. As it was, the move attracted criticisms from all sides, not least for the way the merger was announced, without any discussion and debate. Ultimately, the Constitutional Court declared Yeltsin's decree illegitimate in January 1992.

The result was yet another reorganisation. The SVR remained the same, but the MBVD was again broken into a distinct MVD, under Viktor Erin, and a new Ministry of Security (MB – Ministerstvo bezopasnosti) under Barannikov. For all the reshuffles, though, the security services had changed but little. The KGB's espionage arm, the First Chief Directorate, had always been a service within a service, keeping itself at arm's length from its less élite colleagues, and the SVR was little more than the First Chief Directorate under a new name and with a new chief, Academician Evgenii Primakov. Primakov was an astute and effective foreign affairs analyst, but his role in determining Middle East policy has meant that many have suggested that he had already had more than a passing acquaintanceship with the KGB before his appointment. The Russian MVD has simply occupied the role within Russia that the USSR MVD used to fill and its founding ministers, Andrei Dunaev (minister while it was still coexisting with an All-Union counterpart) and Viktor Erin were both stalwarts of the old Soviet apparatus. As for the MB, it assumed many of the internal security roles and assets of the KGB and as of 1993 had a total of 137,900 staff, of whom just under 3,000 worked in the central headquarters in Moscow. In Barannikov it had a founder who had been a senior Soviet MVD official, playing as Azerbaijan's First Deputy Interior Minister a key role in the use of troops to bring Azerbaijan back under Moscow's control in January 1990. He also made it clear, at the 8th Congress of Peoples' Deputies (1993), that he wanted to build upon rather than replace the methods of the Soviet secret police: 'I am not inclined to cast aside the collective experience of our predecessors, built up by Russian special services within the framework of the former KGB, merely in order to pander to some transient circumstances.'

Government statements trumpeted a massive reduction in the size of the security services, from half a million to 40,000 staff. Yet what lay behind these figures? Of the reduction, around a quarter of a million were accounted for by the transfer away of the Border Troops, while the Government Communications Troops represented another 100,000; yet these men were not sacked, merely transferred to new organisations. With another 100,000 or so KGB officers lost to the new security services in other republics of the former Soviet Union, it is clear that the only real reductions were in the purge of senior figures closely involved in the August Coup. Post-Soviet Russia thus retained a huge intelligence and security apparatus, and one built soundly upon the basis of the KGB and merely reorganised and redirected to suit the needs of the times. This is not, necessarily, a concern, but it throws into the sharp relief two basic questions. First, the usual one of *quis custodiet custodies*, who guards the guardians, who ensures they obey their titular masters? Secondly, who are their masters? In other words, who establishes the policies and the laws which they are meant to uphold?

As it was, they allied themselves with Yeltsin against parliament and in doing so protected themselves from any genuine reform. When Yeltsin looked to the support of the security forces in March 1993, Grachev's Defence Ministry re-emphasised its desire to remain outside internal politics. With Erin pledging the support of the Interior Ministry, Yeltsin turned finally to Security Ministry. While he had been appointed by Yeltsin, Barannikov was unprepared to break the law and the constitution for his patron, and in doing so secured his downfall. In July the poor performance of Border Troops under his jurisdiction in fighting rebels on the Tajik–Afghan frontier was used as a pretext for his replacement by his deputy, Nikolai Golushko. A career KGB officer, with a background suppressing dissidents in the Soviet Ukraine, Golushko proved to have none of Barannikov's scruples.

On 21 September, Yeltsin issued a Presidential decree dissolving parliament. The Supreme Soviet reacted with defiance, and made the mistake of encouraging an anti-Yeltsin mob which rampaged across central Moscow. Although parliament had the law on its side – the constitution clearly stated that the President had no right to dissolve parliament – as well as Vice President Rutskoi, the mob provided the perfect excuse for the armed suppression of parliament. On 4 October, tanks from the army's 2nd and 4th divisions, Interior Troops from the MVD's 1st 'Dzerzhinskii' Division and anti-terrorist commandos shelled and then stormed the 'White House' – the parliament building. The decisive and ruthless strike which had eluded the 'August Coup' plotters of 1991 was executed, ironically enough, by the same leader who had defied them from that very building.

The Defence Ministry, it must be said, had hung back from involving itself in Yeltsin's 'October Coup'. Grachev was worried that this might stretch his authority over his own troops beyond the limit, and had a genuine wish not to introduce the army to the heady joys of kingmaking. As it was, Yeltsin had to visit him in person to plead for his backing. By his determination and thanks to his alliance with the 'Power Ministries', Yeltsin was able to arrest his main rivals and call new elections, while revising the constitution to give the Presidency greater powers relative to the parliament. Not only did the elections of December fail to give him the mandate for which he had hoped – they resulted in a sharp swing towards the communists and the neo-fascist Russian Liberal Democrats – but Yeltsin became increasingly reliant upon his new allies. Interior Minister Erin was made a Hero of the Russian Federation, and Grachev and Golushko were both awarded medals 'for personal valour'. More important were the political pay-offs: the MVD was promised an increased budget, the MB was once again reshuffled, but with Golushko still at its head, and the Defence Ministry was at long last granted the military doctrine it wanted.

RUSSIAN MILITARY DOCTRINE: A NEW CONCEPT?

In 1990 a new Soviet military doctrine had been presented to the world as proof of Gorbachev's commitment to 'defensive defence' and 'reasonable sufficiency'. When the Russian Defence Ministry unveiled its own draft doctrine in 1992, though, this proved a far more hawkish document. There were five main points of interest:

1   that the Commonwealth of Independent States should be kept as a military alliance, but that Russian security concerns should have primacy within it (this would effectively have made the SNG an organisation of military satellites like the old Warsaw Pact);
2   that a threat could come from any direction, requiring Russia to maintain large, mobile forces and base them outside her own borders;
3   that a nuclear first strike may be a sensible strategy under some conditions (although it might have been a propaganda gesture, the Soviets had always ruled this out);
4   that the military had not just a right but a duty to protect Russians living abroad; and
5   that as a result, and in part also given the unstable state of Russia, low-intensity conflict – police actions, limited military operations and anti-guerrilla war – became a new area of importance.

In much of this, it stood in absolute contradiction with what Yeltsin himself had said about doctrine:

We do not consider a single country or coalition in the West or East to be our enemy. Our foreign policy is to create a belt of good-neighbourly, friendly states. The new military doctrine and new military ideology of Russia should proceed from these premises.

Boris Yeltsin, 1993

Yet Yeltsin's draft doctrine never saw the light of day, given that as a price for the army's support in October 1993, the Defence Ministry demanded acceptance of its own version. In December, the Security Council approved the ministry's draft, which closely echoed the 1992 version, albeit with a much greater emphasis placed upon the army's future role in anti-guerrilla warfare and keeping the peace in Russia and on her borders. The implications were serious. Where Gorbachev had wanted to be everyone's friend, Russia's generals have been given licence to assume that they might find potential enemies anywhere – and build up armed forces to match this 'threat'. The whole territory of the former USSR could conceivably become their playground and basing area, while any nation with a Russian minority could expect military intervention if those expatriates seem to be slighted or discriminated against. With twenty-five million Russians living outside the Russian Federation, especially in northern Kazakhstan and eastern Ukraine, this opens to the Russian armed forces a new range of conflicts and confrontations with which they may be forced to deal, from rescuing hostages like the Israelis at Entebbe to pacifying border regions and putting political pressure on neighbouring regimes.

If anything, the demands being placed upon the armed forces have been increased, and this led before the end of the year to the High Command looking again at the defence cuts it had planned. Of course, the size of the armed forces would still have to be reduced from their original level of 2,800,000, but no longer to the 1,500,000 figure mentioned in mid-1993. Instead Grachev began talking of 2,100,000 as a credible figure. Yet these forces would be increasingly drawn from volunteers and would have to be structured and equipped in such a way as to be able to deal with the whole range of conflicts, from low-intensity operations to high-intensity conventional wars, and to do so in battlefields from the plains of Eastern Europe to the mountains of northern Transcaucasia. The response was to divide the Russian army into the élite Mobile Forces (MS – Mobilnye sily) and the Strategic Reserves. The MS were to be further subdivided between the Immediate Reaction Forces (paratroopers and marines who could reach a trouble spot within twenty-four hours) and heavier Rapid Deployment Forces (which could support them within a further forty-eight hours).

On paper this was a dramatic change, reflecting the new line. It nonetheless drew very heavily upon established Soviet practice. The eight paratroop divisions had always been seen as a special strategic reserve and had been used for just such 'power projection' missions in the past, whether capturing Prague in 1968 or Kabul in 1979 or restoring Moscow's control over Baku in 1990. Afghanistan had taught the General Staff the value of the helicopter, and led to the expansion of the DShV air-mobile troops as another such emergency force. The organisation of the MS, which was made up of various brigades which could bring together different types of troops to meet each mission's specific needs was another idea with its roots in the 1980s. Indeed, in his book, *Soviet Military Art in a Time of Change* (London: Brasseys, 1991), Robert Hall dates such ideas back to the 1930s.

THE SOVIET INHERITANCE

No one in the world needs a strong Russia, except Russians themselves . . . [and] a great country cannot have a cheap army.

Ruslan Khasbulatov, 1993

If the new doctrine is to a considerable extent the product of Soviet-era generals trying to apply their old ways to a post-Soviet world, this goes some way to explaining the importance they place upon maintaining under their control as great as possible a share of the old USSR's strategic assets. Of course, the paratroopers count as such, and of the six fully combat-ready divisions, four went to Russia (and one each to Ukraine and Belarus), along with almost the entire DShV force of 40–45 battalions of helicopter-lifted assault troops, most of the USSR's 14,000–strong Naval Infantry (marines) and eight of thirteen Spetsnaz commando brigades. The USSR's 'power projection', her ability to bring her military influence to bear across the globe, also depended upon her navy. The tenure of Admiral Sergei Gorshkov, commander of the Soviet navy from 1956 until his death in 1988, saw the USSR acquire for the first time a genuine 'blue water' capability, with fleets which did not just patrol the country's sea frontiers but roam the oceans, developing naval bases in Cuba, the Middle East, Africa and Vietnam. His legacy was the second most powerful navy in the world, largely divided between four fleets: the Baltic, Northern, Pacific and Black Sea. The struggle between Russia and Ukraine for control of the only fleet not undisputedly under Moscow's aegis is clear evidence of the debt post-Soviet doctrine owes its predecessor.

This Black Sea Fleet was smaller than the Pacific or Northern Fleets and by no means the most modern, but with 400 vessels and around 75,000 officers and sailors it is larger than any NATO navy save the USA's, and possessed its own air arm of over 250 aircraft and a Naval Infantry Brigade of 3,000 marines. A powerful force, to be sure, but also an extremely expensive one, with ships designed for the prosecution of a war against NATO and all too many already obsolete or in need of a costly refit. It is perhaps not surprising that at first the Ukrainian government showed little enthusiasm to control more than a token share of the fleet, until Kiev became wary of Russia's resurgent imperial pretensions. Besides, Ukrainian President Kravchuk, a clever manipulator of nationalist sentiment, saw room to shore up his position by a nicely-judged dispute with Moscow. In 1992 various deals were agreed and broken between Moscow and Kiev whereby the fleet would be divided, to the satisfaction of no one, yet Russia consistently demanded that it retain control over all 'strategic' components of the fleet, a term which it used rather generously to mean not just nuclear-capable vessels but also all major warships, combat aircraft and heavy coastal artillery.

This ambition of becoming the sole inheritor of the USSR's strategic forces and regional dominance is perhaps best illustrated by Russia's position on nuclear weapons. The Soviet Union had left behind a force of 27,000 nuclear warheads, a mix of intercontinental ballistic missiles either housed in underground silos or mobile, mounted on huge lorries or railway carriages, intermediate-range missiles, both land-based and carried by submarines, missiles and bombs to be launched from aircraft and finally, the 'tactical' battlefield weapons – nuclear artillery shells, missiles and charges. The overwhelming majority had been based in Russia, especially ICBMs, with over a thousand missiles; there were a further 176 in Ukraine, 54 mobile ICBMs in Belarus and 104 missiles in Kazakhstan. Of the eight main airbases for nuclear bombers, two were in Ukraine, one in Kazakhstan and five in Russia, while all the USSR's nuclear submarine bases were in Russian ports. As for the short-range, tactical weapons – and if these sound fairly innocuous, it is worth noting that many had warheads several times the power of the bombs which destroyed Hiroshima and Nagasaki – they had been assigned to ground units and were thus scattered largely wherever the Soviet army had been based, but they had already been withdrawn from the more politically volatile regions of Transcaucasia and the Baltic.

Table 4: Distribution of nuclear forces after the fall of the USSR

Type of nuclear force	Location
Intercontinental Ballistic Missiles (ICBMs)	Russia, Ukraine, Kazakhstan, Belarus
Intermediate Range Missiles (IBMs)	Russia, Ukraine, Belarus
Nuclear Submarine Bases	Russia
Nuclear Bombers	Russia, Ukraine, Kazakhstan
Short-Range ('Tactical') Nuclear Weapons	Russia, Ukraine, Kazakhstan, Belarus

Nuclear forces are expensive to maintain and modernise and only of use to nations with pretensions to a global role. Put very crudely, all anyone can do with them is to threaten to blow up the world: they could not force Argentina from the Falklands, they could not bring peace to former Yugoslavia and, from the point of view of the successor states, they could certainly not keep the streets clear of criminals or help bring in the harvest. Thus it is not surprising that Ukraine, Belarus and Kazakhstan all initially pledged to divest themselves of their nuclear forces, gratefully transferring them to SNG and ultimately Russian control. As with the Black Sea Fleet, though, as Russia began to regain her confidence and assert what she saw as her rights as major partner within the Commonwealth, all three governments began to question their commitment. They had chosen to abandon their nuclear capabilities simply because they could not see any threat worth deterring at such cost; those nuclear weapons increasingly became seen as a useful symbol of their independence of Russia.

Thus, by 1993, Ukraine had effectively declared herself a nuclear power until she could negotiate a suitable price and security guarantees from the West and Russia. Kazakhstan, while reaffirming its commitment to eventual non-nuclear status, declared in 1992 that it would take at least fifteen years for this to be achieved. With neighbouring China and nearby India and Pakistan all nuclear powers, it is clear that Kazakhstan was concerned to send a signal not just north to the Russians but also south and eastward. Only Belarus, a nation feeling rather more comfortable with its larger neighbour, had carried out its commitment and sent its mobile SS-25 missiles and tactical weapons back to Russia.

Moscow, by contrast, reorganised the former Strategic Rocket Forces into the new Strategic Deterrence Forces (SSS – Strategicheskie sily sderzhivaniya). By signing the START-2 arms treaty with the USA in June 1992, Russia committed itself to reducing its long-range forces from 21,000 warheads to 3,800–4,250 by the year 2000 and then 3,000–3,500 by 2003. While this is at first a long-awaited exercise in taking obsolescent missiles out of service, the importance of this treaty cannot be understated. Yet in a way it was possible simply because the old model of a world divided between two superpowers is no longer relevant. Russia's new potential enemies are no longer to be found in Western Europe and North America. They may be in China or the Middle East, or they may be their neighbours of the SNG; either way, though, nuclear warheads have become more than anything else a symbol of Russia's desire to be seen as a global power and first nation of Eurasia, rather than a deterrent against any clear potential enemy.

For Russia to seek to maintain its control over the significant, strategic components of the USSR's forces is neither evil nor dishonest. It simply proves the extent to which today's Russia remains dominated by the perennial dilemmas outlined in Chapter 1, and retains a belief in itself as a global power. Thus it could be said that October 1993 did not mark a new beginning but instead completed the circle. As will be discussed in the final chapter, Russia must still come to terms with its new place in the world, to decide whether it is prepared to pay the price for remaining a great world military power and look more clearly as to where the real threats to its security lie. In so many ways, Russia is back to where the USSR was in 1985: despite 1991's intentions to demilitarise the nation, the generals and security interests seem largely to have regained their old pre-eminence and clawed back many of the political losses suffered during the Gorbachev era. In 1985 Gorbachev's election to the General Secretaryship promised a long, cool look at the USSR's future and place in the world – arguably Russia needs to take up this challenge, too.

8   RUSSIA AND THE WORLD

Russia considers herself to be a great power and the successor to the Soviet Union and all its might. Everyone clearly understands that Russia cannot and does not want to wait in the entrance hall of 'the European home' and to ask permission to enter.

Presidential spokesman during Yeltsin's visit to Brussels, December 1993

The beginning of the 1980s had seen the USSR in a state of crisis, its élite desperately looking for a means of reversing its decline. While there are those who would place responsibility for the fall of the Soviet Union and its superpower status upon Gorbachev and his ill-judged reforms, it is clear that retreat predated reform. A study in Robbin Laird and Erik Hoffmann's *Soviet Foreign Policy in a Changing World* (New York: Aldine, 1986) assessed Soviet influence outside its own borders as covering 31 per cent of the world's population and 9 per cent of the world's Gross National Product (GNP) in 1958. By 1979 this had fallen to 6 per cent and 5 per cent, respectively. Another way of looking at Soviet decline is in terms of perceptions. In the period immediately following the Second World War, it was possible to see Stalin's USSR as the ideal of the industrial state, a nation which had dragged itself from agrarian backwardness to military superpower by its own efforts alone. For many newly decolonised countries, the Soviet model seemed to promise rapid modernisation. To the West, Soviet successes in developing its own atomic bomb and then beating the US to putting a satellite in orbit suggested that Moscow was pulling ahead. When Khrushchev told the West 'we shall bury you', this was not so much a threat as a genuine belief – then also held by many outside the Soviet bloc – that history was on the Kremlin's side.

By the 1980s, though, the opposite seemed true. Developing World nations were moving away from the crude collective approach to modernisation, realising that while it was an effective way of building a war-fighting economy in a hurry, it had little to offer in an age when the need was for food, not guns, and when national prosperity was to be found in microchips and motorcars, not yet more coal and pig iron to swell a glutted market. American humiliations over Sputnik had been more than avenged with the Space Shuttle and plans for the 'Star Wars' Strategic Defence Initiative. Once GIs had been dying in Vietnam while back in the USA the campuses protested beneath the icons of Che Guevara and Jane Fonda. By 1980, Private Ivanov was fighting and dying in Afghanistan, while back home the talk was of Bruce Springsteen or, more worrying, the Ayatollah Khomeini.

States and nations naturally seek to preserve and expand their power, their spheres of influence and their autonomy of action. The USSR for most of its existence adopted foreign and security politics which, stripped of the rhetoric of the moment and the personalities at work, were driven by *realpolitik* and pragmatism, not ideology. Just as the USSR found itself facing the same dilemmas as the Tsarist empire and, often, came up with the same responses, so too does post-Soviet Russia often find itself following in the footsteps of its Soviet predecessor. Not only are there many old faces from the Soviet era actively engaged in policy-making today, but the mass public consensus is equally rooted in past expectations and beliefs. In a poll taken in 1992, for example, 69 per cent of Muscovites agreed with the proposition that 'Russia must remain a great power, even if this leads to worse relations with the outside world.'

WHAT IS RUSSIA?

What is the need of the future seizure of Asia? What is our business there? It is necessary because Russia is not only in Europe, but also in Asia; because the Russian is not only a European, but also an Asiatic . . . . In Europe, we were hangers-on and slaves, whereas in Asia we shall go as masters.

Fedor Dostoevsky

This return to traditional attitudes reflects deeper dilemmas: what is the new Russia? Should it forget seventy years of 'building socialism' or look for and retain those positive features of this heritage? Admittedly, these can largely be found in the original ideals of the revolution – sexual and racial equality and freedom from want and oppression – rather than in much actual practice. Does the restoration to Russia of its tsarist past mean that it has to adopt the imperial and military expectations of that age? There is talk of making Russia's last tsar, the decent but severely flawed Nicholas II, a saint and martyr. Need reverence for the man and office also extend to his view of Russia as rightful leader and protector of all Slavs (a major factor behind Russia's disastrous entry into the First World War) or his desire to see Japan challenged for Asian mastery (which saw Russia humbled in the 1904–50 war)?

To a considerable extent this debate has become simplified into the struggle between the 'Atlanticists' and 'Eurasians' touched on in the previous chapter. While taking place in a contemporary context, this dialogue has – as Dostoevsky's words from the nineteenth century attest – long troubled Russia. Its closest parallel, after all, is the ideological debate of the 1840s and 1850s between the Slavophiles and the Westernisers. The 'Atlanticists' clearly dominated the Russian Foreign Ministry. Foreign Minister Andrei Kozyrev, a relatively young career diplomat, English-speaking and a disciple of Shevardnadze's, from the first sought to identify Russia more closely with the West. He argued that the new Russia shared with it certain basic values: capitalism, democracy, a respect for human rights. In many ways this simply reflected George Bush's notion of a 'New World Order', which implicitly divided the world not between East and West, but between the rich North and the poor, non-European, non-Christian South. The 'Atlanticists' wanted to make sure Russia was accepted as part of the new 'Christendom' of the North.

It is thus striking to what extent this is but an evolution of Gorbachev's line of a 'Common European Home'. As such, the 'Atlanticists' suffer many of the same problems. To many, they seemed too eager to abandon Russian interests whenever there was a chance of winning Western approval. While hardliners opposed Russia's support for UN action against Iraq on general principles, for example, others regretted the fact that, so as to please the West, Russia was losing a valued ally and trading partner in the Middle East. And for what? The West has proved little more prepared to support Yeltsin than Gorbachev with the material assistance to ease Russian doubts. While in April 1992 the IMF assembled a package of aid measures worth $24 billion, in practice little of this was of immediate use or was even to be released to the Russians until they themselves had adopted various measures demanded by the Fund. Very little of this money thus reached Russia; the country is still too unstable and the economy too fragile for Western governments, themselves doggedly working their way out of recession, to regard such aid as a worthy investment. Inevitably, then, these radicals found themselves identified with the Westernised *nouveaux riches* mafiosi and entrepreneurs seen as prospering from the misery and hardship of the masses, a resentment which could build upon Soviet and Russian traditions of popular anti-Westernism.

Over time, then, the 'Atlanticists' began losing ground to the 'Eurasians'. Strongly influenced by a debate which took place within Russian emigré circles in the 1920s, they warn against too hasty an identification with the USSR's former enemies in Europe and North America. For a start, if the conflicts of the future are to be between the North American/European 'North' and the Afro-Asian 'South', then Russian would be likely to be on the front line. Besides, is it really better to be a poor and obedient member of the 'North' or an independent player able to work with both camps and develop existing links with China, Asia and the Middle East? Given that the Pacific Rim will become increasingly dominant in the next century, why link Russia with the declining powers? Like Dostoevsky, the 'Eurasians' see Russia's future in the East, or at least as a power able to bridge East and West, Europe and Asia.

There is, of course, much common ground between the two schools of thought. Both are essentially driven by Russian nationalism, the desire to create a new, strong, stable and legitimate state recognised as a world power. Although this new Russia cannot – for the foreseeable future – seek to remain a global superpower, it will certainly retain many of the old USSR's trappings and status, such as its permanent seat at the United Nations and its nuclear capability. In addition, while the 'Eurasian' camp also includes more than its share of national chauvinists, anti-semites, neo-fascists, racists, neo-Stalinists and similar unsavoury fringe extremists, most would share with the 'Atlanticists' a general belief in the need to create viable, democratic institutions and move away from the hidden and élitist politics of the past. After all, the difference between 'Atlanticists' and 'Eurasians' was in part one of factional politics – the former were largely younger diplomats, academics and radicals closer to Boris Yeltsin, the latter Supreme Soviet parliamentarians and older figures with a background in the Soviet élite. Although at first Yeltsin clearly identified himself with the 'Atlanticists', the centre of politics gradually shifted towards the centre through autumn 1992 and into spring and summer 1993.

The flow of senior politicians once regarded as 'democrats' – a term often used to mean 'Westernisers' – to the 'Eurasian' and nationalist camp swelled from trickle to torrent. One was Sergei Stankevich, Yeltsin's own political adviser. Another was Evgenii Ambartsumov, chair of the Supreme Soviet's Foreign Affairs Commission. Yeltsin himself began forging closer links with older, more traditionalist and technocratic politicians, culminating in his symbolic replacement as Prime Minister of Egor Gaidar – a radical thirty-six-year-old economist – with fifty-four-year-old Viktor Chernomyrdin, a former industrial manager and Party bureaucrat. Thus, the 'industrial technocrats' – former Party *apparatchiki* now interested more in steady reform and good governance than Marxism–Leninism – came to dominate the executive arm and the Prime Minister's office. Kozyrev and his 'Atlanticist' Foreign Ministry increasingly took second place to Yeltsin's Security Council, which had a much more 'Eurasian' complexion.

The 'Eurasian' ascendancy soon bore fruit. Early in 1993, Russia hardened its stance over the fighting in Yugoslavia, calling for sanctions against the Croats as a means of lessening the pressure on the (fellow Slav) Serbs, while closing an eye to the smuggling of food, fuel and weapons to the Serbs. Having supported the war against Saddam Hussein's Iraq in 1991, Russia began restoring relations with Baghdad, while thawing the previous freeze on contacts with the PLO. The desire for the nations of East/Central Europe to be integrated into the West European economies and NATO began to receive an ever more frosty response. Perhaps most striking, though, was the impact and implications of Boris Yeltsin's decision in the course of 1993 to throw his weight behind the 'New Imperialism'.

THE 'NEW IMPERIALISM' IN THE 'NEAR ABROAD'

If we want to be a strong state, if we want other states to respect and reckon with us, then we must realise that it is not just generals and servicemen who need the army, we must realise that it is our army. There are already other states which, sensing that we are giving up our military salience, are beginning to talk to us in a completely different way. A country's military prestige is not a political but an economic and moral issue. A strong army raises the self-respect of a people.

Defence Minister Grachev, 1992

The potentially aggressive and expansionist new military doctrine discussed in the previous chapter does not just reflect the prejudices, fears and institutional self-interest of the generals. It also reflects a current in Russian foreign and security policy which became increasingly marked through 1992 and into 1993, as the idealism and optimism which accompanied the fall of the USSR gave way to a sober and sombre realism. Indeed, this 'New Brezhnev Doctrine' seems to have more in common with the rhetoric of the August Coup than with Gorbachev's New Political Thinking. Nationalism is often a safe haven in a time of chaos and hardship: people can find in it some hope for the future, and leaders can use it to provide some common dream and language through which to communicate with the led.

This has certainly been true for Russia. Economic restructuring is always a painful process. Poland, for example, started its 'shock therapy' in 1990. Its industrial output fell by 37 per cent before beginning to recover in late 1992, but even then 1993 saw the problems of inflation and economic management returning to haunt Poland's leaders. Although there are grounds for long-term optimism for Russia, the early years of independence have brought economic collapse, mass poverty and widespread alienation. In 1992 inflation reached 1,450 per cent. Gross National Product and industrial production both fell by 19 per cent, food production by 15 per cent. By the middle of 1993, Russians had experienced a 25–30 per cent decline in their standard of living since the fall of the USSR. There was little the government could do given that the Russian budget deficit by mid-1992 was the equivalent of 15 per cent of GDP. On the other hand, not everyone was suffering: a headlong rush towards the market had created a new class of rich entrepreneurs, the *biznismen*, who could benefit fully from their new economic freedoms, and indulge to the full their taste for Mercedes cars and fine living. Just as Gorbachev had suffered from his failure to match popular expectations, so too did Yeltsin and the democratic government.

Although the December 1993 elections to the new Russian parliament (now called the Duma, after its tsarist equivalent) saw a swing towards the so-called Liberal Democratic Party of the extreme nationalist and neo-fascist Vladimir Zhirinovskii, this largely reflects popular unrest and dismay. As will be discussed later, it certainly need not mean that there are serious dangers of Russia turning fascist, and in part this is because the government itself has moved to absorb some of these tendencies, modifying its policies to incorporate many of the demands of the extreme nationalists. To an extent this reflected the stalemate in politics between parliament and president in 1992–93, such that these fringe groups could exert a disproportionate role in decision-making. Yet it is also the result of a clear shift in government policy, to safeguard Russian democracy and the Russian state, even at the expense of some of the radicals' ideals.

Even such convinced liberals as Foreign Minister Kozyrev changed their approach in 1993, a year in which it became clear that Russia's policies towards the world in general and the so-called 'Near Abroad' (*blizhnee zarubezh'e*) – the other territories of the former Soviet Union – still owed much to the old USSR. For all that Boris Yeltsin had claimed in his 1993 New Year Address that 'the imperial period in Russia's history is over', it had always been unlikely that Russia could so easily and quickly disentangle itself from its new neighbours and from the bonds of decades or centuries of empire. The Tsarist empire and, especially, USSR had encouraged Russian colonisation, which had left around twenty-five million Russians living in the 'Near Abroad'. The Soviet Union had also been marked by a considerable degree of regional economic specialisation and integration, which meant that few of the successor states inherited anything like an independent and viable economy. Only 15 per cent of Russia's GNP is represented by trade with the other republics of the former USSR; for the other successor states this ranged from 32 per cent (Ukraine) to 76 per cent (Turkmenistan).

The naive days in which Kozyrev could state – as he did, in late 1991 – that 'in general it does not matter of which republic you are a citizen' were clearly long since gone. By 1992–93, all the states of the former USSR were engaged in desperate struggles to build genuine economic and thus political independence, often at the expense of their neighbours. Members of the Russian diaspora of the 'Near Abroad', for example, could find themselves facing official suspicion or downright disenfranchisement. In Estonia, new citizenship laws meant that some 42 per cent of the electorate – predominantly of Russian extraction – were barred from voting. Russia also became aware of its geographical position. Its ships, trains and lorries were now having to pay closer to world prices to transit on the way to the lucrative and vital markets to the west and south. Her under-policed frontiers were looking worryingly 'soft' and vulnerable to cross-border flows of refugees, drugs and guns. With the states of East/Central Europe petitioning for membership of NATO, historical fears of encirclement and exclusion from the 'civilised world' reared their heads. An academic writing in the authoritative military journal *Voennaya mysl'* (*Military Thought*) in 1992 gave a feel of the new view held in Moscow of Russia's interests:

> Like any living organism, the Heartland lives as long as it breathes. Its 'lungs' are the seas connecting it with the outside world: . . . the Far Eastern waters, which open up an outlet to the Pacific . . . [and] the Baltic, Northern and Black Seas, which give access to the Adriatic and Mediterranean. Take away one and Russia will begin to suffocate; take away both and it will die.

Traditional fears of marginalisation, the need to defend what was left of Russia's economy, a need to placate nationalists, Moscow's established arrogance, all contributed to creating this 'New Imperialism', which began to manifest itself in a much more aggressive stance towards neighbouring states. In the name of 'peacekeeping', the Russian government accepted many of the generals' demands for a forward and assertive policy in the 'Near Abroad'. In 1993 a constant refrain in Russian communications with the West and the UN was that the world community should acknowledge that it had a rightful 'sphere of influence' in the region. To a large extent, this was phrased in terms of giving Russia free rein to act as a regional policeman in the interests of stability and a status quo which worked implicitly to Moscow's advantage:

> *The moment has come when responsible international institutions including the United Nations should grant Russia special powers as guarantor of peace and stability in the regions of the former Union.*

Boris Yeltsin, March 1993

The sad irony was that Russian involvement was at the heart of much war and instability in Eurasia. A refusal to reign in General Lebed' and his Fourteenth Army in Moldova ensured that the civil war there would continue to run. By late 1993, the Moldovan government was having to adopt a much more accommodating line, following Russia's imposition of crippling taxes on all imports from Moldova. By December, the government was even talking of granting Russia the right to base troops on its soil, effectively legitimising the role of the Fourteenth Army. When the elected Georgian President, the fiery nationalist Zviad Gamsakhurdia, became too much of an irritant to Moscow, Russia indirectly encouraged the coup which toppled him in 1991. Former Soviet Foreign Minister Eduard Shevardnadze was elected in his place, but when Shevardnadze also proved more interested in defending Georgian rights than acknowledging Russian supremacy, Moscow stepped up support for rebels in the northern and western regions of Ossetia and Abkhazia. Shevardnadze was bitterly critical of what he called an 'imperialist Russia', but eventually he was forced to back down, accepting Russian assistance and thus Russian influence. Tajikistan has likewise been forced to accept the presence of Russia's 201st Motor-Rifle Division on its soil following the explosion of a civil war which some say owed something to Moscow's secret services, and in doing so granted Moscow an increasing say in its affairs. Kozyrev bluntly admitted that Russia was not prepared to risk 'losing geopolitical positions that took centuries to conquer'.

RUSSIA'S INTERESTS IN THE GLOBAL AGE

The Russian Federation's foreign policy must be based on a doctrine which proclaims the entire geographical space of the former Soviet Union as a sphere of vital interest (following the example of the US Monroe Doctrine in Latin America).

Academic and parliamentarian Evgenii Ambartsumov, 1992

It is important to note just how many of the leaders of the new Russia stubbornly refuse to fit into any neat left–right or liberal–conservative spectrum, reflecting the consensus which in 1992 began developing between – and far from – the banner-waving antics of the tsarists and communists on the one extreme and the libertarian excesses of the radicals on the other. The majority of the 'new' politicians are men used to compromise as well as confrontation, whose careers were largely formed in the very heart of the Party state. They understand the deals and alliances struck behind closed doors and the shabby but vital arts of managing imperfection more than grand ideals and stirring dreams. Their influence has been visible in the retreat from – disastrous – crash marketisation of the economy, in the more gradualist line adopted in by Chernomyrdin and also in a more robustly assertive foreign policy. This shift in policy reflected a new vision of Russian national interests. For what are the new threats facing Russian national security? If one takes this term as broadly as the Soviets defined it, to include political and economic interests, there appear to be four main concerns looming over the new Russia: regional instability, economic collapse, organised crime and outright fragmentation.

Russia claims to have a clear interest in the stability of Eurasia. This is, however, only part of the truth. It is certainly true that there are many dangers for Moscow in regional instability. Given the essentially artificial nature of so many borders of the post-Soviet states, unrest and fighting could easily spill over into Russia, especially were ethnic Russians to be involved. Russian Cossacks, for example, have already been involved in fighting in Moldova and Georgia, while were Kazakhstan to succumb to civil war – a moderately distant but by no means impossible scenario – the Russian majority of the north would expect and probably receive aid from the Russian state. Moscow can also ill-afford to lose these markets for its goods, suppliers of its raw materials and routes for its trade with the outside world. At the same time, there are also advantages for Moscow in chaos. Scope for 'New Imperialism' would be severely limited if it could not be hidden in deals with dissident factions (such as the anti-Gamsakhurdia forces in Georgia in 1991 and the Ossetians and Abkhazians in 1993) or cloaked in the colours of 'Commonwealth peacekeeping'. The problem is to balance the two: some chaos gives Moscow room for manoeuvre, too many risks inflaming world opinion or turning all Eurasia into a war zone.

Russia's preparedness to spend money on developing its Mobile Forces and other military structures capable of intervening in the 'Near Abroad' reflects this perception that there is not only political but economic value in retaining a dominant role in the region. The economics of empire will prove critical, since Russia's dreams for its future will depend on its ability to resuscitate its economy. As over foreign policy, there is a fair deal of consensus on economic development, to the extent that most key groups and actors support a steady shift towards a market economy, with a continued role for the state in subsidising and developing key sectors of the economy and cushioning – as far as an overstretched budget will allow – the social costs involved.

This is a massive undertaking. Capitalism is not such a natural state; it requires a complex support environment of skills, laws, institutions and attitudes. It needs a viable currency and although through 1993 the rouble began to stabilise against the dollar, for some time to come, barter and foreign currencies will underpin the Russian economy. The legal and social framework lags behind, though, especially in the process of privatisation and the opportunities it provides to create private monopolies. Real capitalism, after all, is not simply about private ownership but competition. Arguably the old Soviet system was marked by the private ownership of most official means of production, distribution and exchange by a corrupt class of bureaucrats. The point was that through the state they protected their little monopolies and thus grew fat and lazy.

Capitalism also requires the skills and abilities to use that economic freedom effectively, learning a new range of skills, from managing to marketing, business accountancy to insurance. It also requires an appreciation of the importance of the long term over the short term, of production over trading. The immediate post-Soviet era has been marked for too many by a belief that capitalism means get-rich-quick wheeling and dealing, bazaar economics where a sharp deal today is better than nurturing a growing relationship or reputation because no one knows what could happen tomorrow. If nothing else, this has had a disastrous effect on investment in research and development, an area in which ex-Soviet science and technology had much that it could offer the world.

This has a significant international dimension. The Foreign Ministry's 1992 programme for discussion noted that Russia's economic linkages with East/Central Europe were likely to be threatened by the closer integration of these nations with Western Europe. Instead, it proposed that Russia should look to cultivating new relationships with moderate regimes in the Middle East as well as rising Developing World nations such as Brazil, Argentina, Mexico, Nigeria and South Africa. In particular, these were vital potential buyers of Russian arms; by 1992, hopes of scaling down the defence industrial sector had to be shelved, and instead the government turned to the aggressive export of weapons as a way of generating vital state revenue. With almost a quarter of the country's industrial workers – around 5,500,000 – directly employed by the defence sector, it could not afford to shut these plants, nor to re-tool. International organisations such as the OPEC petroleum-producers' alliance would also be vital structures through which to protect and advance Russia's economic interests. Although the Supreme Soviet rejected the document, it is clear that this was largely because its overall thrust was far too 'Atlanticist' – and, besides, parliament wanted to flex its political muscle. The economic portion of the document has effectively become policy, in looking to the industrialised nations for joint venture partners, companies willing to invest money in developing Russia and teach it the new skills of capitalism, and to the stronger Developing World economies – including China – for markets and resources.

THE RUSSIAN MAFIAS

> *My feeling is that comparisons between Italy and Russia have some value, but must be taken in context. In Russia, the criminals are better armed than the state, better organised than the state and in many cases are the state. Italy is a country beset by organised crime. Russia is a country increasingly built on organised crime.*

Italian magistrate, 1993

Ironically, the fastest growing area of international cooperation between Russians and the rest of the world – and, indeed, the most dynamic sector of the Russian economy as a whole – has proved to be organised crime. The USSR had always been a deeply corrupt country, ruled by cliques of self-serving Party *apparatchiki* who represented an exploitative ruling class, against which the police were largely powerless. Organised crime in the USSR was able to establish itself during the lax Brezhnev era and spread under *perestroika*, thanks to Gorbachev's anti-alcohol campaign (which did for the Soviet gangs what Prohibition had done for their US counterparts in the 1920s) and economic liberalisation. In the new era of anarchic pseudo-capitalism, though, they acquired a new independence and official estimates of the number of organised crime groups rose from 2,900 in 1989, through 3,500 in 1990 to 5,100 in 1991. From 1991, the numbers of gangs began to fall, but this represented not a decline in the power of organised crime but rather a process of consolidation, as larger groups began taking over or wiping out smaller rivals. The turnover of the black economy they controlled reached 130–150 billion roubles in 1992 – equivalent to 15–18 per cent of the entire Russian defence budget – and might have reached two trillion by the end of 1993. The rise of these 'mafias' has definite implications for the national security of the post-Soviet states and, indeed, their neighbours near and far.

For a start, organised criminality has penetrated deeply into the armed forces. Soldiers' morale is at rock-bottom, coping with appalling living conditions and a pervasive sense of a lack of purpose. In late 1993, 92 per cent of officers polled lacked confidence in the future, and 80 per cent of conscripts wanted to get out of the army. Five soldiers were dying every day, a quarter by their own hand, and nineteen deserting. Inevitably there are soldiers prepared to be seduced by easy money. Allegations predated the fall of the USSR, with Vitalii Urazhtsev, chair of the unofficial radical soldiers' union Shchit ('Shield'), claiming in 1991 that there were a number of military 'mafia clans', including one led by Defence Minister Yazov which specialised in smuggling stolen cars from Europe and drugs from Afghanistan. This was a rather fanciful smear, but it is certainly true that even senior officers have become involved in institutionalised military criminality that has reached such a level that it has genuine national security implications.

This begins to cast doubt upon the government's and Defence Ministry's genuine control over their own troops; the collapse of military discipline also contributes to the spread of guns and other military equipment throughout Russia and the rest of the world. In 1989 around 1,000 guns were stolen from the military; in the first half of 1992 some 25,000 firearms went missing, including more than 135 machine guns, rocket launchers and cannon. This haemorrhage of military weapons has armed militant groups, nationalist partisans and criminal gangs throughout the former Soviet Union: Cossacks in Russia, Ukraine, Kazakhstan and Moldova, Georgians loyal to both Shevardnadze and Gamsakhurdia, Abkhazians, North and South Osetians, Azeris, Armenians, Dneistr Russians, Chechens, Ingushetians. Who is next? Some reports would suggest Tyvinian nationalists keen to dispute Moscow's control over their Central Asian territory. Others, Kazakhs ready to resist any attempt by ethnic Russians of the north to dominate or secede from their homeland. Whoever they may be, they will certainly not lack suppliers for all their military needs. In addition, weapons have passed to fighters in Central Asia and the former Yugoslavia and, further, into the hands of criminals and terrorists in the West, including surface-to-air missiles found by the Italian police in mafia arsenals.

One obvious fear has been the threat that criminals could acquire and trade nuclear materials and technologies. There have

185

certainly been attempts to steal and smuggle fissile materials, but to date these have essentially been 'amateur' operations. There are good reasons why the main Russian 'mafias' have steered clear of this potentially lucrative market. Under heavy Western pressure, the authorities have put considerable effort into controlling their stockpiles, while any attempts to trade in thermonuclear death on any systematic scale would also arouse the sort of response from the Russian and international authorities that no amount of political clout and backstreets muscle could avert.

This reflects the way that Russian organised crime is becoming an international issue. Russian criminals are opening up new drug smuggling routes from Central Asia to Europe, and Russia's overstretched and under-supervised airports represent an ideal transit point for couriers from Latin America and the Far East alike. Russian 'mafias' also have all the imperial pretensions of their culture, and have already developed a powerful presence in East/Central Europe, notably Bulgaria, Hungary and Poland. Thus, they also pose a threat to the emerging democracies and free markets of the region. To expect new, weak states, many with leadership structures already thoroughly compromised by association with organised crime, to face up to these threats alone is almost certainly a fond, vain hope. Beyond that, Russian organised crime has forged alliances with the established syndicates. The four major Italian mafia combines (the Sicilian mafia, Neapolitan Camorra, Calabrian 'Ndrangeta and Puglian Sacra Corona Unita–La Rosa alliance) have all acquired footholds in Russia. There they are trading drugs and hard currencies for rubles, and acquiring a huge new market while providing new opportunities for the Russian organisations. Elsewhere, the unification of Germany and the disaffection of ex-Soviet troops being withdrawn from there has opened up new routes into the north European markets and criminal networks. The Russian mafias have been able to draw on their connections in the former East Germany to develop profitable opportunities in currency dealing and the theft of cars for resale in Moscow.

Perhaps the most infamous of these criminal groupings is the 'Chechen mafia', based around the small and turbulent southern Russian region of Chechnia. Russia's Sicily, Chechnia is a land of traditional clan loyalties and blood feuds which has always been only superficially under Moscow's control. As relations between Moscow and Chechnia worsened through 1992, alarmist rumours began to circulate about the Chechens in Moscow. It was claimed that they controlled organised crime throughout the capital, with some 1,500–3,000 'soldiers', a vast crime syndicate and a fifth column ready to spread chaos and terror throughout the city were the Russian leadership to attempt to suppress Chechen nationalism. This mighty shadow empire is a myth. While there are powerful Chechen mafiosi – just as there are Azeris and Georgians – who control many gangs in the city, there are more home-grown Russian criminals. But this does illustrate the extent to which the spread of criminal organisations carries with it potential political and military power. Thus, the issue of organised crime leads into a wider one: just how far is Moscow still able to control Russia?

CAN THE CENTRE HOLD?

The fragmentation of the USSR created fifteen new states, of which Russia is the largest and strongest. Yet this giant, spanning eleven time-zones and with a population of just under 150 million, is itself a rather ungainly multinational composite of a hundred different ethnic groups. Along with the heartlands of European Russia, there are the non-Russian regions, such as Tyva (formerly Tuva), Kalmykia, Tatarstan, Bashkiria, Udmurtia and the Jewish Autonomous Region. There are the small, border regions of Transcaucasia, such as Dagestan, Chechnia and Ingushetia, where Moscow's writ is especially weak. There is the fortified enclave of Kaliningrad, a Russian territory now separated from the rest of Russia by the Baltic states and Poland. In such a huge country, even mighty Moscow can often seem very far away; to the governor of the Far Eastern island of Sakhalin, even the shelling of parliament in October 1993 was but an irrelevance, 'a struggle between clans'.

In March 1992 Yeltsin managed to persuade all the constituent republics of the Russian Federation except Tatarstan and Chechnia to sign a Federation Treaty which was meant to establish a new basis for these regions to stay together. Russia had apparently been kept whole, but in order to make it palatable, the treaty was left woolly and vague. Beneath the facade of unity, there developed a rolling struggle between Moscow and the local power structures, as well as between individual republics, regions and cities to define the new relationship, each keen to assert its own prerogatives and champion its own interests. As with the central politics between parliament and president, by the end of 1993 the result was still a stalemate.

1 MORDVINIA	6 BASHKIRIA	11 CHECHNIA
2 CHUVASHIA	7 ABKHAZIA	12 INGUSHETIA
3 MARI	8 ADZHAR	13 DAGESTAN
4 TATARSTAN	9 KABARDINO-BALKARIA	14 KALMYKIA
5 UDMURTIA	10 NORTH OSETIA	15 NAKHICHEV

Figure 5: Regions of the Russian Federation

Few regions really want or could cope with genuine political independence, with the possible exception of Chechnia. Udmurtia's arms industries, for example, account for over half its total employment, and depend upon raw materials and components from other parts of Russia and Moscow's defence contracts. It could not afford to pay hard currency and world prices for the former, and could not survive without the latter. Of course, there is a danger in assuming that economic common sense can avert nationalism and regionalism – there is, for example, little economic logic in the Slovaks' desire to divorce the Czechs, as happened when Czechoslovakia was divided in 1993, still less in the wars wracking Yugoslavia and Transcaucasia. On the whole, the aim of Russia's regions is rather to achieve greater economic autonomy, the freedom to use local resources to local advantage.

This is certainly the case in Siberia, which accounts for two-thirds of the nation's energy resources, most of its minerals and over half the country's hard currency revenue. In the Soviet era, the people of Siberia came to depend upon Moscow to provide them with the food, benefits and salaries to make up for their appalling working conditions and to reflect their importance to the nation. With the collapse of the state, many of these supplies dried up; Tyumen, rich in oil and gas (70 per cent and 90 per cent of national production, respectively), had by mid-1993 become the region with the lowest standard of living in the country. It is hardly surprising that Siberia came increasingly to demand greater control of its economy. These demands are inevitable and almost irresistible, and Siberia is certain to become an important power base within future Russian politics. It is easier to envisage the Russian Far East seeking a more permanent divorce from distant Moscow. There is a precedent, in the Far Eastern Republic of 1918–21, yet it is present and future economic prospects which are driving regional self-assertion. While accounting for only 4.5 per cent of national GDP, it provides 15 per cent of national mining output. The Republic of Sakha – Yakutia – is Russia's last remaining source of diamonds. Perhaps most important, though, is its proximity to Japan, China and the developing economies of the Pacific Rim in general.

The traditional Soviet approach was based on the classic four tools of empire: force; a dominant majority nation to provide the key soldiers, policeman, administrators and workers; buying off local élites; and a state ideology to provide some sort of legitimacy. The new Russia has adopted similar strategies. Expanding the

Interior Army was made an early priority of Russian security policy, with a billion rubles allocated to hiring professional contract recruits and a commitment from parliament in autumn 1993 to swell it by a further 28,000 men. The Russians are still clearly dominant in their own country, accounting for 82 per cent of the citizens of the Federation. This is not evenly spread, though. While only Chechnia, Chuvashia, North Osetia and Tyva possess majorities of their 'own' nationality, in several other regions 'indigens' outnumber Russians: Dagestan, Kabardino-Balkaria, Kalmykia and Tatarstan. Here the Russians must rely especially on co-opting local leaders and élites. Yet the question which arose was, quite simply, what could Moscow offer?

To a considerable extent, the answer would seem to be increased freedom to rule as they will. While concessions over local autonomy may manage to pacify the regions, it raises the difficult question of when and where the centre draws the line. This also involves more than just the relationship between central and local government. It is also an open question how far policing and even defence and foreign policy are being determined or influenced at a local level. In particular, this means taxation. 'No taxation without representation' was the battle cry of the American rebels against British rule – if Moscow seriously intends to continue to fund the armed forces to carry out the missions outlined in their doctrine, will the regions be prepared to provide the resources for it? Arguably it was the question of taxation and thus control over the central ministries which made Gorbachev's Union Treaty so unpalatable to the August Coup plotters. Will taxation shatter the Russian Federation, too?

A GLANCE TO THE FUTURE

There is no security, no stability, no law, no food and no money. What do I need freedom for? If we have a choice only between anarchy and dictatorship, I choose dictatorship. Let a strong leader restore order.

Azeri academic, quoted in *Time*, July 1993

When first elected, Gorbachev hoped to save the Soviet superpower. In his view, it was essentially sound, both economically and politically, and needed only to be stripped of certain deformations of the past – notably the industrial and cultural legacies of Stalinism and the time-serving cynicism of the Brezhnev years – to return to its rightful place as a world superpower and the standard-bearer of the socialist ideal. In this respect, Gorbachev was a characteristic Soviet leader of his time, in whom were intermingled a deep sense of Russian patriotism and a genuine, if in many ways naive belief in Marxism–Leninism. His understanding of the state of the nation came, after all, from Party and KGB reports, from *Pravda*, from glimpses snatched through the windows of his Zil limousine as it sped him from his comfortable, high-security Party flat to his Party offices. What did he, could he, know about the real country? It is to his credit, though, that he retained his idealism. As he faced increasing resistance from an élite reluctant to relinquish any of its privileges or perks, he held true to his beliefs, to his conviction that Marxism–Leninism was the ideology of the masses, to his optimism that the USSR had a future, to his refusal to accept mass coercion as a tool of government.

> *The tragedy is that Gorbachev hates to use violence. As he said at the Army conference, 'I will never use violence. I rule out violence ahead of time.' Such a person can follow the teachings of Lev Tolstoi, but he cannot be engaged in politics. Real human lives are behind his policy of non-violence against evil . . And all that Gorbachev has to offer is his conscience . . . . Is it a kind policy to pretend that nothing is happening, that everything is all right? That policy, unfortunately, brings about the opposite result.*

Conservative hardliner Colonel Viktor Alksnis, in M. McFaul and S. Markov, *The Troubled Birth of Russian Democracy* (Stanford: Hoover Institution Press, 1993)

Past Russian and Soviet leaders have rarely shied away from the use of violence. It may have made Gorbachev a better human being, but it also made him a failure as a politician. His decision to introduce some form of democracy to the USSR proved disastrous. The people not only failed to endorse his brand of Marxism–Leninism, they also proved all too willing to elect, alongside convinced and honest reformists, clever and plausible Party hacks prepared to mouth the rhetoric of democracy and nationalism, even while protecting their positions. His failure to appreciate the concerns, both personal and professional, of the generals and secret policemen made the August Coup almost inevitable, even if his reforms had also ensured its failure. His refusal to sanction more than limited and sporadic use of state violence, while admirable, has been characterised by some as self-indulgence. Whatever its failings, the USSR's survival did ensure that interethnic and intercommunal violence was limited to the odd street brawl or sublimated into political or sporting rivalries. In 1992 alone, the territories of the former Soviet Union witnessed war between Armenia and Azerbaijan and civil wars in Georgia, Moldova and Tajikistan. This was certainly not the agenda Mikhail Gorbachev had set himself in 1985.

Yet Gorbachev cannot simply be judged as a politician. He was also a symbol of the irreconcilability of traditional Russian security concerns and the Western model of modernity. Too Western to win Russian hearts and souls, but not Western enough to appreciate and enact the sort of reforms which might have won their stomachs and their minds, his failure is the failure of any attempt to cross-breed from these traditions. In many ways Yeltsin is a far more recognisably Russian figure, something to which he must owe much of the genuine respect and even affection with which he is held even by Russians who decry his economic policies. He is also, on paper at least, a far more powerful president than Gorbachev. The new 1993 constitution grants him sweeping new powers, as well as absolute control of the armed forces and Security Council. The problem is that Russia needs to complete the process Gorbachev began, of breaking out from the vicious circle of limited reform and authoritarian modernisation dictated by the challenges of its history and position. If Yeltsin cannot find new answers, will Russia turn to those who can?

One cannot exclude the possibility of [fascism] in Russia. We can see too many parallels between Russia's current situation and that of Germany after the Versailles Treaty. A great nation is humiliated, many of its nationals live outside the country's borders. The disintegration of an empire at a time when many still have imperialist attitudes . . . all at a time of economic crisis.

Galina Starovoitova, former adviser to Boris Yeltsin,
October 1992

In the context of the strong showing by Zhirinovskii's neofascists in the December 1993 election, Starovoitova's words seem prophetic. As early as October 1991, Zhirinovskii was giving the world a taste of his rhetoric:

> I will gain power and I'll give the people everything they need. And it will be very simple: I'll send troops to the former GDR and do a bit of sabre-rattling, including the nuclear threat, and we'll get everything we need.

Yet Zhirinovskii's vote reflects dissatisfaction with Yeltsin more than a real constituency for his random array of policies, which range from threatening to bomb Japan through to on-the-spot firing squads for burglars and rapists. Besides, unlike Italy in the 1920s and Germany in the 1930s, Russia does not have an élite unhappy with the government and worried for its survival. Hitler and Mussolini, after all, were invited into office by élites which thought they could control and use them. The secret police, the military, the *apparatchiki*-turned-entrepreneurs, even the burgeoning Russian 'mafias' all have a stake in the existing order.

Above all, Russia must thus come to terms with herself and her geopolitical position. She is not an advanced, industrial Western country, but nor is she purely of Asia. Mother Russia has always been a singular character with manners and interests all her own. In part this reflects the fact that Russia has never had an opportunity to develop a clear notion of its own statehood, even of its own boundaries. Over the centuries, Russians and thus the Russian state slowly spread east and south into Asia and Transcaucasia, colonists replacing or settling alongside native populations to create what has been called a 'patchwork nation'. Centuries of the tsarist empire and then decades of the USSR's own type of 'socialist imperialism' have done nothing to help clarify the simple question of where Russia's boundaries should be drawn.

Capitalism does not necessarily mean working liberal democracy, good neighbourliness and prosperity. Indeed, for many Russians capitalism will mean poverty and exploitation, and its creation may yet require authoritarian methods along the lines of Singapore and South Korea. Yet ultimately Russia may be forced to make a choice. Will she develop slowly as a backward but earnest and obliging second cousin to Europe and North America? Or will she aspire once again to build a mighty Eurasian empire, to establish a new sphere of influence to her south and east? After all:

Russia remains. Its population is over 150 million, and its people are educated, hard-working and capable of great endurance. They are still in control of land abounding in natural resources . . . . The genes of the Russian state bear the memory of past greatness and of the ways of attaining it.

Russian journalist Boris Bazhanov, 1992

CHRONOLOGY

1979
December   Invasion of Afghanistan.

1980
July   Strikes spread in Poland.
August   Soviets resume jamming of Western radio
                     broadcasts.

1981
December   Martial law declared in Poland.

1982
November   Brezhnev dies; Andropov elected to succeed him.

1983
September   Korean Airlines KAL 007 shot down in Soviet
                     airspace: 269 dead.

1984
February   Andropov dies; Chernenko elected to succeed
                     him.
December   Defence Minister Ustinov dies: Marshal Sokolov
                     replaces him.

1985
March   Chernenko dies; Gorbachev elected to succeed
                     him.
April   Central Committee plenum meeting launches
                     programme based upon *perestroika*. Gorbachev
                     announces a unilateral moratorium on the
                     deployment of intermediate-range nuclear
                     weapons and nuclear weapons tests.
May   Several senior military conservatives retire.

July	Gromyko becomes President; Shevardnadze replaces him as Foreign Minister.
October	USSR proposes 50 per cent cut in US and Soviet long- and medium-range nuclear forces.
November	Geneva summit between Gorbachev and Reagan.

1986

January	Gorbachev proposes complete elimination of nuclear weapons by the year 2000.
February/March	XXVII Party Congress: Gorbachev affirms need for major reform, and launches the concept of 'reasonable sufficiency'.
April	Chernobyl' disaster.
June	USSR 'uncouples' INF and START talks, offering compromises on the former.
July	'Vladivostok initiative': Gorbachev proposes new spirit of cooperation in Asia and the Pacific and announces a limited withdrawal of troops from Afghanistan.
October	Reykjavik summit between Gorbachev and Reagan opens way for INF treaty.
November	'Delhi declaration': Gorbachev affirms commitment to a 'non-violent' and nuclear-free world.

1987

January	Central Committee plenum meeting: Gorbachev accuses the Party of resisting reform.
April	Visiting Prague, Gorbachev calls for the denuclearisation of Europe.
May	New Warsaw Pact military doctrine announced. Matthias Rust's landing in Red Square opens the way for a purge of the High Command: Defence Minister Sokolov replaced by Yazov.
July	Soviets table proposed new START treaty at Geneva.
October	Yeltsin attacks Gorbachev at Central Committee plenum.
December	Gorbachev visits Washington: INF treaty signed.

1988

February	Agreement on withdrawal from Afghanistan

	announced. Boris Yeltsin sacked from the Politburo. Struggle for Nagorno-Karabakh begins.
March	In declaration over Yugoslavia, Gorbachev renounces the 'Brezhnev Doctrine'.
April	Agreement on withdrawal from Afghanistan concluded.
May	Moscow summit between Reagan and Gorbachev.
June	XIX Party Conference: Gorbachev's general line of reform approved.
July	Warsaw Pact Political Consultative Committee meets in Warsaw and issues proposals for arms cuts in Europe.
September	'Krasnoyarsk speech': Gorbachev outlines proposals to increase security in the Asia–Pacific region.
October	Gromyko resigns as President: Gorbachev adds that title to his own.
November	Constitutional reforms, creating an elected bicameral parliament and a strong executive Presidency approved.
December	Speaking at the UN, Gorbachev announces a unilateral cut of 500,000 troops, including the withdrawal of 50,000 from Eastern Europe. Marshal Akhromeev resigns as Chief of the General Staff.

1989

February	Withdrawal from Afghanistan completed.
March	Elections for Congress of People's Deputies. MBFR talks in Vienna replaced by CFE process.
May	Gorbachev elected President of the Supreme Soviet.
April	Georgian protesters in Tbilisi attacked by troops: twenty killed. Unilateral troop withdrawals from Hungary begin.
May	Gorbachev visits Beijing.
May–June	First session of new Congress of People's Deputies: Gorbachev is elected to the new Presidency.
August	East Germans begin to take advantage of

	Hungary's decision to end border controls with Austria to flee to the West. Solidarity forms new government in Poland.
October	Gorbachev visits East Berlin: warns GDR government of need to reform.
November	Malta summit between Gorbachev and Bush. Berlin Wall falls. Czech government falls in 'Velvet Revolution'.
December	Romanian dictator Ceauşescu toppled and killed.

1990

January	Civil war between Azerbaijan and Armenia: military intervention in Baku.
March	Gorbachev elected President of the USSR.
May	Yeltsin elected President of Russia. Washington summit between Gorbachev and Bush.
July	XXVIII Party Congress.
October	Germany reunited.
November	Second CSCE summit in Paris: CFE treaty signed.
December	Boris Pugo becomes Interior Minister. Shevardnadze resigns as Foreign Minister.

1991

January	Troops attack pro-independence protesters in the Baltic states: fifteen killed in Lithuania, four in Latvia.
February	Warsaw Pact Foreign Ministers meet in Budapest: agree to dismantle the alliance by the end of March 1992.
June	CSCE Foreign Ministers meet in Berlin: Cold War officially over.
July	Warsaw Pact formally dissolved.
August	'August Coup' ends in failure.
December	Russian, Belarussian and Ukrainian governments proclaim the formation of the Commonwealth of Independent States – USSR declared dead.

1992

February	Minsk Summit of Commonwealth of Independent States.
May	Tashkent Summit of Commonwealth of

	Independent States: Ukraine and Belarus fail to attend; security accord signed which effectively ended thought of retaining joint armed forces.
July	Second Tashkent Summit: peacekeeping accord signed.
October	Boris Yeltsin sounds out 'Power Ministries' on anti-parliament coup.
December	7th Russian Congress of People's Deputies sees open split between President and parliament.

1993

January	Moscow summit between Yeltsin and US President Bush: START-2 arms treaty signed.
April	Vancouver summit between Yeltsin and new US President Clinton. National referendum endorses Yeltsin's leadership, but not his policies.
July	Barannikov replaced by Golushko as Security Minister.
September	Yeltsin dissolves parliament.
October	When parliament defies Yeltsin, troops dissolve it by force ('October Coup').
December	Parliamentary elections to new parliament sees swing to Communists and neo-fascist Liberal Democrat Party.

GLOSSARY

ABM	Anti-Ballistic Missile – an ABM Treaty limiting such weapons was signed by the USA and USSR in 1972.
Achalov, Vladislav	Commander of Airborne Forces, then Deputy Defence Minister during August Coup.
Akhromeev, Sergei	Chief of the General Staff from 1984 until his resignation in 1988, then Gorbachev's military adviser until his suicide in 1991.
Andropov, Yurii	Former Chair of the KGB, who succeeded Brezhnev in November 1982 and died in February 1984, though not before introducing reform to the agenda and establishing a power base for his protégé Gorbachev.
apparatchiki	Slang term for members of the Party and state bureaucracies.
Arbatov, Georgii	Head of the USA and Canada Institute.
Atlanticists	'Westernising' school of thought in post-Soviet Russia, opposed to the **Eurasians**.
Bakatin, Vadim	Reformist ally of Gorbachev's; Interior Minister 1989–90; briefly Chair of the KGB in 1991.
Baklanov, Oleg	One of the August Coup plotters; identified with the defence industries.
Barannikov, Viktor	Head of the Russian Interior Ministry, then Security Minister 1992–93.

Bogomolov, Oleg	Head of the Institute of the Economics of the World Socialist System.
Brezhnev, Leonid	General Secretary of the Party between 1964 and his death in November 1982.
Central Committee	Leading body of the **CPSU**, which also controlled the Secretariat, the Party's own civil service.
CFE	Conventional Forces in Europe negotiations – replaced **MBFR** in March 1989.
Chebrikov, Viktor	Chair of the KGB, 1983–88.
chekisty	Slang term for KGB officers (from the Bolsheviks' first political police force, the Cheka).
Chernenko, Konstantin	Short-lived General Secretary, succeeding Andropov in February 1984, dying in March 1985.
CIS	Commonwealth of Independent States, the loose and almost non-existent union which replaced the USSR. Its original members were Russia, Ukraine and Belarus, to which joined Armenia, Azerbaijan, Moldova, Kazakhstan, Kyrgyzstan, Tajikistan, Turkmenistan and Uzbekistan. Azerbaijan and Moldova later left, while Georgia joined in late 1993. Also, **SNG**.
Comecon	The Council for Mutual Economic Achievement, 1949–91, a Soviet bloc economic zone.
Congress of People's Deputies	The largely elected parliament established in 1988. It met only a few times each year, electing from within itself a smaller standing parliament, the **Supreme Soviet**.
CPSU	Communist Party of the Soviet Union.

CSCE	Conference for Security Cooperation in Europe.
dedovshchina	'Grandfatherism', age- and seniority-based bullying within the armed forces.
DOSAAF	Military sports and activities organisation.
DShV	Desantno-shturmovye voiska, Assault-Landing Troops: helicopter-mobile forces.
Erin, Viktor	Russian Interior Minister.
Eurasians	School of thought which held that Russia should not simply associate itself with the West but develop an independent role. Opposed by the **Atlanticists**.
Foreign Intelligence Service	See **SVR**
GDR	German Democratic Republic (East Germany).
gensek	Abbreviation for General Secretary (of the **CPSU**).
GKChP	Gosudarstvennyi komitet chrezvychainogo polozheniya, State Committee for the State of Emergency in the USSR, the junta of the 1991 August Coup.
glasnost'	Usually translated as 'openness', but this policy also had overtones of 'speaking out' and 'publicity'.
Gorbachev, Mikhail	Reformist General Secretary (leader) of the Communist Party 1985–91, the first and last elected President of the USSR in 1991.
Gosplan	State Planning Committee.
GOU	Glavnoe operativnoe upravlenie, Main Operational Directorate (of the General Staff): the planning think-tank.

Grachev, Pavel	Paratrooper: Hero of the Soviet Union for service in Afghanistan; Russian Defence Minister from 1992.
Gromov, Boris	Charismatic general: last commander of Soviet forces in Afghanistan, First Deputy Soviet Interior Minister 1990–91, then Deputy Russian Defence Minister from 1992.
Gromyko, Andrei	Veteran Soviet Foreign Minister until 1985 when he was temporarily made President and replaced by Eduard **Shevardnadze**.
GRU	Glavnoe razvedyvatelnoe upravlenie, Main Intelligence Directorate (of the General Staff): military intelligence.
IEMSS	Institute of the Economics of the World Socialist System.
IMEMO	Institute of World Economics and International Relations.
INF	Intermediate Nuclear Forces treaty, 1987.
institutchiki	Slang term for members of the academic foreign policy think-tanks, such as **IMEMO** and **ISKAN**.
IRBM	Intermediate range ballistic missile.
ISKAN	US and Canada Institute also, ISShAiK.
KGB	Komitet gosudarstvennoi bezopasnosti, Committee of State Security: the USSR's espionage and internal security agency.
Kokoshin, Andrei	Academic expert on arms control, made Russian First Deputy Defence Minister in 1992.
konversiya	'Conversion', the process of reorienting military-related industries to civil purposes.

Kozyrev, Andrei	Liberal Russian Foreign Minister from 1990.
Kryuchkov, Vladimir	One of the 1991 August Coup junta; Chair of the **KGB** 1988–91.
MB	Ministerstvo bezopasnosti, **Ministry of Security.**
MBFR	Mutual and Balanced Force Reduction talks – replaced by **CFE** negotiations in April 1989.
MBVD	Ministerstvo bezopasnosti i vnutrennykh del, Ministry of Security and Internal Affairs: short-lived attempt to agglomerate all security agencies into one, 1991–92.
MID	Ministerstvo inostrannykh del, Ministry of Foreign Relations.
Ministry of Security	Established 1992 to replace the KGB as Russia's internal security agency (**MB**).
Moiseev, Mikhail	Hawkish Chief of the General Staff, 1989–91.
MS	Mobilnye sily, Mobile Forces, part of the post-Soviet Russian army.
MVD	Ministerstvo vnutrennykh del, Ministry of Internal Affairs.
NATO	North Atlantic Treaty Organisation.
NKAO	Nagorno-Karabakh Autonomous Oblast (region) – a part of Azerbaijan populated predominantly by Armenians and thus the immediate cause of the Armenian–Azerbaijan war.
nomenklatura	The system of lists used by the Party to ensure that key jobs were held by people deemed trustworthy – by extension, the term came to be used for the whole Party élite.

NPM — Novoe politicheskoe myshlenie, New Political Thinking: Gorbachev's rethink of foreign policy.

OMON — Otryad militsii spetsial'nogo naznacheniya, Special Purpose Militia [Police] Unit: these 'black berets' were élite riot police forces established in and from 1987.

OMSN — Otryad militsii osobennogo naznacheniya, Specialised Purpose Militia [Police] Unit; anti-terrorist commando forces.

Opnaz — Contraction for 'Operational Designation' – mobile elements of the Interior Army (**VV**).

perestroika — 'Restructuring', Gorbachev's generic term for his reforms of the USSR.

Politburo — Inner leadership of the **CPSU**, officially elected by the **Central Committee**.

Primakov, Evgenii — Academic who became Director of the Foreign Intelligence Service in 1992.

Prokhanov, Aleksandr — Nationalist writer, closely affiliated with the military.

Pugo, Boris — 1991 August Coup plotter; former head of the Latvian KGB; Interior Minister 1990–91; committed suicide, 1991.

PV — Pogranichnye voiska, Border Forces, controlled by the KGB during the Soviet era and then made into an independent service.

Rodionov, Igor' — Commander of the Transcaucasian Military District who used force to disperse Georgian protesters in 1989; then made Head of the General Staff Academy.

Rutskoi, Aleksandr	Much-decorated military pilot (Hero of the Soviet Union) who ran as Yeltsin's Vice President in 1990 yet then became increasingly critical of him and was arrested for his support of parliament during October 1993.
Ryzhkov, Nikolai	Prime Minister 1985–90.
SDI	'Strategic Defense Initiative', the USA's so-called 'Star Wars' programme.
Security Council	An institution developed by Gorbachev and retained by Yeltsin which united the key security ministers; always a rather shadowy and little-understood but very powerful body.
Shaposhnikov, Evgenii	Commander-in-Chief of the Soviet Air Force who was made **CIS** Commander-in-Chief 1991–93.
Shevardnadze, Eduard	Georgian Party leader who became Soviet Foreign Minister 1985–90 and later President of an independent Georgia, 1992–.
SND	Soyuz narodnykh deputatov, **Congress of People's Deputies.**
SNG	Sodruzhestvo nezavisimykh gosudarstv, Commonwealth of Independent States (**CIS**).
Sokolov, Sergei	Soviet Defence Minister 1984–87.
Spetsnaz	Short for *spetsial'noe naznacheniya*, 'of special designation': commando-style special forces.
START	Strategic Arms Reduction Talks.
Stavka	'Staff': a term which came to be used for the Supreme High Command (**SVGK**).

Supreme Soviet	Soviet parliament, which became democratised – after a fashion – in 1989 and survived to become the Russian parliament after the fall of the USSR. It was elected from the much larger **Congress of Peoples' Deputies**. From December 1993, it was replaced by a new body, the Duma.
SVGK	Stavka verkhovnogo glavnokomandovaniya, 'Supreme High Command', the wartime overall agency of military command (also simply **Stavka**).
SVR	Sluzhba vneshnoi razvedky, **Foreign Intelligence Service**.
tormozhenie	'Braking mechanism', an image Gorbachev used to describe resistance to change from within the Soviet system and society.
uskorenie	'Acceleration', the approach to reform used by Andropov and, at first, Gorbachev, which presupposed that the Soviet system was essentially sound and merely needed minor adjustment.
Ustinov, Dmitri	Soviet Defence Minister 1976–84.
Varennikov, Valentin	Commander-in-Chief of Ground Forces 1989–91; arrested for his role in the 1991 August Coup.
VDV	Vozdushnye-desantnye voiska, Air Assault Troops: paratroopers.
VO	Voennyi okrug, Military District.
vosmerka	'Octet': the term for the eight leaders of the August Coup.

VPK	Either 'Military-Industrial Commission', the body with overall control over the Soviet defence industries, or the broader term 'military-industrial complex'.
VV	Vnutrennye voiska, Interior Forces: the Interior Ministry's security troops.
Warsaw Pact	The USSR's East European military alliance, 1955–91. Also known as the **WTO**.
WTO	Warsaw Treaty Organisation – see **Warsaw Pact**.
Yazov, Dmitri	Member of the 1991 August Coup junta; Soviet Defence Minister 1987–91.
Yeltsin, Boris	Party first secretary in Sverdlovsk and then Moscow, sacked by Gorbachev in 1987, who went on to be elected Russian President in 1990.
Zhirinovskii, Vladimir	Neo-fascist populist leader of the Russian Liberal Democratic Party, which won around a quarter of the vote in the December 1993 parliamentary elections.

GUIDE TO FURTHER READING

This is a general overview of some of the more useful and accessible sources bearing upon foreign and security policy in this era. My apologies to the many authors and analysts slighted by omission; this should be seen very much as an introductory and skeletal guide to the field. Broadly speaking, the journals of greatest importance to the field are *Orbis*, *Europe–Asia Studies* (formerly *Soviet Studies*), the *Journal of Soviet* (later, *Slavic*) *Military Studies* and the (now defunct) *Problems of Communism*. For day-by-day and month-by-month analysis, the BBC *Summary of World Broadcasts* and Radio Liberty's *RFE/RL Research Bulletin* (formerly *Report on the USSR*) are invaluable.

PRIMARY SOURCES

Gorbachev, Mikhail, *Perestroika* (London: Collins, 1987).

Gorbachev, Mikhail, *The August Coup* (London: Harper Collins, 1991).

Shevardnadze, Eduard, *The Future Belongs to Freedom* (New York: The Free Press, 1991).

Yeltsin, Boris, *Against the Grain* (London: Jonathan Cape, 1990).

Zaslavskaya, Tat'yana, *A Voice of Reform* (London: M.E. Sharpe, 1989).

GENERAL READING ON THE USSR

Aslund, Anders, *Gorbachev's Struggle for Economic Reform* (London: Pinter, 1989).

Brown, Archie, 'Gorbachev: new man in the Kremlin', *Problems of Communism* 34, 3 (1985).

Lane, David (ed.), *Elites and Political Power in the USSR* (Aldershot: Edward Elgar, 1988).

Sakwa, Richard, *Soviet Politics: an introduction* (London: Routledge, 1989).

Sakwa, Richard, *Gorbachev and his Reforms* (Hemel Hempstead: Philip Allen, 1990).

GENERAL READING ON THE NEW RUSSIA

Bremmer, Ian and Taras, Ray (eds), *Nations and Politics in the Soviet Successor States* (Cambridge: CUP, 1992).

Sakwa, Richard, *Russian Politics and Society* (London: Routledge, 1993).

White, Stephen, Pravda, Alex and Gitelman, Zvi (eds), *Developments in Soviet and Post-Soviet Politics* (Basingstoke: Macmillan, 1992).

FOREIGN POLICY

Light, Margot, *The Soviet Theory of International Relations* (Brighton: Harvester Wheatsheaf, 1988).

MccGwire, Michael, *Military Objectives in Soviet Foreign Policy* (Washington: Brookings Institute, 1987).

Malcolm, Neil, *Soviet Political Scientists and American Politics* (Basingstoke: Macmillan, 1984).

Parrott, Bruce, 'Soviet national security under Gorbachev', *Problems of Communism* 37, 6 (1988).

Pravda, Alex, 'Is there a Gorbachev foreign policy?', *Journal of Communist Studies* 4, 4 (1988).

Sestanovich, Stephen, 'Gorbachev's foreign policy: a diplomacy of decline', *Problems of Communism* 37, 1 (1988).

THE ARMED FORCES

Allison, Roy (ed.), *Radical Reform in Soviet Defence Policy* (Basingstoke: Macmillan, 1992).

Donnelly, Chris, *Red Banner* (Coulsdon: Jane's, 1988).

Hall, Robert, *Soviet Military Art in a Time of Change* (London: Brasseys, 1991).

Herspring, Dale, *The Soviet High Command* (Princeton: Princeton UP, 1990).

Leebaert, Derek and Dickinson, Timothy (eds), *Soviet Strategy and New Military Thinking* (Cambridge: CUP, 1992).

Nation, R. Craig, *Black Earth, Red Star* (New York: Cornell UP, 1992).

Schofield, Caroline, *Inside the Soviet Army* (London: Headline, 1991).

THE SECURITY SERVICES

Galeotti, Mark, 'Perestroika, perestrelka, pereborka: policing Russia in a time of change', *Europe–Asia Studies*, 45, 5 (1993).

Knight, Amy, *The KGB* (London: Unwin Hyman, 1990).

Knight, Amy, 'The future of the KGB', *Problems of Communism* 39, 6 (1990).

THE MILITARY-INDUSTRIAL COMPLEX

Cooper, Julian, *The Soviet Defence Industry: conversion and reform* (London: Pinter/RIIA, 1991).

Wulf, Hubert (ed.), *Arms Industry Limited* (Oxford: OUP/SIPRI, 1993) – Part III relates to the former USSR.

SPECIFIC INCIDENTS AND ISSUES

Afghanistan

Galeotti, Mark, *Afghanistan: the Soviet Union's Last War* (London: Frank Cass, 1994).

Urban, Mark, *War in Afghanistan* (Basingstoke: Macmillan, 1988 and 1990).

Eastern Europe

Dawisha, Karen, *Eastern Europe, Gorbachev and Reform* (Cambridge: CUP, 1990).

Swain, Geoffrey and Swain, Nigel, *Eastern Europe since 1945* (Basingstoke: Macmillan, 1993).

Conscript vs professional army

Arnett, Robert and Fitzgerald, Mary, 'Restructuring the armed forces: the current Soviet debate', *Journal of Soviet Military Studies* 3, 2 (1990).

The Instituchiki

Conner, Albert and Poirier, Robert, 'The Institutes of the USSR Academy of Sciences: an examination of their roles in Soviet doctrine and strategy', *Journal of Soviet Military Studies* 4, 1 (1991).
Holden, Gerard, *Soviet Military Reform* (London: Pluto Press, 1991).

Eurasians vs Atlanticists

Riasanovsky, Nicholas, *The Emergence of Eurasianism* (Berkeley: University of California Press, 1967).
Tolz, Vera, 'Russia: Westernizers continue to challenge National Patriots', *RFE/RL Research Report* 1, 49 (11 December 1992).

Terrorism and organised crime

Galeotti, Mark, 'Organized crime and Russian national security', *Low Intensity Conflict and Law Enforcement* 1, 3 (1992).
Serio, Joseph, 'Organized crime in the Soviet Union and beyond', *Low Intensity Conflict and Law Enforcement* 1, 2 (1992).

The August Coup

Putsch: the diary (Stevenage: SPA Books, 1992). The complete collected releases and reports from *Postfactum* and *RIA* news agencies from the three days of the coup.
Radio Liberty Report on the USSR 2, 36 (1991). A special issue on the coup, strongly to be recommended.

INDEX

Entries in **bold** represent notes in the concluding Glossary.